PRAY**40**DAYS

Complete 40-Day Pray

PRAY**40**DAYS

The Personal Relationship with God You Have Always Wanted

FR. MICHAEL J. DENK

Edited by Dr. Michelle Bussard

The Prodigal Father
Publishing
Cleveland, Ohio

Nihil Obstat: Msgr Michael Heintz, PhD, Censor Librorum
Imprimatur: Most Rev Kevin C Rhoades

The *Nihil Obstat* and the *Imprimatur* are declarations that the work is considered to be free from doctrinal or moral error. It does not imply that those who have granted the *Nihil Obstat* or *Imprimatur* agree with the contents, opinions, or statements expressed.
21 December 2017

Printed January 2016, Revised January 2018

Contact: FrMichael@TheProdigalFather.org

I am Father Michael J. Denk, a priest of the Catholic Diocese of Cleveland. I am a contributor of content to The Prodigal Father Productions, Inc., a non-profit corporation functioning in accord with the traditions and the teachings of the Roman Catholic Church. The corporation and I are separate, it doesn't speak for me, the parish, or on behalf of the Diocese of Cleveland, and I do not speak for it.

IN LOVING MEMORY

Fr. Thomas Tifft who taught me how to be present to God during daily Holy Hour and present to others in my daily interactions.

ADVANCE PRAISE

"Fr. Michael Denk offers a very good method of praying our way through Lent this year. His reflections and method of guided meditation are simple, clear, concise and encouraging and realistic. They invite everyone to try this way of praying and experiencing the presence of God in their busy lives. They help us to pray meditatively and contemplatively with our eyes fixed on Jesus, the goal of our Lenten journey. Fr. Denk reminds us that prayer, Scripture, religious images and daily devotions and meditations are necessary companions along the journey. Ultimately it is the Holy Spirit who leads and guides us in the silence of our hearts. But we need companions and guides along the way! I encourage you to use this prayer guide along your Lenten journey. It is a source of consolation and strength for the blessed 40 days of Lent."

- Fr. Thomas Rosica, CSB, CEO Salt and Light Catholic Media Foundation

"What an inspirational and practical beginning to give people a deeper experience of various forms of prayer. This provides them an opportunity to deepen their relationship with God – to experience the real, active, loving, and transforming presence of the Father, Jesus, and the Holy Spirit. I think the first several lines to the introduction say it powerfully and well. Those lines grab your attention and bring you in right away. Also, the practical preparation tips and calendar get people to focus immediately on actually following through on these guided prayer experiences during Lent. Inspirational, insightful, uplifting, resourceful, practical, great specific examples, and good humor. It is well written. Prayer guidelines are specific enough, rich sources of meditation, and not too long for people to follow through on. Encouraging people to journal is a must. I will go back and use these meditations for my own Lenten experience. I recommend this wonderful spiritual opportunity for growth for everyone. What is offered here is valuable for beginners and for people steeped in prayer, who can benefit from these rich sources of reflection – meditation – contemplation, grounded in Sacred Scripture and the best of the Catholic Christian tradition on prayer."

- Fr. Norm Douglas, Executive Director Heart to Heart Communications

"For those beginning to pray or desiring to deepen their prayer life, this book is a comprehensive and doable way both to learn about, and enter into, many different ways of praying."

- Fr. Patrick Anderson

"Fr Michael Denk's challenge: 'What if I told you that in the next 40 days, God could become "real" to you?' has resulted in an approachable, practical guide to deepening your relationship with God. Think of it as a call to reignite the loving joy Jesus wants so much for us!"

- Dr. Eugene Gan, Professor at Franciscan University of Steubenville, and Author of Infinite Bandwidth: Encountering Christ in the Media

"A few years ago, I attended a 30 day silent retreat where I prayed the Spiritual Exercises of St. Ignatius. In praying the exercises, I encountered the Lord in a new and real way. After having experienced Pray40Days, which embraces the heart of St. Ignatius, I found that I was given a similar, beautiful experience that enabled me to once again encounter Jesus in a very new and real way! Thank you Fr. Michael."

-Fr. Jeremy Merzweiler, Parochial Vicar, St. Gabriel Parish, Concord, Ohio.

FOREWORD

by Father Robert L. McCreary OFM Capuchin. 19 January 2016.

Every Christian community must become a "genuine school of prayer." These words were written by Pope John Paul II in his letter on spirituality for the 21st century, *The Beginning of the New Millennium, 2001.* These are some of his extended expressions of passionate desire for holiness in the Church: "...our Christian communities must become genuine schools of prayer, where the meeting with Christ is expressed not just in imploring help but also in thanksgiving, praise, adoration, contemplation, listening and ardent devotion until the heart truly falls in love." Certainly John Paul's ardent love for Christ was seen by multitudes, and no one would be surprised to hear him say that not only religious communities but parishes should express an "all pervading climate of prayer."

Education in prayer should become in some way a key-point of all pastoral planning. Certainly many priests have done marvelous service in the Church by their depth of preaching, the devout celebration of the Eucharist and sacraments. But, have parish priests grasped the importance of formation of the faithful in meditative prayer, in forms of contemplation which become a genuine dialogue of love rendering the person wholly possessed by the divine beloved Lord? The genuine Christian has the gift and responsibility of a prayer life which can show the depths to which the relationship of Christ can lead. These are the exact sentiments expressed by John Paul II.

As if to echo John Paul II, Pope Benedict gave a series of teachings on prayer published as: *The School of Prayer.* In this book, Pope Benedict follows the inspired teaching of John Paul II by his marvelous and succinct teachings on prayer in the Old Testament, the Psalms, the New Testament and also in typical forms of meditation.

John Paul II also spoke of other religions which offer responses to the call of genuine spirituality and prayer in appealing ways. He so desired, as did Benedict, that the faithful Christian, who deeply believes in Christ, would know the "Spirit's touch". Both Holy Fathers yearn for faithful, prayerful Christians to deeply believe in Christ and know the "Spirit's touch" resting as a child in the Father's heart.

Our present Holy Father, Pope Francis, though profoundly given to tasks for the world, makes it abundantly clear that the genuine disciple of Christ is called to a life of ever deepening, personal and loving prayer.

A Cardinal who works very closely to the Holy Father told me that Pope Francis left a meeting unexpectedly, and said in plain terms: "It is time for my holy hour, from seven to eight!"

Although this man is clearly a worker, he is also a prayerful man! His fear is that we will not be able to assist the world, to serve the immense needs of our brothers and sisters, if we have a shallow and weak heart. He wished to stir up a new enthusiasm for evangelization full of joy, of fervor, generosity, courage and boundless love. He desires that we put infinite love and joy where there seems to be infinite hatred and sadness. In the *Joy of the Gospel,* he says: "What is needed is the ability to cultivate an interior space which can give a Christian meaning to commitment and activity." "Without prolonged moments of adoration, of prayerful encounter with the word, of sincere conversation with the Lord, our work easily becomes meaningless; we lose energy as a result of weariness and difficulties and our fervor dies out. The Church urgently needs the deep breath of prayer."

Fr. Michael Denk enters now into this story with his questions: How can I, just an ordinary Catholic priest come to a newness of life in the way these dear Popes have spoken? How can I come to experience the depth of prayer and apostolic love in the way these Popes explain, promise and hope for? Fr. Michael has been on this quest for the inner life of love for God which is concrete, personal and real. Fr. Michael has come to know the depth of the Catholic Church's Tradition, and now he wishes to give a parochial form to the promise of divine intimacy and the promise of renewed apostolic love. I encourage you, dear reader, to go on this pilgrimage of prayer for the 40 days that echo the 40 days of Moses and other saints. May Fr. Denk's questions become your questions. Allow this enthusiastic young priest to stir up in you the promised graces of our Lord, and the beautiful and gracious hopes that John Paul II, Benedict XVI, Pope Francis, and Fr. Michael Denk have for you, for the Church, and for the world.

FOREWORD

by Father Fred Pausche, Pastor, St. Gabriel Parish, Concord, Ohio. 29 November 2016.

For over forty years as an ordained minister of the Church, I have constantly heard myself counseling individuals, couples, and even groups about the absolute importance of good communication for healthy relationships that are growing and life-giving. I have experienced this in my own personal life, and I have observed it in the lives of others, along with the very detrimental effects of the lack of good communication. If that is true among persons, and I know it is, it is especially true when it comes to good communication with God. We commonly call that prayer, and talk about it in many ways and in many contexts. To know this is one thing. To believe it is another. But, to actually do it is quite another.

People seem to think that priests and ministers of the Church have an inside track on praying. I have often had people ask me to pray for them because, "my prayers are more powerful than theirs" and "God listens to you more." I really don't believe that nor have I ever experienced that in my life. I want prayer to be the most important part of my life, but like most people, I struggle to make that a reality. There are always excuses, distractions, good intentions that fall flat, and most often, just a lack of spiritual discipline. It is not for lack of trying, but probably because I, like everyone, am very human and experience all the challenges that get in the way of good prayer. I continually look for new ways to enhance my prayer life, and pray that I will never stop searching and being open to those ways.

I believe that Fr. Michael Denk's *Pray40Days* has been one of God's ways of answering my prayer. When I first reviewed the content of *Pray40Days* I was very impressed with the simplicity, spiritual depth, and practical aspects of incorporating this into my struggling but growing prayer life. I was excited to enter into this simple "fifteen minutes a day," and wondered what effect it might have. I was even more excited to support Fr. Michael sharing this with our whole community, because I firmly believe that other than loving our people, the most important thing a pastor and staff could do for the community is to help them to pray in a deeper and more fervent way.

I have experienced a lot so far by entering into this spiritual journey of prayer. I learned that it is not always easy to have the discipline I need, the focus I desire, and to attain the benefits I hope for. However, I can honestly say that this spiritual practice has already been very valuable. But what I believe and know deeply in my heart is that this is not so much about me as it is about God. I know that if I at least try and am willing to stick with this and be open to deeper ways of praying, God will do the rest. God has, will in the future, and continues every day to manifest His loving and generous presence. My relationship with the Lord continues to grow—thanks be to God. *Pray40Days* continues to teach me that, "it is all about communication; it is all about prayer; it is all about God." I encourage you to make the most of this wonderful opportunity and pray that this beautiful spiritual tool will help your prayer life to grow, and your relationship with God to blossom and bear much fruit.

JOIN THE PRAY**40**DAYS PROGRAM

Pray40Days is much more then just a book.

To enjoy the benefits of the entire program, go to
TheProdigalFather.org/Pray40Days
and sign up for the program.

Many additional resources are available.

TABLE OF CONTENTS

PREFACE **14**

INTRODUCTION **17**

Preparation Day 1 21
Preparation Day 2 26
Preparation Day 3 32

PRAY40DAYS
Day 1 Praying with Guided Meditation - The Lord's Prayer 36
Day 2 Praying Like a Pirate - The Announcement of the Birth of Jesus 39
Day 3 Praying with Lectio Divina - Psalm 23 43
Day 4 Praying With Your Senses - The Parable of the Lost Son 48

Praying with Sunday Mass 54
Day 5 Praying with Contemplative Prayer - The Father's Plan of Salvation 56
Day 6 Praying with Scriptural Relaxation - Psalm 139 59
Day 7 Praying with Guided Meditation - The Walking on the Water 65
Day 8 Praying Like a Pirate - The Washing of the Disciples' Feet 68
Day 9 Praying with Lectio Divina - Promises of Redemption and Restoration 72
Day 10 Praying With Your Senses - The Return of the Twelve and the Feeding of the Five Thousand 77

Praying with Sunday Mass 81
Day 11 Praying with Contemplative Prayer - Abraham's Visitors with Rublev Trinity Icon 86
Day 12 Praying with Scriptural Relaxation - The Vine and the Branches 91
Day 13 Praying with Guided Meditation - The Baptism of Jesus 96
Day 14 Praying Like a Pirate - What will separate us from the love of Christ? 99
Day 15 Praying with Lectio Divina - Dependence on God 102
Day 16 Praying With Your Senses - The Lord's Supper 107

Praying with Sunday Mass..111
Day 17 Praying with Contemplative Prayer - Praying with Nature..... 113
Day 18 Praying with Scriptural Relaxation -
The Calming of a Storm at Sea 115
Day 19 Praying with Guided Meditation - The Pardon of the Sinful
Woman 119
Day 20 Praying Like a Pirate - The Rich Official............................122
Day 21 Praying with Lectio Divina - Psalm 46 127
Day 22 Praying With Your Senses - The Appearance to the Seven
Disciples..131

Praying with Sunday Mass..136
Day 23 Praying with Contemplative Prayer -
Last Supper Discourses and the Advocate 138
Day 24 Praying with Scriptural Relaxation - Psalm 63 141
Day 25 Praying with Guided Meditation - The Blind Bartimaeus 145
Day 26 Praying Like a Pirate - The Call of Simon the Fisherman 148
Day 27 Praying with Lectio Divina - The Parable of the Lost Sheep..151
Day 28 Praying With Your Senses - The Healing of the Paralytic.......155

Praying with Sunday Mass..160
Day 29 Praying with Contemplative Prayer - San Damiano Cross 161
Day 30 Praying with Scriptural Relaxation -
The Gentle Mastery of Christ..166
Day 31 Praying with Guided Meditation -
A Woman Caught in Adultery 170
Day 32 Praying Like a Pirate - The Wedding at Cana 173
Day 33 Praying with Lectio Divina - The Way of Love 176
Day 34 Praying With Your Senses - The Crucifixion of Jesus 182

Praying with Sunday Mass..187
Day 35 Praying with Contemplative Prayer - Pray with Nature 189
Day 36 Praying with Scriptural Relaxation - The Call of Jeremiah 191
Day 37 Praying with Guided Meditation -
The Appearance on the Road to Emmaus 196
Day 38 Praying Like a Pirate - Jesus and Peter 201
Day 39 Praying with Lectio Divina - Thomas....................................204
Day 40 Praying with Contemplative Prayer - The Prayer of Jesus......209

Praying with Sunday Mass..212

CONCLUSION **213**
ACKNOWLEDGMENTS AND GRATITUDE **215**

APPENDIX I **217**
Types of Prayer 217
Prayer Exercises 221
Guided Meditation 221
Contemplative Prayer 222
Lectio Divina 228
Praying like a Pirate 230
Praying With Your Senses 230
Scriptural Relaxation 232

APPENDIX II **235**
Scripture Passages 235
Scripture Passages by Prayer Type 237

BIBLIOGRAPHY **239**

PREFACE

If you are holding this book, God knows that you have a deep desire to pray. Or maybe you don't, but you will! That desire to pray is a gift from God. Anytime God gives you a gift, He will bring it to fulfillment. If in these next 40 days, you give God your time, there will be a transformation not only in your relationship with Him but also in your relationship with others. You will grow a love for God that will become a desire to give your life in service to helping others know, love, and serve this wonderful Father that loves you more than you could ever imagine.

The greatest adventure we have in life is learning to pray. Pope Benedict XVI, the former Cardinal Ratzinger, said that the entire purpose for Jesus coming into the world was to show us God the Father (*Ratzinger Report*). Some great spiritual masters also suggest that all we ever need to know about God is captured wonderfully in the Parable of the Lost Son (Luke 15:11-32). Over the years, this parable (often known as the Prodigal Son) has become a central theme in my personal prayer life and in my priesthood. What I have come to realize is that the key figure in the parable is not so much the prodigal son, but the father. I have discovered that the father outdoes the son in being prodigal. Let me explain.

The original meaning of the word prodigal comes from the Latin *Prodigus* which means "lavish." Here are more uses to help us define it:

prod·i·gal \ˈprä-di-gəl\ (adjective) (*Merriam-Webster Dictionary*, 2016)

1. Spending money or resources freely and recklessly; wastefully extravagant.

2. Having or giving something on a lavish scale.

3. A person who spends money in a recklessly extravagant way.

In the Parable of the Lost Son, we normally associate prodigal with the son, and rightfully so. However, something pretty amazing happens if we associate this word with the father and his grace. In Luke 15:12, we hear the son demand: '*Father, give me the share of your estate that should come to me.*' And what does the father do? He *divided the property between* his two sons. He almost recklessly and wastefully gives his sons their inheritance.

We all know how the prodigal son goes on to waste everything until he comes to his senses and realizes how good he had it. Now watch how, once more, the father gives everything prodigally to his son: *"So he got up and went back to his father. While he was still a long way off, his father caught sight of him, and was filled with compassion. He ran to his son, embraced him and kissed him. His son said to him, 'Father, I have sinned against heaven and against you; I no longer deserve to be called your son.' But his father ordered his servants, 'Quickly bring the finest robe and put it on him; put a ring on his finger and sandals on his feet. Take the fattened calf and slaughter it. Then let us celebrate with a feast, because this son of mine was dead, and has come to life again; he was lost, and has been found.' Then the celebration began"* (Luke 15:20-24).

The celebration is definitely on a LAVISH scale! As mentioned previously, the word prodigal comes from the Latin word for 'lavish.'

lav·ish \ˈla-vish\ (adjective) (*Merriam-Webster Dictionary, 2016*)

1. Sumptuously rich, elaborate, or luxurious. "a lavish banquet" - synonyms: sumptuous, luxurious, costly, expensive, opulent, grand, splendid, rich, fancy, posh; "lavish parties."

2. Of a person - very generous or extravagant. "He was lavish with his hospitality" - synonyms: generous, liberal, bountiful, openhanded, unstinting, unsparing, free, munificent, extravagant, prodigal; "lavish hospitality" or "given in profusion."

3. "Lavish praise"- synonyms: abundant, copious, plentiful, liberal, prolific, generous; literary plenteous; "lavish amounts of champagne."

4. Bestow something in generous or extravagant quantities upon - synonyms: give freely to, spend generously on, bestow on, heap on, shower with, cover something thickly or liberally with; "She lavished our son with kisses."

Can you see that it is the father who is prodigal? It is the father who lavishes his grace on both of his sons. The father lavishes his son with love as he runs to this lost son, embraces him and kisses him. He also goes out to the older brother who is angry and upset. He pleads with him: *"My son, you are here with me always; everything I have is yours. But now we must celebrate and rejoice, because your brother was dead and has come to life again; he was lost and has been found"* (Luke 15:31-32). This father's astounding words also describe God the Father's love for us and the way that He so lavishly, generously, and prodigally offers His Grace to all of us, His children.

God the Father is so generous, so loving, so unsparing, so lavish, so extravagant, so bountiful, so openhanded, so prolific, so giving without counting the cost, that we can truly call Him "The Prodigal Father." The Father gives the kingdom of heaven away freely and almost recklessly to the good and bad alike. *"He makes his sun rise on the bad and the good, and causes rain to fall on the just and the unjust"* (Matthew 5:45).

And, He wants to give it all to you freely. *"And everyone who has given up houses or brothers or sisters or father or mother or children or lands for the sake of my name will receive a hundred times more, and will inherit eternal life"* (Matthew 19:29). All you have to do is desire and receive His Son, the Holy Spirit, Mary, all the saints in heaven, and all the companions on earth; and, above all, His very self. He loves you that much that He wants to give you everything, not only in eternal life but right now.

The Father delights in you and says, "My son. My daughter. Everything I have is yours, and now we must rejoice because you who were lost, now have been found; you who were dead, now have been brought to life!"

Pray40Days will help you experience God "for real." By end of this great adventure, hopefully, you will have encountered God in a way that you never have before! You will have experienced the personal relationship with God that you have always wanted. If you offer Him your time in prayer, He will not be outdone in generosity. He will lavish you with grace in such extravagant ways that you will learn and love to pray beyond anything you ever expected. As you pray through *Pray40Days* with Sacred Scripture and the wonderful Traditions of our Church, may you come to know this unconditional love of the Father who delights in you. May Jesus be a real person to you, your closest and most intimate friend; not just an idea or a person in history. May the Holy Spirit bring you a sense of wonder and awe. May you behold Mary as your mother and experience her beholding you as her child.

Do you have any desire to grow in your prayer life? I hope for all of us that the answer is a resounding YES! Now, let Jesus show you to His Father and yours.

- Fr. Michael

INTRODUCTION

What if I told you right now that, in these next 40 days, your prayer life could be set on fire? What if I told you that within our own Catholic faith tradition, we have all the tools that can allow us to receive the Holy Spirit and experience God the Father as a tender, caring, deeply personal presence in our lives? What if Jesus were actually real to YOU? What if the Holy Spirit was not just some abstract idea, but a real personal force of inspiration, presence, and overwhelming joy in your life? Sounds pretty amazing, doesn't it?

Welcome to *Pray40Days*. Whether you are a beginner in prayer, want to grow in your prayer life, or have a very advanced prayer life, the exercises in *Pray-40Days* will help you experience God, "for real." My purpose for writing *Pray-40Days* (with corresponding App and online resources) is to help you grow in your prayer life so that you will come to know God the Father, the Son, and the Holy Spirit in a deep, personal, and profound way. It is written especially for people who want to grow in their prayer life but just don't know how. It is also for people who don't even know they want to grow, but will soon discover how much deeper they can really go!

Pray40Days will guide you through different types of prayer that will immerse you in the life of Christ, fill you with the Holy Spirit, and allow you to be held and loved by the Father. By the end of *Pray40Days*, you will come to love spending time with God and look forward to the wonder that awaits you every time you enter into this quality time with God who loves you more than anyone else ever could.

Over my years as a priest, I have learned that many people are content with their prayer life. But when they get a glimpse of a new and deeper way of praying, they actually want "more." The following real experience brings a great deal of insight into this different way of praying and illustrates the idea.

I was working with three men in a marketing firm to discuss how to use new media to enhance prayer life. They didn't seem to really "get" what I was trying to accomplish, so I asked each of them: "How do you pray? Think of the last 24 hours and any time you spent praying." The first man said: "Father, I don't really have a prayer time. My prayer time is on the way to work, especially if I have a tough situation and need God's help." I encouraged him, saying: "That's wonderful. That's prayer of petition. Do you ever set aside other time for prayer?" He replied: "No, that's my time." Going around the table, I asked the second guy to share how he had prayed yesterday. He said: "Father, I don't set time aside for prayer either, but I am simply grateful. I'm grateful for all that God has given me. I am very grateful for my wife and kids, I have a good job, a good family. Father, I've got everything I need." Again, I encouraged him, saying: "That is a prayer of thanksgiving." Finally, the third man said: "Father, I do set time aside..." He then went on to describe very genuinely and sincerely: "Every night before I go to bed, I kneel down next to my bed and say the Our Father, Hail Mary, and Glory Be. And then I go to sleep." "Wonderful," I said, "It' so great that you have that nightly rhythm of prayer."

Then, I asked the men if they wanted to grow in their prayer life. Their response: "Nah, we're good…" (All three said "NO" - with a priest sitting there, pitching them the idea!) They were all content with their prayer life without any real desire to grow. I jokingly said: "Do you realize that you are praying at the same level you learned in second grade?!" They laughed but didn't understand what I meant. So I told them all to close their eyes and listen ....

"Imagine you are walking on the Sea of Galilee. There is a fire: you can see the hot coals and embers flying into the air; you can hear the waves crashing and smell the sea water. Then, you realize Jesus is sitting next to the fire. Try to picture Him. All of a sudden, He looks at YOU and invites you to come and sit by the fire with Him. You realize this is real. Jesus is talking to you. You can see Him and hear Him. You walk over and take a seat; and before you know it, you are having a real conversation. You feel the warmth of the fire and hear it crackling in the silence. You smell fresh bread baking; you look down at it cooking on the fire along with fish. Then you look back up right into Jesus' eyes. He looks deep into your eyes and asks the most important question you will ever be asked: "Do you love me?" "Do you love me?" "Do you love me?" [There was silence in the room.] I told the men: "Go ahead, answer Him; tell Him from your heart." After sensing that each one of them had, I spoke the words that Jesus did: "Feed my sheep." I instructed them one last time: "Spend a moment in silence now with Jesus by the fire at the Sea of Galilee."

This experience only lasted about ten minutes, but at the end, I could tell it had had an effect on the men. They did have an experience of Christ. I could see it on their face and in their eyes. In that meditation, they encountered God like they had never encountered God before. The president of the company looked at me and said: "Father, I get it. I've never experienced anything like that before!"

I think that most of us have not moved beyond a second grade level of praying. Yes, vocal prayer (such as the men's prayers) is a necessary and good form of praying, but there is a deeper prayer life that we are called to grow into - meditative and contemplative prayer. My deepest desire is for Catholics, Christians, and all people to grow in this prayer life. As a priest, I have been tremendously gifted with many opportunities to grow in prayer. I make an annual directed Ignatian eight-day spiritual retreat with wonderful priests, have had great spiritual directors both in the seminary and in priesthood, and experienced The Spiritual Exercises of St. Ignatius (a 30 day silent retreat; a kind of spiritual marathon). I get to spend time every day praying a Holy Hour, and continue to read truly wonderful spiritual books by the greatest saints and mystics. All of these blessings have helped me grow in my prayer life. But, this prayer experience is not just for religious people. I want all people to have access to the blessings and prayer life so often only available to priests and the religious. St. Francis de Sales wrote a book in the early modern era entitled *The Introduction to the Devout Life* because he wanted lay (ordinary) people to have a powerful prayer life. I look at *Pray40Days* as a modern day *Introduction to the Devout Life* so that you, too, can experience the powerful prayer life that comes with meditation and contemplation.

The Jesuit theologian, Karl Rahner, once said: "In the days ahead, you will either be a mystic (one who has experienced God for real) or nothing at all." My desire for *Pray40Days* is for everyone to share in the mystical prayer life where we can "experience God for real" and encounter Him in a way that we never have before! May *Pray40Days* be just what you need to go deeper into your prayer life and grow closer to God.

- Fr. Michael

PRAY**40**DAYS

The Personal Relationship with God You Have Always Wanted

PREPARATION DAY 1

Pray40Days will set you on fire! Over the next 40 days, you will discover the prayer life you have always wanted. Most of us do go our entire lives praying like we were taught in the second grade. What you learned was not wrong, but have you grown? Has your prayer life deepened and evolved each and every day, week, month and year since second grade? If it has not, you may be spiritually out of shape, spiritually dead, and possibly on the verge of losing eternal life. The prayer exercises in *Pray40Days* (very similar to an intense, insane workout program for your body) can help transform your heart, mind, soul and entire being!

HOW TO USE THIS BOOK

Pray40Days is designed to be read on a daily basis and will guide you through an amazing 40 day journey using inspirational prayer exercises. It is best to start this program on a Sunday (see calendar in this chapter for an accountability chart). First, read Preparation Days 1-3 of the book which will prepare you for your new prayer life. Then, starting with Day 1, I will lead you through 40 days of prayer using six prayer types: Contemplative Prayer, Guided Meditation, Lectio Divina, Praying like a Pirate, Praying with the Senses, and Scriptural Relaxation. I describe each prayer method in the Prayer Exercises section of Appendix I.

In the Appendices, there are additional resources to help you learn more about prayer as well as an index of Scripture passages used in *Pray40Days*. Also go to the website at TheProdigalFather.org/Pray40Days to sign up for the program.

Note: The first edition of *Pray40Days* was intended to be used during Lent, however, the Scripture verses are not specific to Lent and are appropriate to use any time you need spiritual renewal throughout the year. I do recommend that you start Preparation Day 1 on a Sunday, whether during Lent or any other time (see Accountability - Calendar).

PRAYING WITH SUNDAY MASS

Every time we go to Mass, we get to encounter God. It is really an extraordinary and amazing experience, if we only realize it. Praying with Sunday Mass is not a prayer type exercise in *Pray40Days* but it is a day to reflect and help us prepare for Mass just like we prepare for prayer. Praying with Sunday Mass encourages us to enter into Mass in unique ways and experience the risen Christ, at that moment. Journaling your experience after Mass is also a wonderful exercise.

SILENCE IS ESSENTIAL

You are given a time of silence following each meditation. This silence can last a few minutes or as long as you need to reflect on the prayer experience. It is extremely important that you make a firm resolution and commit to a certain amount of time for silence each day. Maybe it is 10 minutes, 15 minutes, 30 minutes, or even one hour. Whatever the time commitment is, do not leave a moment early "come hell or high water!" Make a resolution at the beginning of *Pray40Days* that you will stick to the entire program. There will be a thousand and one different excuses and distractions. If you do not remain firm and committed, the enemy will win in distracting you. However, if you are resolute and firm, the enemy will take flight and God will reward you for your generosity and trust in Him. After the time of silence, you will want to journal the experience. So get a journal and a pen so you can write about your feelings and what you heard God say to you after each day's prayer. You will be surprised at how much you learn when writing down your thoughts. You only have to keep your commitment for 40 days but, when you are done, you may find yourself wanting more time with God!

ACCOUNTABILITY

Accountability in your prayer life is important. That is why *Pray-40Days* can be done individually, as a family, or within a group of friends. I recommend that you form a "prayer group" that meets weekly so you can reflect upon the week's prayers and pray the daily experience together whenever you meet.

To help you remain on track, I have included the calendar below. Please use it as an aid to track your progress throughout the pray days. You may want to bookmark the pages so that you can refer daily to the calendar in order to "check mark" each day's prayer that you have completed. You can also swap days, such "Praying with Sunday Mass" on Saturdays if you plan to attend the Saturday Vigil Mass instead. Remember, it is not a race. The journey is the most important part!

PRAY40DAYS CALENDAR

☐ Prep Day 1 Sunday	☐ Prep Day 2 Monday	☐ Prep Day 3 Tuesday	Start 40 Days ☐ Day 1 Wednesday	☐ Day 2 Thursday	☐ Day 3 Friday	☐ Day 4 Saturday
☐ Sunday	☐ Day 5	☐ Day 6	☐ Day 7	☐ Day 8	☐ Day 9	☐ Day 10
☐ Sunday	☐ Day 11	☐ Day 12	☐ Day 13	☐ Day 14	☐ Day 15	☐ Day 16
☐ Sunday	☐ Day 17	☐ Day 18	☐ Day 19	☐ Day 20	☐ Day 21	☐ Day 22
☐ Sunday	☐ Day 23	☐ Day 24	☐ Day 25	☐ Day 26	☐ Day 27	☐ Day 28
☐ Sunday	☐ Day 29	☐ Day 30	☐ Day 31	☐ Day 32	☐ Day 33	☐ Day 34
☐ Sunday	☐ Day 35	☐ Day 36	☐ Day 37	☐ Day 38	☐ Day 39	☐ Day 40
☐ Sunday	*Pray40Days* can be used during Lent and other Liturgical times throughout the year.					

HOW IS YOUR PRAYER LIFE?

How is your prayer life? Think about your last 24 hours, last week, last month - how have you been praying? Are you moving closer to God every day or growing more distant every day? There is no such thing as staying the same; you either grow, or you die. Your prayer life is either bringing you closer to God, or you are growing more and more numb to Him. What is your prayer life like? Is it boring? My spiritual director once told us in the seminary that "prayer should never be boring." If it is boring, you are doing it wrong! My hope is that while reading *Pray40Days*, you will be far from bored. That you will stand in awe and wonder when you discover through prayer just how real God is and how much the Father loves you.

The God of all creation says this: *"I know your works; I know that you are neither cold nor hot. I wish you were either cold or hot. So, because you are lukewarm, neither hot nor cold, I will spit you out of my mouth. For you say, 'I am rich and affluent and have no need of anything,' and yet do not realize that you are wretched, pitiable, poor, blind, and naked. I advise you to buy from me gold refined by fire so that you may be rich, and white garments to put on so that your shameful nakedness may not be exposed, and buy ointment to smear on your eyes so that you may see"* (Revelation 3:15-18).

Is your prayer life hot or cold? If you responded that your prayer life is simply "ok," "fine," or "good", you may be lukewarm. God says that the worst thing for you is to be lukewarm. Likewise, it is better for your prayer life to be either hot or cold; whereas, the worst thing is to be "lukewarm."

This "lukewarm" could also be translated as: "I am fine," "I am doing all right," or "I have got everything I need." But God also says that we have no idea how completely poor, spiritually weak, and completely blind we are. We have plenty of jewelry, but do we have the "gold refined by fire"? We have closets full of clothes, but are we shamefully naked when it comes to our "wearing" a life of deep prayer? We have glasses, contacts, and now even laser eye surgery, but are we spiritually blind?

Mother Teresa, who was canonized in September 2016 by Pope Francis, warns: "The greatest disease in the West today is not tuberculosis or leprosy; it is being unwanted, unloved, and uncared for. We can cure physical diseases with medicine, but the only cure for loneliness, despair and hopelessness is love. There are many in the world who are dying for a piece of bread, but there are many more dying for a little love. The poverty in the West is a different kind of poverty; it is not only a poverty of loneliness but also of spirituality. There's a hunger for love, as there is a hunger for God" (Mother Teresa, 1995).

If this is true, then the greatest disease that we face in the western world is a spiritual one. It is a poverty greater than any other because it impacts the way we relate to God through the greatest and first commandment: *"You shall love the Lord your God with all your heart, with all your soul, with all your mind"* (Matthew 22:37).

Do you love God with ALL your heart, with ALL your soul, with ALL your mind, and with ALL your strength? Or is your heart divided? Is your soul cast down? Is your mind scattered? Is your strength spent, leaving you tired? Do you find yourself constantly exhausted? Lazy? Slothful? Complacent? Numb? Lonely? There is a hunger for love, a hunger for God, a poverty of loneliness, and ultimately a poverty of spirituality. The poverty is that not only have we stopped growing in prayer, but we have even lost a desire to grow in our spiritual life.

What if the spiritual poverty in our souls that Mother Teresa talks about could be transformed? What if the next 40 days could - like an intense workout for your body - transform your heart, mind, and soul? Think about it. In our world, we have great physical workout exercises like the P90X Insanity Workout that can transform our bodies. The fruits of an intense physical workout are that our bodies look different, get stronger and are healthier. The spiritual workout of *Pray40Days* will transform your Spirit! And the evidence of that will be in the gifts and fruits that the Holy Spirit brings.

"The seven *gifts* of the Holy Spirit are wisdom, understanding, counsel, fortitude, knowledge, piety, and fear of the Lord..." (CCC, 1831).

"The *fruits* of the Spirit are perfections that the Holy Spirit forms in us as the first fruits of eternal glory. The tradition of the Church lists twelve of them: "charity, joy, peace, patience, kindness, goodness, generosity, gentleness, faithfulness, modesty, self-control, chastity" (CCC,1832).

Who doesn't want these gifts and fruits? They do not come to those who are bored, lukewarm or are spiritually poverty stricken. They come to those whose prayer life is on fire. They come to those who hunger for God and know, love, and remain in union with their Father.

PREPARATION DAY 1: Prepare for the 40 days of prayer by reading Types of Prayer and the Prayer Exercise: Guided Meditation found in Appendix I.

PREPARATION DAY 2

The 5 P's of Prayer is an excellent exercise that can be used every day. This very practical method of praying was given to me by a very wonderful Jesuit priest, Fr. Bob Welsh, who led my first ever eight-day silent retreat over a decade ago. It changed my life and the way I pray. My hope is that you will follow these 5 P's of prayer before you sit down to pray.

THE 5 P'S OF PRAYER

PREPARATION: It is important when we go to pray that we are already prepared in some way to enter into prayer. Let me give you a few analogies.

I love having the time to run and exercise while listening to music, audiobooks, or podcasts. It gives me focus, keeps me entertained, and allows me to listen to things I might otherwise not have the time for. But, I discovered that if I don't prepare things before a run, half of my time is spent trying to cue up a playlist, search for and download an audiobook, or find the right songs to run to. Needless to say, these are not very effective runs and, sometimes, I end up not even running. However, if I spend time beforehand creating the playlist or downloading a podcast, I actually look forward to running just to listen to my music. Running then becomes less frustrating and an enjoyable experience, and I actually finish the run. Once I put my shoes on and go to the place where I want to run, there has never been a time I haven't run - if I'm prepared.

The same is true with prayer. If we go to our "place of prayer" (just like going to a track or gym), we go to pray. When we are there, we want to be actually praying and not trying to figure out what we are going to pray. Ninety percent of prayer is just doing it - if we are prepared with what we are going to pray, not only will we be ready when we get there but we will actually look forward to the quality time with God.

Another example of preparation is to read the Scripture passage you will be praying with early in the day, and then meditate on it throughout the day. Fr. Welsh once told the story of a husband and wife who were celebrating an anniversary and made preparations to celebrate it that evening. So, in the morning before the husband went to work, he kissed his wife on the cheek and said, "I will see you tonight." Guess what they both thought about throughout the day? Both husband and wife thought all day about how they were going to get together that evening! Likewise, with joyful anticipation, we should prepare for our prayer time by taking time at the beginning of our day to look at the Scripture we are to pray with. We then think about it throughout the day so that when we go to pray, we are ready for it.

There is nothing I love more than a bonfire on the beach at sunset; God's beauty is in the waves, sand, and sun. I love comparing the image of prayer as sitting before a bonfire. There is something mesmerizing about a bonfire and the same is true for prayer. But, both require preparation. Before enjoying the fire, I have to spend the time gathering the driftwood and kindling, stacking the wood together, then starting with a small flame fanning it slowly into a blazing fire. If timed just right, I can sit there watching the sunset, listening to the waves, with the crackling fire keeping me warm. There is a ritual and a rhythm to it. We need this same ritual, rhythm, and routine with our prayer.

To help you prepare as you go through *Pray40Days*, it is a good idea to review the specific type of prayer for that day found in Appendix I. Finally, when we prepare to enter into prayer, it is a good time to just relax, slow down, breath, and rest with God. Let the Father hold you, the Good Shepherd comfort you, and the Holy Spirit enkindle the fire of this wonderful time with God.

PLACE: The most sacred place where we can pray is before the Eucharist. Consider spending your prayer time in a quiet church near the Blessed Sacrament. If you have a church near by with Perpetual Adoration, you can pray in the Exposed Presence of Jesus in the Eucharist. A church, however, may not always be a convenient place as sometimes it is locked or there may be some activity happening in the church. So it is good to have a "go to" prayer place at home. Every home should have a place to pray that is sacred. This place could be a "chapel" which is a whole prayer room with sacramentals (for example: candle, Bible, or crucifix) or it could simply be a "prayer corner" or a "prayer chair". When you are in this place, you know it is time to pray. Others will also know you are praying and are less likely to disturb you. (Go to TheProdigalFather.org/Pray40Days for some examples of preparing your "place").

POSTURE: We pray with our bodies. Therefore, it is important to realize that what we do with our bodies has an impact on our prayer. There are four traditional postures for praying: standing, sitting, kneeling, and prostrating. When we stand, it is symbolic of standing before God in wonder and awe with great attention. When we sit, it is a more relaxed posture which allows us to receive God's Word. When we kneel, we are humbling ourselves before God in a very intense and deliberate way. By kneeling, we are inviting God to bless us. Father McCreary once told me: "Whenever we are doubting, the sheer act of kneeling says to God, 'I believe.'"

Finally, there is prostrating, which is lying face down and surrendering to God. This posture is perfect for when we feel completely at a loss and all we can do is literally lay our bodies and our lives down before God. It is a very powerful form of prayer and surrender. There is nothing more powerful then surrendering your whole body, mind, and soul to God and laying it all down before Him.

PASSAGE: Passage means the actual Scripture text that you will be praying with. It is important to have this ready and prepare with it ahead of time so that when you go to the passage you can actually begin your prayer time. In *Pray40Days*, we will pray using passages from the Bible, however, during contemplative prayer, we may also be praying with an icon or nature.

PRESENCE: Take some time to enter into the presence of God. This may be simply closing your eyes, making the sign of the cross, and inviting God to be present to you and you to be present to God. It may be helpful to imagine yourself being held by God the Father. Imagine Jesus, the Good Shepherd, comforting you or the Holy Spirit breathing into you. If you are close to the Blessed Mother, Mary can also be a wonderful way to draw us into the presence of God with her maternal care. It may only be a brief moment, but it is essential to enter into this personal prayer of experiencing God in a very real and wonderful way.

PLACE

Ninety percent of prayer is just being "there" in that "place." If you don't have a place to pray, it won't happen. If you do have a place to pray and you physically place yourself there, prayer will happen! Every home should have a sacred space: a prayer room, a prayer corner or, at least, a prayer chair. If you do have a place like this, then the first thing you need to do is "get it ready!" If you don't have a place like this, treat yourself. You are worth it. God is worth it.

The greatest and first commandment is: "*You shall love the Lord your God with all your heart, with all your soul, and with all your mind*" (Matthew 22:37). A very concrete way for this to happen is to have a place in your home dedicated to God. Your entire home should be dedicated to God, but let's start first with a designated sacred space. This will help you realize that when you are there, it is for praying. It will also communicate to other people in your home that when you are in that sacred place, you are praying and under no circumstances are to be disturbed - short of the house catching on fire!

Check out some ideas and layouts at our prayer resource page: TheProdigalFather.org/Pray40Days. Consider ordering sacramentals or something like it. Or, if you have a religious goods store nearby, go there; they will have everything you need. You don't have to go overboard; these are just to give you ideas. You surely have "religious" items already in your home. Use those and arrange them in a way where you can sit comfortably in a chair and see them. It is important to have some sacramentals: "Holy Mother Church has, moreover, instituted sacramentals. These are sacred signs which bear a resemblance to the sacraments. They signify effects, particularly of a spiritual nature, which are obtained through the intercession of the Church. By them men are disposed to receive the chief effect of the sacraments, and various occasions in life are rendered holy" (CCC, 1667). Keep in mind that these are only suggestions. But do "treat" yourself! You are worth it and so is God!

Another great sacramental is a Holy Water font. Consider placing this right by the entryway to your "sacred space" so that whenever you enter it you can make the Sign of the Cross. This is a very powerful sacramental that not only draws you close to God but also protects you from the devil.

Now that you have your "prayer room" or "sacred space" set up, it is important to get comfortable in it. You are going to be spending some great quality time there, and you should feel comfort and a sense of warmth whenever you enter. Consider some kind of ritual to make it sacred, some transition from the ordinary to the extraordinary. Mother Teresa insisted that all of her nuns remove their shoes or sandals before entering the chapel to pray. I have prayed in a number of their chapels throughout the world, and I have to say that it is a very profound experience and "sets you up" to pray. God said: *"Do not come near! Remove your sandals from your feet, for the place where you stand is holy ground"* (Exodus 3:5). The most important thing is that you feel safe and comfortable in your prayer space.

POSTURE

Now that you are in your "sacred place," try different prayer postures. Traditionally, the Church has four postures of praying: standing, sitting, kneeling, and prostrating. You experience most of these at Sunday Mass. Think about how many times you change posture during Mass. Each posture is intentional and has some meaning with a desired effect. Find a posture in which you can relax and be comfortable with so that your body is not a distraction during prayer.

STANDING: When we stand, we can pray at any time - even at the grocery store. When we stand at Church, we are "at attention." We stand during the Processional, the Gospel, the Recessional, the Petitions, and all of the prayers of the Mass (when we are not kneeling). *At that time the*

LORD set apart the tribe of Levi to carry the ark of the covenant of the LORD, to stand before the LORD to minister to him, and to bless in his name, as they have done to this day (Deuteronomy 10:8). *"Be vigilant at all times and pray that you have the strength to escape the tribulations that are imminent and to stand before the Son of Man*" (Luke 21:36).

KNEELING: When kneeling, we enter the presence of God. *The man then knelt and bowed down to the LORD* (Genesis 24:26). St. Paul writes: "*... that at the name of Jesus / every knee should bend, / of those in heaven and on earth and under the earth*" (Phil. 2:10).

SITTING: *Moving on from there Jesus walked by the Sea of Galilee, went up on the mountain, and sat down there* (Matthew 15:29). When sitting, we are prepared to receive God's Word. *The LORD appeared to Abraham by the oak of Mamre, as he sat in the entrance of his tent, while the day was growing hot* (Genesis 18:1).

PROSTRATING: Prostration means lying face down and surrendering to God. *But Moses and Aaron went away from the assembly to the entrance of the tent of meeting, where they fell prostrate... Then the glory of the LORD appeared to them"* (Numbers 20:6). *Then he brought me by way of the north gate to the facade of the temple. I looked—and the glory of the LORD filled the LORD's house! I fell on my face. The LORD said to me: Son of man, pay close attention, look carefully, and listen intently to everything I tell you* (Ezekiel 44:4-5). *And one of them, realizing he had been healed, returned, glorifying God in a loud voice; and he fell at the feet of Jesus and thanked him* (Luke 17:15-16).

Practice these different prayer postures and see how they affect you. You may experiment all you want before prayer, but try to remain in one prayer posture for your entire prayer period unless God moves you otherwise. Spend three minutes (as best you can without hurting yourself) today in each of the postures for a total of 12 minutes. During that time, meditate on any one Scripture passage that you choose.

Journal your experience now. What was it like? Which posture felt most comfortable? Did you feel closer to God with any of the postures? Which posture helped you to "feel" prayerful? Did you sense that you were in God's presence? Did God speak to you?

PREPARATION DAY 2: Continue preparing for the 40 days of prayer by reading Contemplative Prayer - Word, Icon, and Nature, and Lectio Divina under the Prayer Exercises section in Appendix I.

PREPARATION DAY 3

THE DAILY HABIT OF PRAYER

If we want to be "good" at something, we must spend time doing it. If we want to get in shape, we have to get into a routine, and it has to be consistent. If we want to "fall in love with someone" (in this case, God Himself), we must spend time with that person. The same is true for prayer. Like anything else, it takes time. Time is the greatest gift God has given to us, and so often we waste it. Ah, but there is nothing better than "wasting time" in prayer with God. We just have be dedicated because if we are not dedicated, like anything else, it will fall to the wayside.

"The choice of the *time and duration of the prayer* arises from a determined will, revealing the secrets of the heart. One does not undertake contemplative prayer only when one has the time: one makes time for the Lord, with the firm determination not to give up, no matter what trials and dryness one may encounter" (CCC, 2710).

The reality is that we need a time to pray just like we need a place to pray. Our Jewish ancestors and Jesus himself prayed traditionally three times every day. *But I will call upon God, / and the LORD will save me. / At dusk, dawn, and noon, / I will grieve and complain, / and my prayer will be heard* (Psalm 55:17-18). [Daniel] *"continued his custom of going home to kneel in prayer and give thanks to his God in the upper chamber three times a day"* (Daniel 6:11).

The hope and desire is that every moment of every day we are in union with Jesus and God the Father. *Rejoice always. Pray without ceasing. In all circumstances give thanks, for this is the will of God for you in Christ Jesus. Do not quench the Spirit* (1 Thessalonians 5:16-19).

Jesus teaches us to pray every day and gives us a perfect prayer: The Lord's Prayer. *"This is how you are to pray: / Our Father in heaven, / hallowed be your name, / your kingdom come, / your will be done, / on earth as in heaven. / Give us today our daily bread"* (Matthew 6:9-11).

If we want to pray all the time, we have to start by praying at some particular time. It must be every day. It must be made out of a determined act of will. We must not miss it for anything "come hell or high water." The Church in her great wisdom gives us 40 days and 40 nights every year during Lent to form a new habit or break an old one. *Pray40Days* can help you form the new habit of a daily, deep, and profound prayer life.

And he said to them, "Suppose one of you has a friend to whom he goes at midnight and says, 'Friend, lend me three loaves of bread, for a friend of mine has arrived at my house from a journey and I have nothing to offer him,' and he says in reply from within, 'Do not bother me; the door has already been locked and my children and I are already in bed. I cannot get up to give you anything.' I tell you, if he does not get up to give him the loaves because of their friendship, he will get up to give him whatever he needs because of his persistence (Luke 11:5-8).

It is important, every time you pray, that you always pray through, with, and in Christ. He is the way to the Father. It is a good practice to keep your Bible with you. During times of silent meditation, you can go back to the actual Scripture to refresh yourself and remember what it is that you were meditating on. This works well especially if you get distracted during prayer.

The Answer to Prayer. *"And I tell you, ask and you will receive; seek and you will find; knock and the door will be opened to you. For everyone who asks, receives; and the one who seeks, finds; and to the one who knocks, the door will be opened. What father among you would hand his son a snake when he asks for a fish? Or hand him a scorpion when he asks for an egg? If you then, who are wicked, know how to give good gifts to your children, how much more will the Father in heaven give the holy Spirit to those who ask him?"* (Luke 11:9-13).

SOME HELPFUL TIPS:

The following helpful tips are merely suggestions (this entire book is actually just a suggested way to learn to pray meditatively and contemplatively.) The Holy Spirit will be your ultimate Spiritual Director. If there is anything in this book or in these meditations that is not helpful for you, don't feel that you have to use it. The most important maxim is "Do no harm." However, I encourage you to try to do the entire program of *Pray40Days*. If at any point you don't want to continue, or find yourself confused, please seek a wise spiritual person to guide you. At the end of *Pray40Days*, keep what is helpful and dismiss what is not helpful to you.

- Go on TheProdigalFather.org/Pray40Days website to follow along with the meditations in the book or listen online.

- Communicate to others that you will be praying. I have a huge Italian family and every Sunday the family gets together for dinner. Thankfully, my parents have kept my bedroom for me so I still have a "prayer room" in my family home. I have communicated to my whole family that when I go up there and close the door, I am praying and do not want to be disturbed for any reason. They all know that when the door is closed, I am praying. Even my nieces and nephews know that when "Uncle Mike" is upstairs, and his door is closed, he is praying. Believe it or not, they understand, and I have NEVER been disturbed by them! One of my nieces, the youngest, said, “We can’t go up there. Uncle Mike is praying now, but sometimes I think he’s really sleeping.” Sometimes I am!

- Take some time to transition into your sacred space.

- Set a goal for yourself of how long you feel God is calling you to pray. It should be something that you are going to be able to do every day. As with every goal, it has to be doable but also challenge you to really grow. I suggest 10-15 minutes for beginners who have never experienced this type of prayer, half an hour for those who have some experience, and a “Holy Hour” for those who have had many years of praying. When you decide what you would like to commit to, make a resolution with God, and share it with a spiritual director or another wise spiritual person.

- Have someone you can be accountable to. Consider forming a prayer group that will meet once a week to pray together, to review and share your experiences of prayer, and to be accountable to.

- NO matter what, DO NOT leave even a moment early. The enemy will try to get you out of that prayer place. He will offer you a thousand and one different excuses to leave prayer early. Remain steadfast and committed to whatever your resolution was.

- Always have your Bible and journal with you.

- If you find yourself distracted at any time by an outside noise or an interior disturbance or thought, that is normal. Be kind and gentle to yourself every time and calmly return to the passage of Scripture that you are praying.

- What if I fall asleep? It is OK; maybe God just wanted you to rest with Him. I say, “I would rather be asleep in God’s presence than awake anywhere else!” But, if it does become a habit, you may want to consider praying at a different time when you are more awake, or changing your posture, or even taking a nap before you pray.

- Begin with the 5 P’s of Prayer.

- At the end of the meditation or contemplation, take your time transitioning out of prayer and just enjoy the experience.

- Journaling is a wonderful experience of prayer. Be sure to keep your journal safe and private so that you can freely and honestly express yourself to God. You will find yourself writing things that He is speaking to you without even realizing it. It is one way that you can really dialogue with God and "hear His voice."

- Consider ending with an Our Father, Hail Mary, and Glory Be. It could also be a vocal prayer, meditative prayer, or a journal reflection.

PREPARATION DAY 3: Finish preparing for the 40 days of prayer by reading about Praying like a Pirate, Praying with Your Senses, and Scriptural Relaxation in the Prayer Exercises section of Appendix I. Also, take a moment and read tomorrow's Day 1 reading: Luke 11:1-4, The Lord's Prayer.

DAY 1

PRAYING WITH GUIDED MEDITATION

PREPARATION:

5 P's of Prayer: Prepare - know your passage ahead of time and meditate on it throughout the day. When you transition into prayer, take time to breathe, relax, slow down, and just rest. Place - go to your prayer place, room or chair. Ninety percent of prayer is just being there. Posture - we pray using our bodies. Try one of the four postures: standing, sitting, kneeling, or prostrating. Presence - make the Sign of the Cross and invite the Father, the Son, and the Holy Spirit into this time of prayer. Invite God the Father to hold you, the Son to be the Good Shepherd to you, and the Holy Spirit to be Christ in you. Passage - hold the Bible in your lap and realize: "The Word of God is alive." The Father will speak to you!

GUIDED MEDITATION:

Find a quiet room, settle into a spot that will be comfortable, and place your body in a relaxed position, usually without crossed arms or legs. Allow your imagination, fueled by your senses, to enter into the story. Close your eyes as you meditate. At the end of the meditation, do not rush to open your eyes. Let your body tell you when you are ready. Review Guided Meditation under the Prayer Exercises section of "Types of Prayer" in Appendix I.

PRAY NOW:

We will be using a prayer of meditation called imaginative prayer. St. Ignatius believed that one of the greatest gifts that God gives to us in prayer is using our imagination, so feel free to use your imagination. Try to see, hear, touch, taste, and smell. Place yourself in the scene. This prayer experience is with The Lord's Prayer, Luke 11:1-4.

He was praying in a certain place, and when he had finished, one of his disciples said to him, "Lord, teach us to pray just as John taught his disciples." He said to them, "When you pray, say: Father, hallowed be your name, / your kingdom come. / Give us each day our daily bread / and forgive us our sins / for we ourselves forgive everyone in debt to us, / and do not subject us to the final test." (Luke 11:1-4)

He was praying in a certain place. Imagine Jesus in prayer. The Scripture passage says that it is *a certain place.* We don't know exactly where it is, but try to imagine the place. Maybe it is in the Holy Land. Maybe it is a desert. Maybe it is a mountain. Maybe it is a cave. Maybe it is on the sea. Try to imagine yourself in that place. If it is the desert, imagine yourself on that dry land. You can feel the dust on your lips. The heat coming off the ground. The sun beating down brightly. You can hear the air roll across the land, and feel the breeze across your skin. It is a deserted place.

Up high in the mountains is a cave; a light is coming through. As you enter the cave, imagine yourself seeing Jesus. He is standing there praying. *And when he had finished, one of his disciples said to him, "Lord teach us to pray just as John taught his disciples."* Imagine yourself watching as that disciple stands up and with great enthusiasm, begs Jesus, *"Lord teach us to pray just as John taught his disciples*." Maybe, as you enter into this meditation, you have that desire to be taught how to pray. What I want you to do is imagine yourself going into the cave and walking up towards Jesus. He sees you, He looks at you, and He is just waiting for you to ask the same question. At first, you find yourself not having the words. But with trembling, you begin to get the words out and you say, "Lord, teach me how to pray." He looks at you with great love. He looks at all of His disciples and tells them to take a seat.

Then, He says, "*When you pray, say: Father*." And you see, when He says the word *Father*, His face completely light up. His whole mission on earth has been to show you, to reveal to all of us, the true God - who the Father really is. This unconditional loving Father, this Daddy, this Abba. This God who just wants to embrace us, delight in us, and be with us. God is so delighted to have this time with you in prayer. Jesus says, "*Father, hallowed be your name."* Just calling His name is such a holy experience. Say it right now. Just stop and say out loud: "Father... Father... Father…" He hears you. He knows that you want to pray. That you want to experience this communion with Him. *Father, hallowed be your name, / your kingdom come*. Jesus, again, gets this look of joy on His face knowing that as we pray this prayer, *your kingdom come*, God's kingdom right now is coming to us. We are in His midst.

Give us each day our daily bread. Whatever you need from God right now to make it through the day, ask Him - right now. Go ahead, there is nothing too small or nothing too great. Whatever you desire of the Father, ask Him. Ask Him for your daily bread and to *forgive us our sins*. Perhaps there is some sin right now in your life that you are struggling with. It is something that you feel you cannot overcome on your own. The most wonderful thing that we can do is to ask God for forgiveness. Because when we ask Him for forgiveness, we humble ourselves and we commend ourselves to His care. All we have to do is ask for His forgiveness and, all of a sudden, we are wrapped in His unconditional love. So whatever it is; if there is anything you need to be forgiven for, ask Him. Ask for forgiveness, right now. In your heart, out loud. Try to express it to Him.

For we ourselves forgive everyone in debt to us. You realize when you pray this statement, as Jesus looks at you with a little bit of a smirk, that He knows that right now in your heart there is someone that needs to be forgiven. You have been hurt in this life. You have been hurt in this world. Until you forgive each and every person, each and every hurt, each and every moment, you cannot be forgiven. So acknowledge that hurt. Acknowledge that person right now before God. Just say the words: "I forgive… I forgive… I forgive…." If you find yourself not able to do that, ask God for the grace. Say, "Father, help me to forgive."

And do not subject us to the final test. Throughout our day, there will be many temptations, many tests; we are asking right now that God spare us from any temptation or task that would take us away from Him. Especially the final test, that final moment, where we go before God. We ask that we will experience His mercy. That His love will take us beyond any temptation. That we will have the courage and desire to choose Him. Not only in eternal life, but right now in this moment. That we will choose to do His will, to desire His Kingdom to come, to call out His name and know that it is holy. To forgive anyone who has sinned against us, and to experience the forgiveness of God. Take a few moments in **<u>silence</u>** and repeat the word "Father." Call on Him: "Father... Father… Father…."

As you come to the end of this prayer session, take a moment now to **<u>journal</u>** your experience. What was it like to meditate? What was it like to use your senses and imagination to try to see the scene? What was it like to actually dialogue with Jesus? With the Father? What was it like for you to speak to God from your heart with whatever it is that you are going through? What was it like to ask God for your daily bread? What was it like to be forgiven by God? Did you hear God's voice? Did you feel God's presence? Did you feel reassured?

PREPARATION FOR TOMORROW:
Read the following Scripture as you prepare for tomorrow:
Announcement of the Birth of Jesus, Luke 1:26-38.

DAY 2

PRAYING LIKE A PIRATE

PREPARATION:

5 P's of Prayer: Prepare - know your passage ahead of time and meditate on it throughout the day. When you transition into prayer, take time to breathe, relax, slow down, and just rest. Place - go to your prayer place, room or chair. Ninety percent of prayer is just being there. Posture - we pray using our bodies. Try one of the four postures: standing, sitting, kneeling, or prostrating. Presence - make the Sign of the Cross and invite the Father, the Son, and the Holy Spirit into this time of prayer. Invite God the Father to hold you, the Son to be the Good Shepherd to you, and the Holy Spirit to be Christ in you. Passage - hold the Bible in your lap and realize: "The Word of God is alive." The Father will speak to you!

PRAYING LIKE A PIRATE:

ARRR: What does it mean and why is praying like a pirate helpful? Let me introduce you to the acronym, ARRR: Acknowledge, Relate, Receive and Respond to God. (Review Praying like a Pirate in the Prayer Exercises section of "Types of Prayer" in Appendix I.) In this type of prayer, you acknowledge whatever is in your heart. After you acknowledge, you relate those feelings to God. After you acknowledge and relate, you need to receive God's message. Once you receive God's message, you respond to Him. Praying like a pirate is an intimate sharing with God the Father, the Son, the Holy Spirit, and with Mary. St. Ignatius always encourages us to go to Jesus through Mary. The wisdom of this is that Mary is truly our spiritual mother and the model for perfect prayer. The Annunciation was a prayer experience that completely changed the course of her life. Let's look at this model of praying ARRR through Mary's experience.

PRAY NOW:

Today's meditation is based on the Announcement of the Birth of Jesus, Luke 1:26-38.

In the sixth month, the angel Gabriel was sent from God to a town of Galilee called Nazareth, to a virgin betrothed to a man named Joseph, of the house of David, and the virgin's name was Mary. And coming to her, he said, "Hail, favored one! The Lord is with you." But she was greatly troubled at what was said and pondered what sort of greeting this might be. Then the angel said to her, "Do not be afraid, Mary, for you have found favor with God. Behold, you will conceive in your womb and bear a son, and you shall name him Jesus. He will be great and will be called Son of the Most High, and the Lord God will give him the throne of David his father, and he will rule over the house of Jacob forever, and of his kingdom there will be no end." But Mary said to the angel, "How can this be, since I have no relations with a man?" And the angel said to her in reply, "The holy Spirit will come upon you, and the power of the Most High will overshadow you. Therefore the child to be born will be called holy, the Son of God. And behold, Elizabeth, your relative, has also conceived a son in her old age, and this is the sixth month for her who was called barren; for nothing will be impossible for God." Mary said, "Behold, I am the handmaid of the Lord. May it be done to me according to your word." Then the angel departed from her. (Luke 1:26-38)

Acknowledge Mary was a virgin engaged to Joseph. She lived in Nazareth and *the angel Gabriel was sent from God* to her. *The angel said to her, "Do not be afraid, Mary, for you have found favor with God."* Mary probably had a lot of different emotions going on upon hearing this. Maybe she was excited, nervous, unsure, or filled with joy. The first step in ARRR is simply to acknowledge whatever we are thinking or feeling. The important thing is to be authentic. It is being aware of the movements in our heart, the thoughts that we are having and the emotions that we are feeling. We have to be honest with ourselves and with God, and acknowledge how we are truly feeling. Notice how Mary acknowledges her true feelings: *She was greatly troubled at what was said and pondered what sort of greeting this might be.*

Two things are going on in Mary's heart. She was greatly troubled and she pondered. How many times do we do this? We get troubled about something and we ponder. Think about it; this is a very real experience and very relatable to us. What are you feeling right now? Just acknowledge it. Take a moment in **silence** to acknowledge how you are feeling. Pay attention to your feelings. Try to be honest and acknowledge whatever it is that is going on in your heart, in your mind, in your soul, and **journal** your feelings.

It is wonderful to acknowledge and realize what is going on in our hearts. So often, we are running from thing to thing without taking time to be aware of the state of our minds and our souls. At times we may acknowledge our feelings, but we try to sort through them ourselves or work out problems on our own. We try to make sense of the situation or stop ourselves from worrying. To be able to acknowledge what we are feeling is a great first step. It is a gift of grace. But for it to become prayer, we can't stop there. If we don't do the next step, we end up trying to do things ourselves, or make decisions without God's help.

Relate The second step which flows from acknowledging is relating whatever is going on in our hearts and in our minds to God. Mary, being told that she will conceive and bear a son, begins to think some things and is aware of what she is feeling. She takes the next step and expresses [relates] her feelings to God; sharing with God that she is greatly troubled. So, acknowledging her feelings, she then relates her question to God: *"How can this be? Since I have no relations with a man."* To relate means to share with God, in some way, whatever is going on. It is one thing to acknowledge it to ourselves, but it becomes prayer when we relate and share what is going on with God. This is the intimate sharing that St. Teresa of Avila speaks of. It may be just telling God how we are feeling. It may be expressing some emotion of anger, joy, sadness, or peace. It may be a question of doubt, concern, or petition. Whatever it is, relate it to God in prayer. Take a moment in **silence** to relate whatever you are experiencing to God and **journal** the experience.

Receive The third step is often the most difficult and the one that we are likely to skip. We must now receive whatever God wants to give us or do to us at this moment. This is the part of the prayer that requires some listening, waiting, and silence. It is always good to do this part with Scripture because Scripture is the inspired Word of God and the way that God most often speaks to us. You can do this prayer with the Sunday Mass readings, the daily readings, your favorite Bible story, or just open your Bible up to any page. Then wait, listen, and be open to God.

Mary gets a response from God. The angel Gabriel spoke to her in reply, "*The holy Spirit will come upon you and the power of the Most High will overshadow you.*" Instead of Mary trying to figure it all out on her own, she asks God and God gives her an answer. She listened, heard, and received what the angel spoke to her.

Having acknowledged our feelings and related them to God, we must now be willing to receive whatever God wants to give to us or do in us. Mary received a message from the angel Gabriel. She actually got an answer to her question. You, too, if you ask God right now and pray with His Word, will receive an answer. When you are ready, take a moment of **silence** to receive whatever it is God wants to give to you, and **journal** your experience.

Respond Finally, hopefully, you will feel moved to respond in some way. This, too, needs to be authentic. For Mary, it was: "*May it be done to me according to your word.*" For us (hopefully we respond like Mary), it may be a different response. It may be another question. We may express hesitation or doubt. But at some point, when God makes His will known to us, hopefully, we will respond with "yes." What is your reaction to whatever it is He has spoken to you? Take a moment in **silence** and respond to God. Be honest. It may be a simple response, it may be a prayer, it may be a further question, or it may be simply saying: "Yes." **Journal** your experience.

You have now experienced a wonderful way of relating to God. Notice how through this simple process of acknowledge, relate, receive and respond (ARRR), you are being consoled. You will have a clearer sense of direction and a felt experience of God. This wonderful type of prayer can be done throughout the day. May you always be in intimate conversation with God like Mary was. As Teresa of Avila once said: "Mental prayer, in my opinion, is nothing else than an intimate sharing between friends; it means taking time frequently to be alone with Him who we know loves us." (Kavanaugh, 1987)

PREPARATION FOR TOMORROW:
Read the following Scripture as you prepare for tomorrow:
Psalm 23.

DAY 3

PRAYING WITH LECTIO DIVINA

PREPARATION:

5 P's of Prayer: Prepare - know your passage ahead of time and meditate on it throughout the day. When you transition into prayer, take time to breathe, relax, slow down, and just rest. Place - go to your prayer place, room or chair. Ninety percent of prayer is just being there. Posture - we pray using our bodies. Try one of the four postures: standing, sitting, kneeling, or prostrating. Presence - make the Sign of the Cross and invite the Father, the Son, and the Holy Spirit into this time of prayer. Invite God the Father to hold you, the Son to be the Good Shepherd to you, and the Holy Spirit to be Christ in you. Passage - hold the Bible in your lap and realize: "The Word of God is alive." The Father will speak to you!

LECTIO DIVINA:

A type of prayer in which one is reading Scripture, meditating or pondering Scripture, praying vocally with God, and contemplating in silence. Review Lectio Divina in the Prayer Exercises section of "Types of Prayer" in Appendix I.

PRAY NOW:

The first step of *Lectio Divina* is *Lectio*, which is to read. Lectio should always be done with Scripture and in the presence of God - that is what makes it divine reading. It should never be forgotten that the Word of God is the subject of divine reading. It is through praying in a very personal way with God that this truly becomes an experience of God. We read in Psalm 119:105: *Your word is a lamp for my feet, / a light for my path.* You can pray with any Scripture when you do Lectio Divina. The Sunday readings or the daily readings are a great source.

It is always good to hold your Bible on your lap; there is something about holding the Word of God that I think helps us focus on it and really reverence it. The same is true for a physical journal. There is nothing like it, so if you have a Bible and a journal, hold on to them now.

As Lectio Divina was developed over the centuries, one of the things that remained consistent was the first step: reading the passage, over and over. The first time slowly, a second time more slowly, then a third time even more slowly. You may read the Scripture passage out loud during one of the times. Finally, you might read it a fourth time until your heart or mind rests on a Word, a phrase, or passage.

For this exercise, we will use Psalm 23.

The LORD is my shepherd;
there is nothing I lack.
In green pastures he makes me lie down;
to still waters he leads me;
he restores my soul.
He guides me along right paths
for the sake of his name.
Even though I walk through the valley of the shadow of death,
I will fear no evil, for you are with me;
your rod and your staff comfort me.

You set a table before me
in front of my enemies;
You anoint my head with oil;
my cup overflows.
Indeed, goodness and mercy will pursue me
all the days of my life;
I will dwell in the house of the LORD
for endless days.
(Psalm 23)

This is a familiar Psalm, but maybe this is the first time you have actually heard it or read it straight through. Read it again a second time, a little bit slower.

Did you enjoy it more the second time around? Read it a third time, even slower.

Read it one last time. Maybe you paid attention to different parts of Psalm 23 or noticed things that you didn't notice the first or second time around. It will probably happen again in this next reading. So read it one last time, very slowly.

Take some time in **silence** with this reading, and then **journal** any Words, phrases, or ideas that called out to you. The Word of God, we believe, is alive; so right now, God is speaking to you as you read this. He is saying something to you right now that He has never said before or will ever say again. Right now, the Word is alive. God speaks to you.

The second step of Lectio Divina is *meditatio*, which is meditation. So let's spend some time meditating upon Psalm 23. When you meditate on this Psalm, it is a time to really use your mind, to use your imagination, to think about it, to ponder, and to apply it to your own life. To wrestle with it, to question it, and to ask God what it really means for you. With that in mind, we will walk through this meditation together.

The Lord is my shepherd. I think this is the part that we all love, that we have this Good Shepherd that will lead us and guide us. *There is nothing I lack.* Wow! Have you ever thought about this before? You lack nothing. Right now, with Jesus as your shepherd, you lack nothing. *There is nothing I lack*, we have everything that we need, we have a good shepherd to guide us.

In green pastures he makes me lie down. Try to think about this, a restful image of the green pasture. Have you ever done that on a warm summer day, laid out in the grass in the sun? Such a relaxing feeling.

To still waters He leads me. Imagine yourself by that water, completely still. There is a beauty in water. Imagine yourself drinking from a spring. Thirsty, and being restored. *He restores my soul.* I think so many times our souls feel beaten up by life - tired. Right now, He is refreshing and restoring your soul.

He guides me along right paths / for the sake of his name. Maybe there is a decision you have to make right now in life, and you just realize that the Good Shepherd is going to guide you. He guides you along the right path. Maybe this passage, right now, just brings you a sense of assurance or trust that He is guiding you.

Even though I walk through the valley of the shadow of death. My grandfather told me before he died that this was a prayer that he would often recite to himself, over and over. When he was in World War II, in the darkest of times, he would repeat this, "*Even though I walk through the valley of the shadow of death, / I will fear no evil, for you are with me.*" What are you going through in life right now that is difficult? Is this a time in your life that is like the shadow of death? Well, even though we *walk through the valley of the shadow of death, / I will fear no evil.* Why? *For you are with me.* He is with you right now. Whatever you are going through in life, whatever dark valley you are walking through, you have the Good Shepherd right with you.

Your rod and your staff comfort me. What does this mean: *Your rod and your staff comfort me.* Shepherds often use the rod and staff for protection, so maybe we can think of that as protection. With His rod and His staff, the Good Shepherd is protecting you from any evil. Our Heavenly Father who governs all things can keep you safe from anything that would do you harm, from anything that would keep you from being with Him. With His rod and staff, He comforts you.

You set a table before me. What is it like to share a meal with God? To have everything that you need? All the food is provided for you. Not only is there food, but there is wine. There is gladness and there is joy. Imagine being at that table with God.

In front of my enemies. Is there anybody that you are afraid of right now? Is there anybody that has been an enemy to you, that has bullied you, or that has been harsh to you? Imagine yourself, right now, being protected. That God has chosen you right now because you are reading this, and praying with this, and meditating on this. There is something special about you. God has chosen you for this.

You anoint my head with oil. Oil is a sign of protection and of being chosen. When you were baptized your head was anointed with oil. If you have been confirmed, your head was anointed with oil and you were sealed with the gifts of the Holy Spirit. Meditate upon this reality. Imagine Jesus right now anointing your head with oil.

My cup overflows. When you look at everything that you have in life and all that God provides for you, gratitude tends to be overwhelming.

Indeed goodness and mercy will pursue me / all the days of my life. What does this mean for you, that all the days of your life, God is going to pursue you with goodness and mercy? Isn't that a wonderful thing? *I will dwell in the house of the LORD / for endless days.* As you come to the end of this part of meditation, take a moment in **silence** to think about what that means to *dwell in the house of the LORD / for endless days.* You never have to leave, you can always be here with Him in His house with this meal. The Good Shepherd protecting you. Lacking nothing.

Take some time now to **journal**. What was most vivid for you? What was most real for you? What was it like to experience and meditate upon the Good Shepherd in Psalm 23?

The third step of Lectio Divina is *oratio* or prayer. Chances are that after meditating upon this passage there is something that stood out for you. Maybe there is a question you want to ask of God or maybe there is something you feel He is saying to you. In some way or another, allow yourself to pray with God. To talk this over with God. To speak to Him, to question Him, and to let Him respond to you. Take a moment of **silence** and **journal** when you are ready. Let whatever comes to mind flow through you and be written out on the page. Often times, without even realizing it, we will write the very thing that God is speaking to us. So spend some time in prayer and journal what God speaks.

The fourth step in *Lectio Divina* is *contemplatio* or contemplation. This fourth step is very simple. Sometimes it is a difficult step for people because it involves silence. It is doing nothing. It is just resting. Take a moment to savor it and take it all in. This is your opportunity to rest. You don't have to say anything or do anything. Just be with God. It might help to look at the Scripture passage once more to contemplate a Word or phrase. Or read through your journal and rest with whatever God is speaking to you. Take a moment now to rest with it, to enjoy this experience and spend some time in **silence**. When you are ready, **journal** your experience.

PREPARATION FOR TOMORROW:
Read the following Scripture as you prepare for tomorrow:
The Parable of the Lost Son, Luke 15:11-32.

DAY 4

PRAYING WITH YOUR SENSES

PREPARATION:

5 P's of Prayer: Prepare - know your passage ahead of time and meditate on it throughout the day. When you transition into prayer, take time to breathe, relax, slow down, and just rest. Place - go to your prayer place, room or chair. Ninety percent of prayer is just being there. Posture - we pray using our bodies. Try one of the four postures: standing, sitting, kneeling, or prostrating. Presence - make the Sign of the Cross and invite the Father, the Son, and the Holy Spirit into this time of prayer. Invite God the Father to hold you, the Son to be the Good Shepherd to you, and the Holy Spirit to be Christ in you. Passage - hold the Bible in your lap and realize: "The Word of God is alive." The Father will speak to you!

PRAYING WITH YOUR FIVE SENSES:

This type of prayer uses your senses, physically and imaginatively (seeing, hearing, smelling, tasting, and touching). Review Praying with Your Senses in the Prayer Exercises section of "Types of Prayer" in Appendix I.

PRAY NOW:

When we use our senses and experience the Word of God, we can enter in a very real, profound, and tangible way into the scenes of the Gospel. Often times, people say they don't experience God in prayer, have never seen Him or heard His voice. This is one of the ways that He can come to you and be very real to you. When we pray with our senses and our imagination through the Holy Spirit, we can enter into God and allow God to enter into us. As with all prayer, the focus is never on us but on God and what God is doing in us and in our world right now.

For this prayer experience, we will pray with our senses using The Parable of the Lost Son, Luke 15:11-32. First, read through this passage using your sense of sight. As you read, ask the Holy Spirit to help you to see what God wants you to see, physically and spiritually.

Then he said, "A man had two sons, and the younger son said to his father, 'Father, give me the share of your estate that should come to me.' So the father divided the property between them. After a few days, the younger son collected all his belongings and set off to a distant country where he squandered his inheritance on a life of dissipation. When he had freely spent everything, a severe famine struck that country, and he found himself in dire need. So he hired himself out to one of the local citizens who sent him to his farm to tend the swine. And he longed to eat his fill of the pods on which the swine fed, but nobody gave him any. Coming to his senses he thought, 'How many of my father's hired workers have more than enough food to eat, but here am I, dying from hunger. I shall get up and go to my father and I shall say to him, "Father, I have sinned against heaven and against you. I no longer deserve to be called your son; treat me as you would treat one of your hired workers."' So he got up and went back to his father. While he was still a long way off, his father caught sight of him, and was filled with compassion. He ran to his son, embraced him and kissed him. His son said to him, 'Father, I have sinned against heaven and against you; I no longer deserve to be called your son.' But his father ordered his servants, 'Quickly bring the finest robe and put it on him; put a ring on his finger and sandals on his feet. Take the fattened calf and slaughter it. Then let us celebrate with a feast, because this son of mine was dead, and has come to life again; he was lost, and has been found.' Then the celebration began. Now the older son had been out in the field and, on his way back, as he neared the house, he heard the sound of music and dancing. He called one of the servants and asked what this might mean. The servant said to him, 'Your brother has returned and your father has slaughtered the fattened calf because he has him back safe and sound.' He became angry, and when he refused to enter the house, his father came out and pleaded with him. He said to his father in reply, 'Look, all these years I served you and not once did I disobey your orders; yet you never gave me even a young goat to feast on with my friends. But when your son returns who swallowed up your property with prostitutes, for him you slaughter the fattened calf.' He said to him, 'My son, you are here with me always; everything I have is yours. But now we must celebrate and rejoice, because your brother was dead and has come to life again; he was lost and has been found.'" (Luke 15:11-32)

Then he said, "A man had two sons." Try and see this man and his two sons. *"And the younger son said to his father, 'Father, give me the share of your estate that should come to me.' So the father divided the property between them."* Try to see the father's face. What did it look like when he did this? Does he look upset, sad, or at peace?

After a few days, the younger son collected all his belongings and set off to a distant country where he squandered his inheritance on a life of dissipation. Try to picture this scene, like a movie scene, of the younger son collecting all his things from the house, all his belongings; whatever is important to him. He takes off for a distant country. Then he squanders it all, loses it on a life of dissipation. *When he had freely spent everything, a severe famine struck that country, and he found himself in dire need.* What does someone in dire need look like?

So he hired himself out to one of the local citizens who sent him to his farm to tend the swine. Try to picture him out there on a farm - with the pigs, in the mud, tending them. *And he longed to eat his fill of the pods on which the swine fed, but nobody gave him any.* Look at his face and see the desperation. *Coming to his senses he thought, 'How many of my father's hired workers have more than enough food to eat, but here am I, dying from hunger.'* He came to his senses. He could see the shape that he was in. Try to picture him, completely destitute, in the mud, completely broken, hungry, and desperate.

'I shall get up and go to my father and I shall say to him, "Father, I have sinned against heaven and against you. I no longer deserve to be called your son; treat me as you would treat one of your hired workers."' So he got up and went back to his father. Now imagine this, try to picture him standing up and beginning the journey back.

W*hile he was still a long way off, his father caught sight of him.* Try to see off in the distance, his young son coming. He *was filled with compassion. He ran to his son, embraced him and kissed him.* Can you see the father running to his son? Can you see what his face must look like? The relief, as he runs to him, embraces him, and kisses him. *His son said to him, 'Father, I have sinned against heaven and against you; I no longer deserve to be called your son.' But his father ordered his servants, 'Quickly bring the finest robe and put it on him.'*

Imagine this beautiful robe being placed on the son. *'Put a ring on his finger and sandals on his feet.'* Picture the gold ring he places on his finger, because he has his son back. He gives his son sandals for his feet so he is not barefoot. *'Take the fattened calf and slaughter it. Then let us celebrate with a feast, because this son of mine was dead, and has come to life again; he was lost, and has been found.' Then the celebration began.*

Take a moment to remember what you saw. What were some of the vivid images you saw of the father, the son, or the brother? Take a moment in **silence** to reflect on that and when you are ready, **journal** your experience.

Now apply your sense of hearing. Not only hearing the people, places, and things, but what God may be saying to you. Imagine you can hear Jesus' voice speaking this parable to you: *"A man had two sons and the younger son said to his father, 'Father, give me the share of your estate that should come to me.'"* Can you hear the tone of the son's voice? Or yours? How does it sound? Listen to the echo.

So he hired himself out to the local citizen who sent him to the farm to tend the swine." Try to hear now - What does it sound like for him to be tending the swine? Can you hear them stomping through the mud? Can you hear the noises that they are making? Can you hear the vicious way that they eat? Can you hear the growling in the younger son's stomach?

Again, *coming to his senses he thought, 'How many of my father's hired workers have more than enough food to eat, but here am I dying from hunger.' So he gets up and goes back to his father.* Try to hear the footsteps.

While he was still a long way off, his father caught sight of him, and was filled with compassion. He ran to his son. What does that sound like? This old man running to his son. You can hear their clothes as they embrace. The sound of a tender kiss on his cheek. Then you hear the son say, *'Father, I have sinned against heaven and against you; I no longer deserve to be called your son.'* Can you hear the agony in his voice?

But his father ordered his servants. Listen to the father's voice. *'Quickly bring the finest robe and put it on him; put a ring on his finger and sandals on his feet. Take the fattened calf and slaughter it. Then let us celebrate with a feast, because this son of mine was dead, and has come to life again; he was lost, and has been found.'* Listen to the father's voice so full of joy. Now you hear the sound of the celebration as everyone is coming together and there is music and dancing. Take a moment in **silence** to listen and hear the sound of that celebration. **Journal** how it felt to sense God in this Scriptural passage.

Now use your sense of smell. Start with the most obvious, when he hired himself out to tend to the swine. Try to imagine what it must smell like to be with the swine, with the pigs in that muck. It is this smell that gets to him when he comes to his senses.

Now move forward as he decides to go home. As we transition from the smell of the swine, imagine him leaving the pig pen, going out into the country, and smelling the fresh air. Maybe he smells the fragrance of flowers or the land. Maybe he smells his home. Sometimes, there is a fragrance to a home that is so inviting; you feel good there. What did it feel like to be back and smell his father's home?

Imagine the transition from smelling the swine to smelling clean again. Smell the clean clothes, clean sandals. Smell the leather on his sandals.

Transition to the celebration. What must that have smelled like? He smells the fattened calf being slaughtered. Can you smell the meat cooking? Can you smell the bread baking? Can you smell the wine? All the smells that come with music, dancing, and celebrating. Take a moment in **silence** to linger on that smell, what it must be like to be home, to have a meal prepared and cooked for you. Engage your sense of smell. When you are ready, **journal** your experience.

What can you taste as you read through this passage? There is not much explicitly that the son tastes. But think of it as an emotional taste, such as a bad taste in your mouth. So think of the son's taste in his mouth as he left the estate, as he took everything that belonged to him and went off to that distant country. At first, everything tasted good. But the longer he was there, the poorer he got, the more destitute he got; and the food began to taste worse and worse until he had no food. We hear that nobody gave him any. Coming to his senses, he tastes that he is dying of hunger. Think a little about the taste in his mouth when he went back home. The humble pie he had to eat. What is the taste like in his mouth as he goes back to his father? Maybe his stomach was anxious and upset. But quickly that taste transforms as his father is not upset with him, but delights in him.

Now the celebration and the tasting begin. Try to imagine everything he must have tasted at that moment. Imagine him eating tender meat after all those months of starving. Imagine the wine; taste the wine. Imagine the desserts. Imagine all the food he got to taste after being so barren. Maybe at this time your mouth is beginning to water as you think about the taste of food. Spend a moment of **silence**, lingering in the taste. When you are ready, **journal** your experience.

Let's focus on our sense of touch that is so powerful in this passage. In the beginning, touch was absent. I imagine as the son took off from his father that he left with no final embrace, no final hug. He probably just took off. There was a time when he did not want anyone to touch him - until he lived this life of dissipation and began to experience the lower pleasures of touch, the lower pleasures of prostitution and the base desires. After he freely spent everything, his next touch would be with the swine. Imagine him bumping into the pigs and walking through the mud. That touch would begin to change him as he comes to his senses and starts to go home. I imagine that on the son's journey home, although he was anxious, there was probably some relief in his body just knowing that he was leaving all that behind and going back to his father.

While he was still a long way off, his father caught sight of him, and was filled with compassion. He ran to his son, embraced him and kissed him. This is the moment where touch is so profound. Try to imagine this sense of touch between a father and son who have been missing each other for so long. This really is an image of God the Father holding us. If you have been away, just let God hold you, let God run to you, let God embrace you and kiss you. What is it like to be held by God? What does it feel like to be in His embrace? What does it feel like to have Him kiss you on the cheek?

Spend some time in **silence** to experience that touch of being held by the Father as He embraces you, kisses you, puts the robe on you, puts the ring on you, and puts sandals on your feet. What is it like to be touched and held by God the Father? At the end of this entire prayer experience, spend some time talking to the Father. Tell Him what you heard, what you saw, what it was like to be held by Him, embraced by Him, and loved by Him unconditionally. When you are ready, **journal** your experience.

PREPARATION FOR TOMORROW:
We will pray with Sunday Mass.

PRAYING WITH SUNDAY MASS

Every time we go to Mass, we get to experience God. It is really a wonderful and amazing thing if we only realize it. Preparing for Mass, just like we prepare for prayer, can really help us enter into Mass and experience the risen Christ, right there at Mass. It is also a wonderful experience after Mass to spend a few moments journaling. Whatever you held onto, whatever you experienced, or whenever you most felt Christ present during the Mass, journal that. That is a wonderful gift that God is giving to you.

PREPARATION BEFORE SUNDAY MASS:

Today's preparation for the Mass will be to realize that at every Mass we have an opportunity to ask God for anything that we want - to present in prayer our greatest hopes and desires. We have the opportunity at Mass to present anything that is going on in our life, anyone that is in need of prayer, anyone that has asked us to pray for them, anything that we want to pray for. So it is important that when we go to Mass, we go with a prayer intention. That we actually go with something we want to ask of God. Either we are praying for ourselves, or for someone else, or for the entire world. What an amazing opportunity we have at every Mass to ask God for anything. So don't hold back, ask for your heart's desire!

You may not know it, but at the beginning of Mass, there is a time for presenting whatever your personal prayer may be. The first time the priest says, "Let us pray," that is not just a cue for the book bearer to come. When he says, "Let us pray," there is supposed to be a moment of silence which is called the Collect. During this moment of silence, the priest is collecting all the prayers of the people, the prayers of the entire congregation there in the church.

Notice that during the Collect, as he gathers everyone's prayers, the priest has his arms in what is called Oran's position. He is praying in the person of Christ, offering the prayers of the people to the Father. But in order for that to happen, you have to have a prayer! You actually have to have an intention. You have to state it in your heart and your mind during that moment. Sometimes it comes and goes so fast that we are not even ready for it. But if you prepare before Mass and know what it is you want to pray for, then, when the priest says, "Let us pray," you will be ready to make your prayer known to God. And, as he lifts his hands and says the opening prayer, your prayers will be joined to that of the general assembly and offered to God. I want you to think about that today before you go to Mass. If you could ask God for anything, what would you ask Him for?

The most amazing thing is that He might even answer your prayer during this Mass. So today, your prayer experience will be to fully, actively, and consciously participate in the Liturgy.

AFTER SUNDAY MASS:

What did you ask God for during Mass? What was your prayer when the priest said, "Let us pray," and collected all the prayers of the assembly? Did He answer your prayer as He spoke to you in Word, Sacrament, Liturgy, songs, chants, prayers, or the Eucharist? Did you sense that He answered you?

Take some time now to **journal** your experience of when you felt most present with God at Mass today. Also journal what you asked of God, what your petition was, because you may find that if He didn't seem to answer it right at this time, He will later on.

PREPARATION FOR TOMORROW:
Read the following Scripture as you prepare for tomorrow:
The Father's Plan of Salvation, Ephesians 1:3-12.

DAY 5

PRAYING WITH CONTEMPLATIVE PRAYER

PREPARATION:

5 P's of Prayer: Prepare - know your passage ahead of time and meditate on it throughout the day. When you transition into prayer, take time to breathe, relax, slow down, and just rest. Place - go to your prayer place, room or chair. Ninety percent of prayer is just being there. Posture - we pray using our bodies. Try one of the four postures: standing, sitting, kneeling, or prostrating. Presence - make the Sign of the Cross and invite the Father, the Son, and the Holy Spirit into this time of prayer. Invite God the Father to hold you, the Son to be the Good Shepherd to you, and the Holy Spirit to be Christ in you. Passage - hold the Bible in your lap and realize: "The Word of God is alive." The Father will speak to you!

CONTEMPLATIVE PRAYER:

Contemplative prayer is a type of prayer that involves silence and simply being in the presence of God. Review Contemplative Prayer and praying with the Word (Prayer Exercises) in "Types of Prayer" in Appendix I.

PRAY NOW:

The Word we will pray contemplatively with is The Father's Plan of Salvation, Ephesians 1:3-12. Read the passage in silence once very slowly. Then begin again and read it slower until you find a Word or a phrase that you feel God is speaking to you. Remain in silence repeating this Word over and over in your heart. If you get distracted, and you will, remember that the virtue is in returning back to the Word, no matter how many times it takes. Continue repeating the phrase over and over again until you come to a place of rest in the Word. Remain in silence, peace, and stillness for as long as the moment lasts. If there is fruit, remain with that Word or phrase. However, if you find the Word or phrase is no longer "working" for you, continue on until God speaks to you in another Word or phrase. It may help to speak it out loud if you are especially distracted. Repeat it over and over again until you become settled and remain in silence.

Contemplative prayer is an intense focused time on the Word. If you notice your self moving back into vocal prayer or meditative prayer, gently try and let that go so that you can remain in this heightened state of contemplative prayer. Remember, that as long as you remain in prayer "all is grace." God will use it all to bring you closer to Him. The Holy Spirit will be your guide into this deep and abiding prayer with Christ and the Father. Read the Word now.

Blessed be the God and Father of our Lord Jesus Christ, who has blessed us in Christ with every spiritual blessing in the heavens, as he chose us in him, before the foundation of the world, to be holy and without blemish before him. In love he destined us for adoption to himself through Jesus Christ, in accord with the favor of his will, for the praise of the glory of his grace that he granted us in the beloved.

In him we have redemption by his blood, the forgiveness of transgressions, in accord with the riches of his grace that he lavished upon us. In all wisdom and insight, he has made known to us the mystery of his will in accord with his favor that he set forth in him as a plan for the fullness of times, to sum up all things in Christ, in heaven and on earth.

In him we were also chosen, destined in accord with the purpose of the One who accomplishes all things according to the intention of his will, so that we might exist for the praise of his glory, we who first hoped in Christ. (Ephesians 1:3-12)

Remember, contemplation is not thinking, rather, it is a state of being; resting with a Word or phrase. Try it now. Spend time in silence and read until a Word or phrase stands out or touches you; simply rest with that. If you are distracted, go back to it and repeat it. If you sense you want to move on, slowly continue reading until the next Word or phrase. Spend time doing this now. The following is an example of what this might look like.

Blessed be the God and Father of our Lord Jesus Christ, who has blessed us in Christ with every spiritual blessing in the heavens. [Take a moment in silence to contemplate how God has blessed us with every spiritual blessing in the heavens.]

As he chose us in him ... [Take a moment in silence to contemplate how God has blessed us with every spiritual blessing in the heavens.]

Before the foundation of the world, to be holy and without blemish before him. In love he destined us for adoption ... [Take a moment in silence to contemplate how God has blessed us with every spiritual blessing in the heavens.]

To himself through Jesus Christ, in accord with the favor of his will, for the praise of the glory of his grace that he granted us in the beloved. In him we have redemption ... [Take a moment in silence to contemplate how God has blessed us with every spiritual blessing in the heavens.]

By his blood, the forgiveness of transgressions, in accord with the riches of his grace that he lavished upon us.

[Take a moment in silence to contemplate how God has blessed us with every spiritual blessing in the heavens.]

In all wisdom and insight, he has made known to us the mystery of his will in accord with his favor that he set forth in him as a plan for the fullness of times, to sum up all things in Christ, in heaven and on earth.

In him we were also chosen, destined in accord with the purpose of the One who accomplishes all things according to the intention of his will, so that we might exist for the praise of his glory, we who first hoped in Christ. We who first hoped in Christ. [Take a moment of silence to contemplate that phrase - *we who first hoped in Christ.*]

Spend time in **silence** contemplating on this or any Word or phrase from this passage. **Journal** your experience of contemplating with God's Word.

PREPARATION FOR TOMORROW:
Read the following Scripture as you prepare for tomorrow:
Psalm 139.

DAY 6

PRAYING WITH SCRIPTURAL RELAXATION

PREPARATION:

5 P's of Prayer: Prepare - know your passage ahead of time and meditate on it throughout the day. When you transition into prayer, take time to breathe, relax, slow down, and just rest. Place - go to your prayer place, room or chair. Ninety percent of prayer is just being there. Posture - we pray using our bodies. Try one of the four postures: standing, sitting, kneeling, or prostrating. Presence - make the Sign of the Cross and invite the Father, the Son, and the Holy Spirit into this time of prayer. Invite God the Father to hold you, the Son to be the Good Shepherd to you, and the Holy Spirit to be Christ in you. Passage - hold the Bible in your lap and realize: "The Word of God is alive." The Father will speak to you!

SCRIPTURE RELAXATION:

The focus of this exercise is Christ healing us and the Word of God helping us to change our thinking patterns. Review Scriptural Relaxation in the Prayer Exercises section of "Types of Prayer" in Appendix I. You can also do the audio version of Scriptural Relaxation found in TheProdigalFather.org/Pray40Days.

PRAY NOW:

The following is a scriptural relaxation based on Psalm 139. Try to find a place that is quiet where you will not be disturbed. Find a position that is comfortable where you will not have to move or adjust. Either sit or lie down. Begin by closing your eyes for a moment. Or just gaze, unfocused. During this time, allow yourself to relax. As I lead you through this relaxation and the Scripture passage, you will find yourself dwelling in great peace because it is the Word of God. Try to be aware of each feeling before moving on to each step; each relaxation step helps the next. Remain in silence, peace, and stillness for as long as the moment lasts. If you fall asleep, that's OK. I always say I would rather be asleep in God's presence than awake anywhere else.

First, begin by reading the Scripture passage. Just meditate upon the Words and listen to them, let them sink in. After you do that, begin to do the relaxation.

LORD, you have probed me, you know me:
you know when I sit and stand;
you understand my thoughts from afar.
You sift through my travels and my rest;
with all my ways you are familiar.
Even before a word is on my tongue,
LORD, you know it all.
Behind and before you encircle me
and rest your hand upon me.
Such knowledge is too wonderful for me,
far too lofty for me to reach.

Where can I go from your spirit?
From your presence, where can I flee?
If I ascend to the heavens, you are there;
if I lie down in Sheol, there you are.
If I take the wings of dawn
and dwell beyond the sea,
Even there your hand guides me,
your right hand holds me fast.
If I say, "Surely darkness shall hide me,
and night shall be my light"—
Darkness is not dark for you,
and night shines as the day.
Darkness and light are but one.

You formed my inmost being;
you knit me in my mother's womb.
I praise you, because I am wonderfully made;
wonderful are your works!
My very self you know.
My bones are not hidden from you,
When I was being made in secret,
fashioned in the depths of the earth.
Your eyes saw me unformed;
in your book all are written down;
my days were shaped, before one came to be.

How precious to me are your designs, O God;
how vast the sum of them!
Were I to count them, they would outnumber the sands;
when I complete them, still you are with me.
When you would destroy the wicked, O God,
the bloodthirsty depart from me!
Your foes who conspire a plot against you

are exalted in vain.

Do I not hate, LORD, those who hate you?
Those who rise against you, do I not loathe?
With fierce hatred I hate them,
enemies I count as my own.

Probe me, God, know my heart;
try me, know my thoughts.
See if there is a wicked path in me;
lead me along an ancient path.
(Psalm 139)

LORD, you have probed me, you know me: / you know when I sit and stand; / you understand my thoughts from afar. / You sift through my travels and my rest; / with all my ways you are familiar. The Lord is familiar with all of your ways. He is sifting through your thoughts right now. He is with you as you sit or lie down. He understands your thoughts. He is able to bring you to rest. He knows what you need.

Feel your body sink down deep.... This body that God has given to you, created, molded, and shaped. [Pause for a moment of silence.]

Begin with your feet.... Imagine these feet that have walked from the very time you were a child. God has taught you to walk upon them. These feet now rest for a brief while.... Allow them to sink down.... Feel the warmth upon them.... Know that the Lord has shaped your feet. He continues to shape and support them. Right now allow God to ease any tension.... Imagine the Lord taking your feet in His hands.... First your left foot, pressing it and blessing it.... Then your right foot.... He squeezes your foot, blesses your foot, and gently lays it down.... [Pause for a moment of silence.]

Even there your hand guides me, / your right hand holds me fast. Breathe in deeply and hold that breathe for a moment.... Release and breathe out.... Breathe in and hold it.... He breathes the Holy Spirit into you.... Breathe out. Breathe in.... He invites you to breathe out any worries or anxieties; breathe out to release them.... One last time He invites you to breathe in the Holy Spirit, deep into your lungs, opening them as deep as you can and holding it for a moment.... Breathe out... You release all of your tensions, all of your worries, all of your anxieties. All of your sinfulness is purified.... [Pause for a moment of silence.]

If I say "Surely darkness shall hide me, / and night shall be my light" - / Darkness is not dark for you, / and night shines as the day. Imagine Him now taking His hand and first blessing your neck and throat.... Pressing and releasing.... You feel very heavy.... All the muscles in your neck and shoulders release.... He has you in the palm of His hand, in complete control.... [Pause for a moment of silence.]

Darkness is not dark for you, / and night shines as the day. / Darkness and light are but one. The Lord takes His two hands and lays them over your entire face, covering your eyes, your nose, and your mouth.... [Pause for a moment of silence.]

Darkness is not dark for you, / and night shines as the day. He lays His hands on your forehead.... Gently pressing, you feel the warmth of His hands.... Heavy, warm, gentle, blessing, cleansing your mind, and purifying your thoughts.... Granting you the peace that only God can give. [Pause for a moment of silence.]

He takes His hands and His fingers and He places them on your eyes.... Gently massaging and rubbing the area around your eyes and your eyebrows.... All the tension releases.... Your eyes once more become His eyes.... Eyes that will see and take in all the beauty of creation.... Eyes that will see as He does and not as you do.... Eyes that will see the light, even in darkness.... [Pause for a moment of silence.]

He then moves down to your nose, presses, and massages.... Strokes the bridge of your nose down to the sides of your cheeks.... Breathe in.... Breathe out.... This nose can now smell so clearly and crisply; a fragrance of God.... The fragrance of the world and the fragrance around you.... He relieves any pressure from any sinuses or allergies. You can breathe clear, gently, and effortlessly.... Breathe in through your nose.... Breathe out.... [Pause for a moment of silence.]

He places His hands upon your mouth now.... He massages your cheekbones and He blesses your mouth.... He forgives any words that you may have spoken against Him or against others.... He signs it with the cross and asks that these lips be used to proclaim His Word.... [Pause for a moment of silence.]

My bones are not hidden from you, / When I was being made in secret, / fashioned in the depths of the earth. He places His hands over your entire face.... This beautiful image of God.... The face of Christ.... Your face is beautiful, created in His image.... Now after He has touched and blessed it, your face begins to radiate once more, with joy and goodness.... [Pause for a moment of silence.]

Your eyes saw me unformed; / in your book all are written down; / my days were shaped, before one came to be. He then takes His fingers and lays them on your temple.... Gently massaging and pressing; easing the tension.... You feel warmth, peace, relief, and rest. [Pause for a moment of silence.]

He takes His fingers and lays them first over your ears.... *How precious to me are your designs, O God; / how vast the sum of them!* He speaks these Words into your ears: “You are my beloved in whom I am well pleased.... I am in you, and you are in me.... I am in you, and you are in me.... I am in you, and you are in me.” Looking up to heaven, He asks God to open your ears once more.... That you may hear and receive His Word.... Your ears feel warm and alive.... You can hear every tiny sound around you; not as distractions, but as part of God's symphony.... Every sound reminding you of His voice in creation....[Pause for a moment of silence.]

He takes His hands and lays them on your head; over your mind.... The warmth of His hand radiates all the way to the back of your head and down your spine.... [Pause for a moment of silence.]

How precious to me are your designs, O God; / how vast the sum of them! / Were I to count them, they would outnumber the sands; / when I complete them, still you are with me. Your whole mind He knows.... He knows all of your thoughts; before ever one of them even came into being He knew them. He is able to sort them and order them.... Make them holy, bring forth those thoughts that are good, and cast out any that are evil.... [Pause for a moment of silence.]

His hands lay upon you.... You can feel His being.... His presence.... It radiates now from the top of your head to the inside of your mind, down your spine, through your chest, into your belly, to your legs, to your knees, to your feet, to your toes.... [Pause for a moment of silence.]

Probe me, God, know my heart; / try me, know my thoughts. Once more He blesses your forehead.... He lays His hand upon your heart.... *Probe me, God, know my heart.* Imagine Him taking your heart gently into His hands.... Taking your stony heart from your chest.... Receiving it into His and taking His most sacred heart and placing it into your chest.... [Pause for a moment of silence.]

See if there is a wicked path in me; / and lead me along an ancient path. He blesses your heart.... His heart and yours beat as one.... "I am in you, and you are in me.... I am in you, and you are in me".... Your heart beats so rhythmically, so purposefully.... Your whole body rests now in Him.... Your mind, your thoughts, your feelings, and your spirit dwell in Him, rest in Him, are at peace in Him.... Hold me, Lord, and know my thoughts.... [Pause for a moment of silence.]

You know when I sit and I stand; / you understand my thoughts from afar. / You sift through my travels and my rest; / with all my ways you are familiar. / With all my ways you are familiar. With all my ways you are familiar. You are loved.... You are blessed.... You are held.... You are constantly being formed and created in Jesus. [Pause for a moment of silence.]

When you are ready, take another deep, slow, long breath.... Breathe in the Holy Spirit and hold it for a moment.... *You have probed me, you know me.* Breathe out slowly.... *Even before a word is on my tongue, / LORD, you know it all.* Breathe in once more.... *Behind and before you encircle me / and rest your hand upon me.* Breathe out.... *Such knowledge is too wonderful for me, / far too lofty for me to reach.* [Pause for a moment of silence.]

Realize now that you have just offered your entire body to the Lord. Whatever you go about to do now, your body is His. You are in Him, and He is in you.... He knows your thoughts.... He knows your ways.... He follows each one of your steps.... He is with you, to lead you, and to guide you.... May the almighty God bless you and keep you. May the Father, the Son, and the Holy Spirit descend upon you and remain with you forever.... Amen. Take some time in **silence** and when you are ready, **journal** your experience.

PREPARATION FOR TOMORROW:
Read the following Scripture as you prepare for tomorrow:
The Walking on the Water, Mark 6:45-52.

DAY 7

PRAYING WITH GUIDED MEDITATION

PREPARATION:

5 P's of Prayer: Prepare - know your passage ahead of time and meditate on it throughout the day. When you transition into prayer, take time to breathe, relax, slow down, and just rest. Place - go to your prayer place, room or chair. Ninety percent of prayer is just being there. Posture - we pray using our bodies. Try one of the four postures: standing, sitting, kneeling, or prostrating. Presence - make the Sign of the Cross and invite the Father, the Son, and the Holy Spirit into this time of prayer. Invite God the Father to hold you, the Son to be the Good Shepherd to you, and the Holy Spirit to be Christ in you. Passage - hold the Bible in your lap and realize: "The Word of God is alive." The Father will speak to you!

GUIDED MEDITATION:

Find a quiet room, settle into a spot that will be comfortable, and place your body in a relaxed position, usually without crossed arms or legs. Allow your imagination, fueled by your senses, to enter into the story. Close your eyes as you meditate; at the end of the meditation, do not rush to open your eyes. Let your body tell you when you are ready. Review Guided Meditation under the Prayer Exercises section of "Types of Prayer" in Appendix I.

PRAY NOW:

This Scripture meditation is based on The Walking on the Water, Mark 6:45-52. I encourage you to have your Bible and journal with you.

Then he made his disciples get into the boat and precede him to the other side toward Bethsaida, while he dismissed the crowd. And when he had taken leave of them, he went off to the mountain to pray. When it was evening, the boat was far out on the sea and he was alone on shore. Then he saw that they were tossed about while rowing, for the wind was against them. About the fourth watch of the night, he came toward them walking on the sea. He meant to pass by them. But when they saw him walking on the sea, they thought it was a ghost and cried out. They had all seen him and were terrified. But at once he spoke with them, "Take courage, it is I, do not be afraid!" He got into the boat with them and the wind died down. They were [completely] astounded. They had not understood the incident of the loaves. On the contrary, their hearts were hardened. (Mark 6:45-52)

Imagine yourself in that scene. You are one of the disciples. Jesus makes you *get into the boat and precede him to the other side toward Bethsaida.* What do you feel like when He makes you get into the boat? Are you apprehensive, are you excited, are you afraid? Try to place yourself in that scene. Imagine being there on the Sea of Galilee with the other disciples and the commotion. The insecurity of realizing that Jesus is asking you to get into the boat. Try to picture yourself there. The rocking of the boat on the water. The waves gently tumbling into the shore. You look around at the beauty of the sea. You smell the fish in the sea. You feel the water. As you climb into the boat, you feel that you are no longer on stable ground. The boat begins to rock, you can hear the creaking of the wood, and the lapping of the water against the boat. As you look around and see each disciple's face, they all convey a different emotion. Some of them are very peaceful, some are excited, some are afraid, some are anxious, some are preoccupied and not even paying attention. What are you feeling right now as you get into the boat?

Then Jesus *dismissed the crowd.* So after all this commotion, the crowd begins to depart. Jesus comes up to the boat. He looks at you and tells you that He is going off to pray for a while. Jesus gives the boat a gentle push and pushes you off into the water. You watch as He goes off to the mountain to pray.

The sun sets and it is evening. At this point, the boat was far out on the sea. Jesus was alone on the shore. *He saw that they were tossed about while rowing, for the wind was against them.* Imagine yourself out in the boat. It is dark. You can't see Jesus. The wind picks up so strongly you can hear it whipping. You can feel the spray from the water, beating against your face. You try to row uncontrollably and without any direction. Feeling like you are not getting anywhere, making any progress, or having any direction to where you are going. Almost in a state of panic.

Imagine now the different things in your life that are outside of your control. Imagine all these things in your life that are like the waves crashing upon you. Imagine your life is like being in that boat, unable to control it, unable to steer it, unable to guide it. You can't see Jesus. The wind is against you. It feels like life is against you. You are completely and utterly helpless.

The fourth watch of the night is the darkest time. Jesus *meant to pass by them. But when they saw him walking on the sea, they thought it was a ghost and cried out.* Imagine you are in that darkness. You are on the boat. You are with the waves and the storm. You look out and you see what appears to be a ghost walking on the water. It is an image of transparency.

There is something there or someone there that you can't quite make out. It doesn't seem to be a person. You can't imagine it is a person. You are terrified. But at once you hear the voice of Jesus. A voice you know so well. He says to you, "*Take courage, it is I, do not be afraid!*" At the moment you hear His voice, your fear completely subsides. His word has so much effect on you. You just hear His voice and you are immediately comforted and assured. *"Take courage, it is I, do not be afraid!"*

Then watch as He gets into the boat with you. He walks over on the water placing one foot into the boat and the wind dies down. Jesus gets all the way into the boat and you look around. The disciples are *[completely] astounded.* You can see the look of surprise on their faces. *They had not understood the incident of the loaves*, the miracle that God had worked and the power that Jesus has over nature. *On the contrary, their hearts were hardened.* You realize that your heart was hardened. That for a little bit of time in your life, you had lost the faith. You let your heart grow hardened to the ability of Jesus to control not only all of nature but everything in your life.

You look at Him as He gets into the boat. He speaks the words to you, *"Take courage, it is I, do not be afraid!"* All of a sudden everything is calm. The water is calm, your heart is calm, your mind is calm, your life is calm, and Jesus is in the boat with you. You don't have to paddle anymore. You don't have to try to direct yourself anymore. You don't have to try to figure anything out anymore. You know that Jesus is with you. You know that He will take control. You know that He will take charge.

Spend a few moments in **silence** and continue to meditate upon whatever image brought you comfort. Whatever image was most vivid to you. When you most felt or experienced Jesus really present to you. Meditate upon that in silence.

When you are ready, take a few moments to **journal** your experience. Write down what was especially vivid for you, when you most felt or experienced some movement of God, where Jesus seemed very real to you. Where your senses and imagination came alive. This was a real experience with Jesus. This experience of Jesus calming the sea can calm the sea in your own life. So journal whatever it is that you may be upset about in life right now. And let Jesus bring calm to you.

PREPARATION FOR TOMORROW:

Read the following Scripture as you prepare for tomorrow:
The Washing of the Disciples' Feet, John 13:1-20.

DAY 8

PRAYING LIKE A PIRATE

PREPARATION:

5 P's of Prayer: Prepare - know your passage ahead of time and meditate on it throughout the day. When you transition into prayer, take time to breathe, relax, slow down, and just rest. Place - go to your prayer place, room or chair. Ninety percent of prayer is just being there. Posture - we pray using our bodies. Try one of the four postures: standing, sitting, kneeling, or prostrating. Presence - make the Sign of the Cross and invite the Father, the Son, and the Holy Spirit into this time of prayer. Invite God the Father to hold you, the Son to be the Good Shepherd to you, and the Holy Spirit to be Christ in you. Passage - hold the Bible in your lap and realize: "The Word of God is alive." The Father will speak to you!

PRAYING LIKE A PIRATE:

ARRR: Acknowledge, Relate, Receive, and Respond to God. Review Praying like a Pirate in the Prayer Exercises section of "Types of Prayer" found in Appendix I.

PRAY NOW:

This meditation is based on The Washing of the Disciples' Feet, John 13:1-20. We will pray like a pirate, ARRR: acknowledge, relate, receive, and respond. I encourage you to use your Bible and open up to this passage. This is a wonderful exercise for journaling, so I encourage you to journal during this meditation.

Before the feast of Passover, Jesus knew that his hour had come to pass from this world to the Father. He loved his own in the world and he loved them to the end. The devil had already induced Judas, son of Simon the Iscariot, to hand him over. So, during supper, fully aware that the Father had put everything into his power and that he had come from God and was returning to God, he rose from supper and took off his outer garments. He took a towel and tied it around his waist. Then he poured water into a basin and began to wash the disciples' feet and dry them with the towel around his waist. He came to Simon Peter, who said to him, "Master, are you going to wash my feet?" Jesus answered and said to him, "What I am doing, you do not understand now, but you will understand later." Peter said to him, "You will never wash my feet." Jesus answered him, "Unless I wash you, you will have no inheritance with me." Simon Peter said to him, "Master, then not only my feet, but my hands and head as well." Jesus said to him, "Whoever has bathed has no need except to have his feet washed, for he is clean all over; so you are clean, but not all." For he knew who would betray him; for this reason, he said, "Not all of you are clean."

So when he had washed their feet [and] put his garments back on and reclined at table again, he said to them, "Do you realize what I have done for you? You call me 'teacher' and 'master,' and rightly so, for indeed I am. If I, therefore, the master and teacher, have washed your feet, you ought to wash one another's feet. I have given you a model to follow, so that as I have done for you, you should also do. Amen, amen, I say to you, no slave is greater than his master nor any messenger greater than the one who sent him. If you understand this, blessed are you if you do it. I am not speaking of all of you. I know those whom I have chosen. But so that the scripture might be fulfilled, 'The one who ate my food has raised his heel against me.' From now on I am telling you before it happens, so that when it happens you may believe that I AM. Amen, amen, I say to you, whoever receives the one I send receives me, and whoever receives me receives the one who sent me." (John 13:1-20)

Acknowledge Take a moment to acknowledge how you are feeling. The great Socrates and Plato once said: "Know thyself." It is so important that we are able to know ourselves. To know what we are experiencing and what we are feeling. Not only that we know ourselves, but that we allow God to know us. How are you feeling right now? What are the emotions that you are experiencing in life? There is no judgment here. There are no good or bad emotions. All emotions are just indicators. They are what they are. But it is important that we are aware of them. So take a moment of **silence** and, when you are ready, **journal** your emotions. Acknowledge what you are feeling.

Relate In this passage of the washing of the disciples' feet, I imagine what Simon Peter was feeling. *He poured water into a basin and began to wash the disciples' feet and dry them with the towel around his waist. He came to Simon Peter.* We hear that Simon *Peter said to him, "Master are you going to wash my feet?"* This might indicate to us that Simon Peter was experiencing confusion. Maybe he felt uncomfortable, awkward, or maybe he felt proud. There could be a number of feelings that were stirring in Simon Peter's heart. How are you feeling right now as you imagine Jesus washing your feet? Simon Peter wonderfully relates his feelings to Jesus; he says to him, "*Master, are you going to wash my feet?*" There is a wonderful dialogue where Jesus responds to him and says, "*What I am doing, you do not understand now, but you will understand later.*" Peter relates to Him again. He says, "*You will never wash my feet.*" That is probably a horrible answer, but again there is no wrong answer. Relate whatever you are experiencing to Jesus. Tell Him how you are feeling or what you are going through. Take a moment in **silence** to relate your feelings to Jesus. Try to express them, to speak to Him, to get them out, to verbalize them. When you are ready, **journal** those feelings.

Receive If we are praying, really praying with Scripture and spending time in silence, Jesus will speak to us. Just like he spoke to Simon Peter. Simon Peter was possibly feeling awkward or uncomfortable. But he acknowledged what he was feeling and then he related to God. He said: "*Master, are you going to wash my feet?*" He would say later: "*You will never wash my feet.*" So now having related whatever your feelings are to God, He's going to respond to you in some way. Jesus' response to Simon Peter was: "*What I am doing, you do not understand now, but you will understand later.*" He says to him again, "*Unless I wash you, you will have no inheritance with me.*" Simon Peter receives this message from Jesus. Spend some time in **silence** and pray with this Scripture, and see if Jesus says anything to you. See if He speaks to you and try to receive whatever it is He wants to say to you, whatever He wants to do in you, however He wants to act in you. Spend some time in silence now and receive. When you are ready, **journal** what you received from Jesus.

Respond After Simon Peter acknowledged what he was feeling, he related that to Jesus with a question, *"Master, are you going to wash my feet?"* Jesus responded, *"What I'm doing, you do not understand now, but you will understand later."* Simon Peter says to Him, "*You will never wash my feet.*" Jesus says back, "*Unless I wash you, you will have no inheritance with me.*" Simon Peter has gone through this whole experience of first acknowledging his emotions; what he's feeling. Then so honestly and candidly relating to Jesus whatever he was feeling. Then he receives from Jesus. The first time he didn't receive so well, so Jesus had to say it to him a second time. Sometimes that happens with us. But after receiving, after we hear what He wants to say to us, it is important that we respond back. Simon Peter said to Him, "*Master, then not only my feet, but my hands and my head as well.*" His response was: "Yes, Lord if you want to wash me, wash my whole body." So maybe you have experienced this progression. You first acknowledged what you were feeling. You related it honestly to God. You received whatever He wanted to say back to you. Now respond to Him. Take a moment in **silence** and respond in your heart or out loud. When you are ready, **journal** your experience.

PREPARATION FOR TOMORROW:

Read the following Scripture as you prepare for tomorrow: Promises of Redemption and Restoration, Isaiah 43:1-5.

DAY 9

PRAYING WITH LECTIO DIVINA

PREPARATION:

5 P's of Prayer: Prepare - know your passage ahead of time and meditate on it throughout the day. When you transition into prayer, take time to breathe, relax, slow down, and just rest. Place - go to your prayer place, room or chair. Ninety percent of prayer is just being there. Posture - we pray using our bodies. Try one of the four postures: standing, sitting, kneeling, or prostrating. Presence - make the Sign of the Cross and invite the Father, the Son, and the Holy Spirit into this time of prayer. Invite God the Father to hold you, the Son to be the Good Shepherd to you, and the Holy Spirit to be Christ in you. Passage - hold the Bible in your lap and realize: "The Word of God is alive." The Father will speak to you!

LECTIO DIVINA:

A type of prayer in which one is reading Scripture, meditating or pondering Scripture, praying vocally with God, and contemplating in silence. Review Lectio Divina in the Prayer Exercises section of "Types of Prayer" in Appendix I.

PRAY NOW:

This meditation is based on Promises of Redemption and Restoration, Isaiah 43:1-5. The first step of *Lectio Divina* is *Lectio* or reading. It is suggested that you read the passage over a number of times. Traditionally it has been four times, so that is what we will do for this exercise. First, read it once straight through. Then a little bit slower. Then a bit more slower. Then even a little slower. Try to pick one Word or phrase that God is speaking to you, that sticks out at you, or strikes you in some way. Hold that Word or phrase in your heart and in your mind.

But now, thus says the LORD, / who created you, Jacob, and formed you, Israel: / Do not fear, for I have redeemed you; / I have called you by name: you are mine. / When you pass through waters, I will be with you; / through rivers, you shall not be swept away. / When you walk through fire, you shall not be burned, / nor will flames consume you. / For I, the LORD, am your God, / the Holy One of Israel, your savior. / I give Egypt as ransom for you, / Ethiopia and Seba in exchange for you. / Because you are precious in my eyes / and honored, and I love you, / I give people in return for you / and nations in exchange for your life. / Fear not, for I am with you. (Isaiah 43:1-5)

Let's read it again. Try reading aloud this time. As you read it again, try to pick one Word or phrase that God is speaking to you, or that sticks out to you, or strikes you in some way. Hold that Word or phrase in your heart and in your mind.

But now, thus says the LORD, / who created you, Jacob, and formed you, Israel: / Do not fear, for I have redeemed you; / I have called you by name: you are mine. / When you pass through waters, I will be with you; / through rivers, you shall not be swept away. / When you walk through fire, you shall not be burned, / nor will flames consume you. / For I, the LORD, am your God, / the Holy One of Israel, your savior. / I give Egypt as ransom for you, / Ethiopia and Seba in exchange for you. / Because you are precious in my eyes / and honored, and I love you, / I give people in return for you / and nations in exchange for your life. / Fear not, for I am with you.

Now let's read it one more time, even slower.

But now, thus says the LORD, / who created you, Jacob, and formed you, Israel: / Do not fear, for I have redeemed you; / I have called you by name: you are mine. / When you pass through waters, I will be with you; / through rivers, you shall not be swept away. / When you walk through fire, you shall not be burned, / nor will flames consume you. / For I, the LORD, am your God, / the Holy One of Israel, your savior. / I give Egypt as ransom for you, / Ethiopia and Seba in exchange for you. / Because you are precious in my eyes / and honored, and I love you, / I give people in return for you / and nations in exchange for your life. / Fear not, for I am with you.

Let's do it one last time and try to hold on to whatever Word or phrase you feel God is speaking to you. Maybe it has been a Word or phrase that has come up over and over again in your heart. Or, maybe this time, it will be something completely new. Remember, every time we pray with Scripture, it is alive.

But now, thus says the LORD, / who created you, Jacob, and formed you, Israel: / Do not fear, for I have redeemed you; / I have called you by name: you are mine. / When you pass through waters, I will be with you; / through rivers, you shall not be swept away. / When you walk through fire, you shall not be burned, / nor will flames consume you. / For I, the LORD, am your God, / the Holy One of Israel, your savior. / I give Egypt as ransom for you, / Ethiopia and Seba in exchange for you. / Because you are precious in my eyes / and honored, and I love you, / I give people in return for you / and nations in exchange for your life. / Fear not, for I am with you.

Take a moment of **silence** and when you are ready, begin to **journal** whatever the Word or phrase was that God spoke to you. Maybe it was something different during each of the readings; maybe it was the same Word or phrase that resounded.

The next step in Lectio Divina is *meditatio* or meditation. During this time, try to use your intellect, your imagination, and your senses. Do whatever it takes for you to meditate. Meditation can allow us to experience God beyond what we physically think is possible. Be free to let your imagination wander, your mind to question, your heart to bring feelings to the surface, and your soul to yearn for whatever it desires.

The first verse strikes me. *But now, thus says the LORD.* Right now, He is saying something to you. It doesn't matter about yesterday or tomorrow. Right now, He wants to tell you something. *Who created you, Jacob, and formed you, Israel.* This God, who created you and formed you says: *Do not fear, for I have redeemed you.* That really strikes me. Does it strike you? *Do not fear, for I have redeemed you.* Jesus has already won the battle. He has redeemed us. He has saved us. We have nothing to be afraid of.

I have called you by name. Do you like your name? Have you ever heard God call you by name? Have you ever heard the call of God or experienced Him calling you to something in life? *You are mine.* You are His special possession. He loves you more than anything else.

When you pass through waters, I will be with you. He is going to be with you no matter what you go through. *Through rivers, you shall not be swept away.* If there are things right now in life that you think are sweeping you away, God says nothing is going to pull you away from Him. *When you walk through fire, you shall not be burned.* We go through these horrible difficult things in life that are so painful; but, they are not going to hurt us forever. They are not going to burn us. *Nor will flames consume you.*

For I, the LORD, am your God, / the Holy One of Israel, your savior. So He is telling you right now: *I, the LORD, am your God.* I think of the commandment, *"I am the LORD your God... / You shall have no other gods besides me"* (Exodus 20:2-3). Sometimes we do that, put other things before God. Sometimes we put our hopes in other people or things to save us. But God, He is our Savior.

I give Egypt as ransom for you, / Ethiopia and Seba in exchange for you. God is willing to do anything for you *because you are precious in my eyes / and honored, and I love you.* Listen to that. So beautiful. God is saying that to you right now. Why does God do all this? *Because you are precious in my eyes / and honored, and I love you.* Meditate on that. *I give people in return for you / and nations in exchange for your life.* Then, He ends with this: *Fear not, for I am with you.*

Take some time in **silence** to meditate and when you feel ready, **journal** whatever you are most moved by.

The third step in Lectio Divina is *oratio* or pray, which means speech, discourse, or dialogue. Take some time now to have a dialogue with God. To talk to Him. To share with Him what is going on in your heart after you have heard these wonderful Words. What is it like to have God say to you, "*You are precious in my eyes / and honored, and I love you.*" Maybe we just want to say back to Him, "WOW! God, that is amazing! Do you really mean it, can I trust that, am I really precious to you?" Or you might just want to say, "Thank you, thank you God, for loving me this much, for honoring me." Or maybe you want to respond back – "I love you!" Or maybe you are afraid and you say to God, "I know you are telling me not to be afraid but I am afraid right now." *Fear not, I am with you.* Take this time in silence to have some dialogue with God. Anytime you don't feel Him speaking to you or hear His voice, just refer back to Scripture because that is how He speaks to us. He speaks to us in Word and also in silence. Speak to Him now. Spend some time in **silence** and **journal** your experience when you are ready.

The final step in Lectio Divina is *contemplatio* or contemplation. This is really the experience of just being with God after you have had this wonderful exchange with Him. So you have read His Word over and over, slower and slower, until it began to sink in. As you read it, something probably stood out to you each time; it was God speaking to you. Think about your meditation. What were the images that were strongest for you? What emotions did you experience? What thoughts went through your mind? What was it like to dialogue with God? To talk to Him? To share with Him? Now simply rest. Rest with whatever Word, phrase, or image seems to be most consoling to you and repeat it over and over in your heart. *Because you are precious in my eyes / and honored, and I love you. Because you are precious in my eyes / and honored, and I love you.*

Spend some time in **silence** now, contemplating. Just resting. **Journal** your experience when you are ready.

PREPARATION FOR TOMORROW:

Read the following Scripture as you prepare for tomorrow:
The Return of the Twelve and the Feeding of the Five Thousand, Matthew 14:13-21.

DAY 10

PRAYING WITH YOUR SENSES

PREPARATION:

5 P's of Prayer: Prepare - know your passage ahead of time and meditate on it throughout the day. When you transition into prayer, take time to breathe, relax, slow down, and just rest. Place - go to your prayer place, room or chair. Ninety percent of prayer is just being there. Posture - we pray using our bodies. Try one of the four postures: standing, sitting, kneeling, or prostrating. Presence - make the Sign of the Cross and invite the Father, the Son, and the Holy Spirit into this time of prayer. Invite God the Father to hold you, the Son to be the Good Shepherd to you, and the Holy Spirit to be Christ in you. Passage - hold the Bible in your lap and realize: "The Word of God is alive." The Father will speak to you!

PRAYING WITH YOUR FIVE SENSES:

This type of prayer uses your senses, physically and imaginatively (seeing, hearing, smelling, tasting, and touching). Review Praying with Your Senses in the Prayer Exercises section of "Types of Prayer" in Appendix I.

PRAY NOW:

Today, we will pray with our senses. This meditation is based on The Return of the Twelve and the Feeding of the Five Thousand, Matthew 14:13-21. I encourage you to have your Bible as well as a journal and pen with you. As you read the passage, let it come to life and ask the Holy Spirit to help you to see.

When Jesus heard of it, he withdrew in a boat to a deserted place by himself. The crowds heard of this and followed him on foot from their towns. When he disembarked and saw the vast crowd, his heart was moved with pity for them, and he cured their sick. When it was evening, the disciples approached him and said, "This is a deserted place and it is already late; dismiss the crowds so that they can go to the villages and buy food for themselves." [Jesus] said to them, "There is no need for them to go away; give them some food yourselves." But they said to him, "Five loaves and two fish are all we have here." Then he said, "Bring them here to me," and he ordered the crowds to sit down on the grass. Taking the five loaves and the two fish, and looking up to heaven, he said the blessing, broke the loaves, and gave them to the disciples, who in turn gave them to the crowds. They all ate and were satisfied, and they picked up the fragments left over—twelve wicker baskets full. Those who ate were about five thousand men, not counting women and children. (Matthew 14:13-21)

The first sense you will be focusing on is sight. Use your imagination to try to see everything in the Scripture passage.

When Jesus heard of it, he withdrew into a boat to a deserted place by himself. The crowds heard of this and followed him on foot from their towns. Use your imagination and try to see Jesus withdrawing in a boat. As He drifts away, down the shore, crowds hear that He is there and they begin to follow Him on foot. Imagine this crowd of people walking along the Sea of Galilee trying to keep up with Jesus in the boat.

Then you see Jesus notice the crowd. And *his heart was moved with pity for them*. So watch as the boat comes to shore and Jesus steps onto the land. The crowd is bringing sick people to Him and He begins to cure them. Watch as He lays hands on the sick. Maybe there is a sickness you have right now. Can you see Him laying hands on you? Maybe it is somebody you love that is going through a difficult time. Imagine that they are in that scene by the shore. Try to picture them with Jesus. Jesus is laying His hands on them and healing them!

When it was evening the disciples approached him and said, "This is a deserted place and it is already late; dismiss the crowds so they can go to the villages and buy food for themselves." Watch Jesus with His disciples and how He responds to them. His disciples are probably getting anxious and overwhelmed. You can see that in their faces. But what does Jesus' face look like?

[Jesus] said to them, "There is no need for them to go away; give them some food yourselves." But they said to him, "Five loaves and two fish are all we have here." Then he said, "Bring them here to me," and he ordered the crowds to sit down on the grass. So watch as this huge crowd of people begins to sit down on the grass. Try to see the grass and the hillside. Watch as their fingers first touch the ground and as their bodies get comfortable in the grass.

Taking the five loaves and two fish. Watch Jesus take these five loaves of bread and two fish into His hands. *And looking up to heaven, he said the blessing, broke the loaves, and gave them to the disciples, who in turn gave them to the crowds.* Try to play this out like a movie; watch Jesus break the loaves of bread and give them to the disciples who then go out into the crowd.

What does the crowd look like? We hear that they are all *satisfied, and they picked up the fragments left over -twelve wicker baskets full. Those who ate were about five thousand men, not counting women and children.*

Take some time in **silence** to visualize this whole scene and meditate upon the part that is most vivid for you. When you are ready, **journal** your experience.

The second sense we will use is hearing. Try to hear the sounds of the people, places and things. Listen to what people might be saying. What God may be saying to you. Listen to the sound of the waves on the Sea of Galilee, Jesus in the boat, and the murmuring of the crowds. The excitement as they followed Him on foot from their towns. Listen to Jesus as He disembarks the boat; the creaking of the wood, the splashing of the water, His foot hitting the dry land. Listen to the people as He begins to cure them.

Then, listen to the disciples as they approach Jesus in the evening. What do they sound like? How do their voices sound? I imagine distressed. *This is a deserted place and it is already late.* Then, maybe even a little bit commanding: *"Dismiss the crowd so that they can go to the villages and buy food for themselves."*

Now listen to Jesus' voice; how different the tone is. *[Jesus] said to them, "There is no need for them to go away, give them some food yourselves."* Just listen to His voice: *"There is no need for them to go away, give them some food yourselves."*

Then, listen to His disciples as they try to explain: "*Five loaves and two fish are all we have here.*" Jesus, confidently and calmly, says: "*Bring them here to me.*" Listen as He says the blessing and breaks the loaves. Can you hear the loaves breaking? The blessing that He says to the Father? The crowd as they sit down? The sound of them all eating and being fulfilled? Spend some time in **silence** just listening to the scene. When you are ready, **journal** your experience.

The third sense is smell. This one is often difficult. But we can do it. Try to take in the scent of the scene. The smells on the shore of the Sea of Galilee, the fragrance of bread, the two fish, and the crowd. What are some of the smells that you have taken in? By using the gift of scent and all the gifts of our senses, we can enter very deeply into this scene, so take a moment in **silence** and just try to smell the scene. When you are ready, **journal** your experience.

The fourth sense is taste. The notion here is to savor and relish the sweetness of God's Word. The part that seems most explicit with taste is the loaves of bread and the fish as Jesus passes them out to the crowd. Imagine yourself taking a fraction of this bread handed to you by one of

His disciples and placing it in your mouth. What does it taste like? Is it hard or soft? Is it fresh or stale? What does the fish taste like to you? Has it been cooked? Is it salty? Does it have crispness to it? Can you taste the juiciness of the flesh? Spend some time in **silence** now trying to taste the scene. When you are ready, **journal** your experience.

The final sense is touch. What does it feel like to be in a crowd? To have people all around you, bumping into you? Maybe when you sit down, somebody is sitting right next to you, touching you. Do you touch other people when you are in the crowd? Are you holding someone in your lap? What is it like to touch the bread and the fish? To put it into your mouth and to feel it in your mouth? How does it feel to be satisfied? To have leftover fragments? Spend some time in **silence** with the sense of touch and try to really feel the Scripture passage. When you are ready, **journal** your experience of praying with your senses.

PREPARATION FOR TOMORROW:
Tomorrow, we will pray with Sunday Mass.

PRAYING WITH SUNDAY MASS

Today's prayer will be celebrating the Sunday Mass and experiencing God the Father in the Eucharist and Liturgy. Prepare before Mass with the following and then journal your experience after Mass.

PREPARATION BEFORE SUNDAY MASS:

As we prepare for Mass today, I would like you to focus on forgiveness. Specifically, on any sins that you may have committed. Now, first of all, if you have been away from Mass or away from the sacraments in a while, we all know that the proper way to receive forgiveness is to go to Confession. If you have not had that experience recently, if it has been months, or a year, or two years, or three years, or five years, or twenty years, or thirty years, or fifty years, or if it has been since grade school since you have been to confession, I encourage you to go. You will experience God's mercy. You will experience the prodigal Father and His great love for you in the sacrament of Confession. If you have any mortal sin or any serious sin, confession is really the way to experience His mercy.

The truth is we all sin, every day. As much as we would like to deny it, we do. At every Mass, we have the opportunity to have our sins forgiven. This is called the Penitential Rite. It comes right at the beginning of Mass and happens very quickly, so if you blink, you might miss it. Just like the opening prayer, sometimes we miss that opportunity. But, again, we have to be prepared beforehand. So it is good to get to Mass a little bit early to spend some time in preparation. My spiritual director at the seminary always said to us, "If you get to Mass on time, you are late." The notion is that we should go early in order to prepare ourselves. Not only to settle down and enter into Mass, but to take some time in prayer.

So today, what I would like you to do in preparation is to reflect on your own sin. Is there any sin that you are struggling with right now? It could be any of the seven deadly sins. Think about the seven deadly sins: pride, greed, lust, envy, gluttony, wrath, and sloth. Chances are that there is at least one that you probably struggle with or have a tendency towards.

Of the seven deadly sins, the greatest is pride. When people come to confession and say, "Father I don't have any sin. I don't do anything wrong, Father," I usually kind of laugh and say to them, "Well, your sin is pride." So if you think that you don't have any sin, chances are your sin is pride because the reality is that we all have sin. The next deadly sin is greed. Could that be the deadly sin you struggle with? Next is lust. Have you had any experiences of lustful actions or desires? Envy - have you envied anyone or anything? Gluttony can be not only eating or drinking but just gluttony in general; taking more than we need or overfilling ourselves. Wrath (also known as anger) - is that your core sin? Sloth, I think, is the one that a lot of people struggle with; many don't realize this sin. This sense of sloth is a spiritual sloth. It is neglecting to do what you know you need to do to be close to God.

So, are you struggling with any of these? They could be what you bring to the Penitential Rite and to experience His forgiveness.

Let's review the Ten Commandments: *I am the LORD your God, ... You shall not have other gods beside me ... You shall not invoke the name of the LORD, your God, in vain ... Remember the Sabbath day - keep it holy ... Honor your father and your mother ... You shall not kill ... You shall not commit adultery ... You shall not steal ...You shall not bear false witness against your neighbor ... You shall not covet ... anything that belongs to your neighbor* (Exodus 20:2-17).

I am the LORD your God, ... You shall not have other gods beside me means that our number one love is God. Jesus says that the first and greatest commandment is, *"You shall love the Lord, your God, with all your heart, with all your soul, and with all your mind"* (Matthew 22:37). That is the first and that is the greatest commandment. But do you love God with your whole heart, your whole mind, your whole soul, and with every fiber of your being? Is He the love of your life? Is He first? Again, a good indication of this will be our daily prayer. Do we spend time in daily prayer? Do we really allow that to be the priority that the rest of our day falls around? I think we brush over that one quickly.

You shall not have other gods besides me. Has there been any idolatry in your life? Have you placed anyone or anything before God? If you have missed Mass for anything, whether it be sports, a party, a concert, or an event, then you have placed that in front of God and that becomes idolatry. So maybe that is what you need to bring to God. The same is true with prayer. I think a good indicator of this is by looking at daily prayer. Do you pray every day? If you don't, if you put something else before prayer, you may not even realize it but you make an idol out of that.

You shall not invoke the name of the LORD, your God, in vain. Do you find yourself using God's name in vain? It is a sacred name. Maybe you don't realize this; some people don't. But, it is such a sacred name that we should never utter it unless it is with prayer and sincerity. I think another way of taking His name in vain is praying in vain. When we pray but really don't believe it or are not really physically there, then you might just be using God. That is another way of taking God's name in vain.

Remember the Sabbath day - keep it holy. Keep holy the Sabbath. Not only when we go to Mass on Sunday, but the day as a whole is a holy day for us. I think the big one, especially in America, is working. We are so focused on working that we don't even have a day of rest. Sunday really should be a day of rest. So if you are working at all on Sunday, that is considered a sin because even God Himself rested for a day and He wants you to be able to rest, too. It is not a punishment. It is, "Hey, take the day off and enjoy it, be with your family, be with your loved ones. Do something that you enjoy that nurtures life. That nurtures your soul and your spirit. Make the whole day of Sunday wonderful." Is your Sunday like that? If it is not, that could be something you bring to the Penitential Rite.

Honor your father and your mother. We are called to show reverence and respect to our earthly fathers and mothers. This can include anyone in authority. If you have any superior, any boss, or anyone above you, show them honor. Do not dishonor them, or disdain them, or disrespect them. If you do find yourself struggling with this, again, this could be something you bring to the Penitential Rite so that you experience forgiveness.

You shall not kill. Everybody knows this one. It is usually the first thing some people say when they come to confession: "Father, I have not killed anyone." However, there are other ways of killing too. We do it all the time; any time that we kill another person's spirit, any time we put somebody down, any time we criticize somebody. This is something that can be brought to the Penitential Rite. There is one sin, however, that is worth mentioning because it is so prolific. I have often witnessed the shame and pain of women who have had an abortion or men who have aided in this. Sometimes going twenty or thirty years, holding it in, maybe too afraid to admit it, or confess it. I want to say first off to those men and women, "I am sorry that we as a Church were not there for you to help you imagine the possibility of life." I also want to say with great reverence and tenderness, "You are so loved by God and by the Church."

Pope Francis addressed this in a historic announcement: "Given this need, lest any obstacle arise between the request for reconciliation and God's forgiveness, I henceforth grant to all priests, in virtue of their ministry, the faculty to absolve those who have committed the sin of procured abortion. The provision I had made in this regard, limited to the duration of the Extraordinary Holy Year, is hereby extended, notwithstanding anything to the contrary. I wish to restate as firmly as I can that abortion is a grave sin, since it puts an end to an innocent life. In the same way, however, I can and must state that there is no sin that God's mercy cannot reach and wipe away when it finds a repentant heart seeking to be reconciled with the Father. May every priest, therefore, be a guide, support and comfort to penitents on this journey of special reconciliation" (Vatican, 11/20/2016).

You shall not commit adultery. Do you find yourself in some kind of affair? This could even be a struggle with pornography, masturbation, or fantasizing. If there is some kind of sin that is taking your mind away from God, then that is something that you probably want to be freed from. Bring it to the Penitential Rite.

You shall not steal. Is there anything that you have stolen? Have you taken anything that is not yours? I think we do this a lot as kids, but the temptation is there even as adults. So if you find yourself doing this, bring it to the Penitential Rite.

You shall not bear false witness against your neighbor. How do we speak about each other? Scripture says, *"Say only the good things men need to hear, things that will really help them"* (iBreviary, 2008). Do we gossip or speak critically of other people? Do we find ourselves putting other people down or speaking badly about people when they are not around? That is bearing false witness. We are not speaking to the truth of who they are; they are a child of God, they are loved by God, and if we can't see them that way, then it is really our mind and our heart that needs to be changed, not that person.

Finally, *you shall not covet ... anything that belongs to your neighbor*. I think this is a great sin in America. There is always this tendency to covet, of wanting more; it is never enough. We all probably struggle with this.

Spend some time going over the seven deadly sins and the Ten Commandments. Maybe there is just something else that comes up that you know is a sin and that you want to be freed from. There is no more powerful time to bring it to God, besides confession, than at Mass. The priest will say, "As we prepare to celebrate these sacred mysteries, let us take a moment to acknowledge our sins." Then there is silence. Now, that is not supposed to be just an uncomfortable silence or like: Why is he waiting so long? That moment of silence is to give you time to concentrate and focus on your sins. When the priest says, "Take a moment and call to mind your sin," call your sins to mind. What do you need to be forgiven for? At that very Mass, you can experience His forgiveness. If you spend time doing this examination of conscience, you will be prepared for the Penitential Rite.

As you go into Mass today, call whatever your sin may be to mind during the Penitential Rite and experience God's unconditional love, mercy, and forgiveness.

AFTER SUNDAY MASS:

So how was Mass? What was it like to actually come to Mass with a sin on your mind or in your heart? To bring it to God and experience forgiveness during the Penitential Rite? What did it feel like for you? What did it feel like to receive Communion and know that at that moment all your sins were forgiven and you were united with Him again? Take a moment to **journal** your experience of this Penitential Rite, this forgiveness, and being reunited with God in the Liturgy of the Eucharist.

PREPARATION FOR TOMORROW:
Read the following Scripture as you prepare for tomorrow:
Abraham's Visitors, Genesis 18:1-15.

DAY 11

PRAYING WITH CONTEMPLATIVE PRAYER

PREPARATION:

5 P's of Prayer: Prepare - know your passage ahead of time and meditate on it throughout the day. When you transition into prayer, take time to breathe, relax, slow down, and just rest. Place - go to your prayer place, room or chair. Ninety percent of prayer is just being there. Posture - we pray using our bodies. Try one of the four postures: standing, sitting, kneeling, or prostrating. Presence - make the Sign of the Cross and invite the Father, the Son, and the Holy Spirit into this time of prayer. Invite God the Father to hold you, the Son to be the Good Shepherd to you, and the Holy Spirit to be Christ in you. Passage - hold the Bible in your lap and realize: "The Word of God is alive." The Father will speak to you!

CONTEMPLATIVE PRAYER:

Contemplative prayer is a type of prayer that involves silence and simply being in the presence of God. Review Contemplative Prayer and praying with Icons (Prayer Exercises) in "Types of Prayer" in Appendix I.

PRAY NOW:

Prepare to pray with the icon Rublev Trinity (see Figure 1 in this chapter) by reading Abraham's Visitors, Genesis 18:1-15.

The LORD appeared to Abraham by the oak of Mamre, as he sat in the entrance of his tent, while the day was growing hot. Looking up, he saw three men standing near him. When he saw them, he ran from the entrance of the tent to greet them; and bowing to the ground, he said: "Sir, if it please you, do not go on past your servant. Let some water be brought, that you may bathe your feet, and then rest under the tree. Now that you have come to your servant, let me bring you a little food, that you may refresh yourselves; and afterward you may go on your way." "Very well," they replied, "do as you have said."

Abraham hurried into the tent to Sarah and said, "Quick, three measures of bran flour! Knead it and make bread." He ran to the herd, picked out a tender, choice calf, and gave it to a servant, who quickly prepared it. Then he got some curds and milk, as well as the calf that had been prepared, and set these before them, waiting on them under the tree while they ate.

"Where is your wife Sarah?" they asked him. "There in the tent," he

replied. One of them said, "I will return to you about this time next year, and Sarah will then have a son." Sarah was listening at the entrance of the tent, just behind him. Now Abraham and Sarah were old, advanced in years, and Sarah had stopped having her menstrual periods. So Sarah laughed to herself and said, "Now that I am worn out and my husband is old, am I still to have sexual pleasure?" But the LORD said to Abraham: "Why did Sarah laugh and say, 'Will I really bear a child, old as I am?' Is anything too marvelous for the LORD to do? At the appointed time, about this time next year, I will return to you, and Sarah will have a son." Sarah lied, saying, "I did not laugh," because she was afraid. But he said, "Yes, you did." (Genesis 18:1-15)

You don't need to know anything about an icon in order to contemplate with it. However, in terms of preparation, sometimes it is helpful to know a little bit of the background. Hopefully, as you look at the Rublev Trinity icon, you will see very clear references to the passage that we have just read. You can see the oak tree of Mamre. You can see the entrance to the tent and you can see the three angels. In the Scripture passage, we are not given any indication of who the angels are, but all three angels have wings and halos which represent their divinity. We are led to believe that one of them is the voice of God.

Traditionally, we have come to understand this icon as the Trinity - the Father, the Son, and the Holy Spirit. Many theologians over the years and people that study iconography have tried to figure out which is which, and in the end it is unsure. The most common view, however, seems to be that it is the Son in the middle. I say this because Jesus is frequently represented in colors and iconography often uses colors to portray meaning. Red is a symbol for humanity and blue is a symbol for divinity. You can see that the angel in the middle is wrapped in humanity with red. On top of the red, He is wrapped in divinity. If you notice at the right hand of the angel, there are two fingers that are pointed outward. If there are two fingers pointed out, that means the other three are tucked under; this has always been known to convey the meaning of the Trinity. Three fingers that are tucked under represent the Father, the Son, and the Holy Spirit. The two fingers that are pointing outward represent Jesus - fully human and fully divine; the two natures of Jesus.

The angel on the right is often thought to be the Holy Spirit because you see the colors of blue and green. Blue represents divinity and green usually represents the natural world. Above this angel, you see a mountain. In icons, a mountain is often seen as the experience of an encounter with God. It also symbolizes a heightened sense of purity which signifies the Holy Spirit.

Finally, some presume that the angel to the left is the Father. The Father is wrapped in gold and the blue underneath is the divinity. It is a sense of divinity, highlighted and wrapped in gold. Notice the tent or the home in the background. It is symbolic and could represent our home and eternal life. Jesus promises us that in His *Father's house there are many dwelling places* (John 14:2). So the angel on the left could very well represent the Father. So there you have the Trinity.

As you gaze upon the icon, notice that the center Angel is the one in front of the tree. Some say the tree is symbolic not only because of the tree in the Scripture reading, but also for the wood of the cross on which Jesus would be crucified. One of the other things you see is the table. It can almost be seen as an altar. Being familiar with the chalice, the cup in the center of the table might look to us like a chalice, which is symbolic for the Eucharist. Another interesting thing is the niche in the front of the table. Some say the niche is placed there for a relic because every altar in the old days had a relic that was placed inside the altar. Others in theology studying this icon say that the niche is an open place for us. That it is a place for you to go to place your heart, so that you can be right there at the altar of God, right in the midst of the Trinity, and right in the middle of this scene.

In the beginning, as you pray with this icon, your eyes will probably go wild as you look around at all the different details. But with contemplation, we are not trying to figure it out or meditating (although there can be a time for that). Ultimately, contemplation is simply being with God. So as you gaze upon this icon, just like you would pray with the Word, let your eyes move around until they settle on something. Then allow your eyes to remain there and to gaze. At some point, hopefully, you will come to silence. To stillness. Where you just simply rest with this icon. Where you enter into the mystery of the Trinity. Where you actually experience a glimpse of this "window into heaven." Where you have this contemplative moment of being with God the Father.

Take some time in **silence** and contemplate the icon of the Trinity. When you are ready, **journal** your experience of contemplating with the icon. What did your eyes settle on? What did you see as you glimpsed into heaven?

Figure 1: Rublev Trinity. Wikipedia (2016)

PREPARATION FOR TOMORROW:
Read the following Scripture as you prepare for tomorrow:
The Vine and the Branches, John 15:1-17.

DAY 12

PRAYING WITH SCRIPTURAL RELAXATION

PREPARATION:

5 P's of Prayer: Prepare - know your passage ahead of time and meditate on it throughout the day. When you transition into prayer, take time to breathe, relax, slow down, and just rest. Place - go to your prayer place, room or chair. Ninety percent of prayer is just being there. Posture - we pray using our bodies. Try one of the four postures: standing, sitting, kneeling, or prostrating. Presence - make the Sign of the Cross and invite the Father, the Son, and the Holy Spirit into this time of prayer. Invite God the Father to hold you, the Son to be the Good Shepherd to you, and the Holy Spirit to be Christ in you. Passage - hold the Bible in your lap and realize: "The Word of God is alive." The Father will speak to you!

SCRIPTURE RELAXATION:

The focus of this exercise is Christ healing us and the Word of God helping us to change our thinking patterns. Review Scriptural Relaxation in the Prayer Exercises section of "Types of Prayer" in Appendix I. This type of prayer may be difficult in the book format and you may find it more beneficial to actually listen to the exercise. You can find the audio version of Scriptural Relaxation at TheProdigalFather.org/Pray40Days.

PRAY NOW:

This Scriptural relaxation is based on The Vine and the Branches, John 15:1-17. Take a moment to find a quiet place where you will not be disturbed. Either sit or lie down and just allow your body, your mind and your heart, a chance to rest from the worries of the day.

Begin by taking a deep breath in. As you breathe in through your nose, imagine breathing in the Holy Spirit deep into your body. Hold it there for a moment. When you are ready, release through your mouth. As you breathe out, breathe out any worries, anxieties, or troubles that you have and just rest.

Take another long, slow, deep breath in through your nose. Breath in all the way, filling your lungs. Breathe in the Holy Spirit. Hold it for a moment. Let a deep breath out and release anything that you are preoccupied with, any concerns that you have, any burdens that you have - give them to God during this time.

Take one more long deep breath in through your nose. Breathe in the

Father, the Son, and the Holy Spirit dwelling in you. Breathe them into your body, your mind, your heart, your soul, and hold it for a moment. Finally, one last time, if there is anything else on your mind, breathe out and offer that to God.

"I am the true vine, and my Father is the vine grower. He takes away every branch in me that does not bear fruit, and every one that does he prunes so that it bears more fruit. You are already pruned because of the word that I spoke to you. Remain in me, as I remain in you. Just as a branch cannot bear fruit on its own unless it remains on the vine, so neither can you unless you remain in me. I am the vine, you are the branches. Whoever remains in me and I in him will bear much fruit, because without me you can do nothing. Anyone who does not remain in me will be thrown out like a branch and wither; people will gather them and throw them into a fire and they will be burned. If you remain in me and my words remain in you, ask for whatever you want and it will be done for you. By this is my Father glorified, that you bear much fruit and become my disciples. As the Father loves me, so I also love you. Remain in my love. If you keep my commandments, you will remain in my love, just as I have kept my Father's commandments and remain in his love.

I have told you this so that my joy may be in you and your joy may be complete. (John 15:1-11)

I am the true vine, and my Father is the vine grower. He takes away every branch in me that does not bear fruit, and every one that does he prunes, so that it bears more fruit. Imagine that your body is a branch.... Connected to God.... Each of your limbs, your legs, your arms, your fingers, your toes, your head; all of these are under the care of the vine grower.... [Pause for a moment of silence.]

You are already pruned because of the word that I spoke to you. Imagine God pruning you, caring for you, taking away from you anything that is dying, or dead, or causing you pain.... Imagine that you are totally in His care. Allow your body to rest in His care.... [Pause for a moment of silence.]

Remain in me, as I remain in you. Just as a branch cannot bear fruit on its own unless it remains on the vine, so neither can you unless you remain in me. Imagine yourself remaining in God.... He is in you and you are in Him.... He is in you and you are in Him.... *Remain in me, as I remain in you.* Imagine yourself full.... Being filled with the Holy Spirit.... Imagine yourself with the indwelling Trinity deep within you.... Each one of your limbs sustained, filled with this life.... Beginning with your toes and your feet, imagine God is within you.... Jesus within you.... The vine grower providing for you.... Totally connected to Him.... Removing from you anything that does not bear fruit.... Removing from you anything that is broken or causes pain.... Removing any blemish.... [Pause for a moment of silence.]

Your feet feel full, heavy, and warm.... Filled, connected to the vine.... Move up to your legs, beginning with your calves. Any emptiness that is there is full.... Then to your knees, the Holy Spirit filling up your body.... The vine grower taking away anything that causes you pain.... You are connected to the source of life.... That life continues to fill you.... As you imagine the life moving up into your thighs and your torso.... You are full.... You are connected.... *Remain in me, as I remain in you.* [Pause for a moment of silence.]

Just as a branch cannot bear fruit on its own unless it remains on the vine, so neither can you unless you remain in me. I am the vine, you are the branches. Imagine yourself connected to the vine and connected to Jesus.... One with Jesus. He is in you and you are in Him.... He continues to fill your being.... Now from your lower body to your upper body.... Filling your stomach, which seems so often empty and hungry.... Quenching any thirst that you have.... Your stomach is full, your stomach is heavy, your stomach is warm.... You are connected to the vine.... You are filled.... [Pause for a moment of silence.]

As you continue to move up, allow the Holy Spirit to fill your chest.... Feel the warmth.... Your upper body is heavy, it begins to sink deeply.... That same vine is connected to your very heart, to your very soul.... You feel the warmth.... You feel the life.... You feel God moving within you, filling you.... Completing you.... [Pause for a moment of silence.]

Just as a branch cannot bear fruit on its own unless it remains on the vine, so neither can you unless you remain in me. I am the vine, you are the branches. Whoever remains in me and I in him will bear much fruit, because without me you can do nothing. Now imagine that vine, that source of life Jesus, spreading to your arms and your hands.... Everything that you do is all because of your connection with Christ.... You can do nothing on your own.... You don't have to do anything on your own.... Why would you want to do anything on your own? You are connected.... [Pause for a moment of silence.]

Fill your fingers and your hands full of the Holy Spirit.... Imagine that warmth and that heaviness spreading up your arms.... Through your veins, to your forearms, and your shoulders.... Imagine your shoulders connected.... Your whole body connected to the vine.... All of your limbs, all of your branches, are one with the vine.... Your body begins to rest.... All the tension and pressure is gone because it is not you who does the growing.... It is not you who does the pruning, it is the vine grower.... It is God working within you.... Jesus and you are one.... He is in you and you are in Him.... [Pause for a moment of silence.]

Whoever remains in me and I in him will bear much fruit, because without me you can do nothing. Without me you can do nothing. Imagine the Holy Spirit now rising up from your shoulders through your neck.... All the tension releasing from your head.... Your head that has tried to control so much.... Your mind that has tried to manage, plan, and work.... Remember, you can do nothing without Him.... [Pause for a moment of silence.]

Anyone who does not remain in me will be thrown out like a branch and wither; people will gather them and throw them into a fire and they will be burned. If you remain in me and my words remain in you, ask for whatever you want and it will be done for you. Imagine now your entire mind being filled with this Word of God.... Your mind, your head, and your imagination.... All of it connected with God.... Remaining in God.... One with God.... Feel that rest now as your head sinks deeply.... Feel the warmth.... The fullness.... The pressure and tension release.... Realizing that without Him, you can do nothing.... [Pause for a moment of silence.]

Whoever remains in me and I in him will bear much fruit, because without me you can do nothing. Imagine the same life radiating through your face and through your eyes.... [Pause for a moment of silence.]

By this is my Father glorified, that you bear much fruit and become my disciples. You are His disciple.... This Word that you have been listening to.... This Word that you have been connected to.... This Word that you have been allowing to grow in you.... By this you will *bear much fruit.* You are His disciple.... [Pause for a moment of silence.]

As the Father loves me, so I also love you. Remain in my love. Your entire body is filled with the Holy Spirit.... Jesus is in you and you are in Him.... The Father and I are one.... Imagine your entire body filled with Christ.... All the way from your feet... To your legs.... To your torso... To your stomach.... To your chest... To your heart... To your arms.... To your hands.... To your shoulders.... To your neck.... To your head... To your face.... Filled, fulfilled, warm, complete.... [Pause for a moment of silence.]

By this is my Father glorified, that you bear much fruit and become my disciples. As the Father loves me, so also I love you. Remain in my love. Remain connected to this vine.... You are the branches.... *Without me you can do nothing.* [Allow yourself to rest for a moment.] Completely connected.... Completely full.... One with Christ.... One with the Father.... The Holy Spirit is dwelling within you..... *As the Father loves me, so I also love you. Remain in my love.* [Pause for a moment of silence.]

As you come to the end of this relaxation, allow the Word to remain in you. As you transition back into your day, remember you are connected to the vine and you are full. Remember that the Father is in you and you are in Him. Remember that Christ is one with you. Remember that you are filled with the Holy Spirit. Remember to remain in His love. *As the Father loves me, so I also love you. Remain in my love. If you keep my commandments you will remain in my love, just as I have kept my Father's commandments and remain in his love. I have told you this so that my joy may be in you and your joy may be complete.* [Pause for a moment of silence.]

Feel how relaxed your body is. *As the Father loves me, so I also love you. Remain in my love.* Let this Word echo in your heart.... *As the Father loves me, so I also love you. Remain in my love.* [Pause for a moment of silence.]

Spend some time in **silence** feeling God's love. When you are ready, **journal** your experience.

PREPARATION FOR TOMORROW:
Read the following Scripture as you prepare for tomorrow:
The Baptism of Jesus, Matthew 3:13-17.

DAY 13

PRAYING WITH GUIDED MEDITATION

PREPARATION:

5 P's of Prayer: **Prepare** - know your passage ahead of time and meditate on it throughout the day. When you transition into prayer, take time to breathe, relax, slow down, and just rest. **Place** - go to your prayer place, room or chair. Ninety percent of prayer is just being there. **Posture** - we pray using our bodies. Try one of the four postures: standing, sitting, kneeling, or prostrating. **Presence** - make the Sign of the Cross and invite the Father, the Son, and the Holy Spirit into this time of prayer. Invite God the Father to hold you, the Son to be the Good Shepherd to you, and the Holy Spirit to be Christ in you. **Passage** - hold the Bible in your lap and realize: "The Word of God is alive." The Father will speak to you!

GUIDED MEDITATION:

Find a quiet room, settle into a spot that will be comfortable, and place your body in a relaxed position, usually without crossed arms or legs. Allow your imagination, fueled by your senses, to enter into the story. Close your eyes as you meditate; at the end of the meditation, do not rush to open your eyes. Let your body tell you when you are ready. Review Guided Meditation under the Prayer Exercises section of "Types of Prayer" in Appendix I.

PRAY NOW:

When you were baptized, you were baptized into Christ. At that very moment you became Christ for the world today. Though you may not remember your baptism, in a very significant way, you were united with Jesus in His baptism. So as you meditate, imagine that you are Christ. This meditation is based on The Baptism of Jesus, Matthew 3:13-17.

Then Jesus came from Galilee to John at the Jordan to be baptized by him. John tried to prevent him, saying, "I need to be baptized by you, and yet you are coming to me?" Jesus said to him in reply, "Allow it now, for thus it is fitting for us to fulfill all righteousness." Then he allowed him. After Jesus was baptized, he came up from the water and behold, the heavens were opened [for him], and he saw the Spirit of God descending like a dove [and] coming upon him. And a voice came from the heavens, saying, "This is my beloved Son, with whom I am well pleased." (Matthew 3:13-17)

Imagine yourself coming from Galilee and you are Jesus. You go to John at the Jordan to be baptized by him. John tries to prevent you saying, "*I need to be baptized by you and yet you are coming to me*?" Try to imagine yourself there, in Galilee, at the River Jordan. Use your senses to imagine what it must have been like to be in that place. Try to hear the sound of the river, of the water flowing.

You see John the Baptist. He is in the middle of the river and he is baptizing people. Taking them in and plunging them into the water. As you watch each person get baptized, you see the look on their face. As they are about to go down under the water, there is uncertainty. They begin to hold their breath. There is a rush of water. They disappear for a moment and, then, they are brought back up. You can see on their faces, as they take in a deep breath, that there is new life.

You walk up to the water realizing your identity in Christ. You look to John and he tries to prevent you. You say to him, *"Allow it now, for thus it is fitting for us to fulfill all righteousness."* And then he allows it. Imagine yourself being baptized by John. As you step into the river, feel the cold water touch your feet. As you go deeper and deeper, it rises up to your knees and your legs. John reaches out his hand to you. You take his hand and he walks you out to where he is. He looks to see if you are ready. Are you ready to be baptized? You look back at John and you give him a nod. He sees in your eyes that you are indeed ready.

John lays one hand behind your back and the other on your head and, slowly, he immerses you into the water. As you plunge into the cold River Jordan, you close your eyes. You hear the sound of the water. You feel the water rush by your skin and you hold your breath. You wait until John brings you back up. As you are brought out of the water, you take a deep breath in and open your eyes. You look and see the heavens are opened, the clouds part in the sky and the bright sun bursts through. Out of this light coming down towards you appears the Holy Spirit, like a dove. It keeps coming towards you until finally the Spirit comes upon you.

As you stand up straight, you hold open your arms. And you hear the voice of the Father from heaven saying, "This is my beloved son. This is my beloved daughter, *"with whom I am well pleased."* Let that sink into you. God the Father, breaking through heaven, sending down His Holy Spirit upon you and saying these words. Booming these words. These words enter into the deepest part of your heart, into your soul. This is my beloved son. This is my beloved daughter, *"with whom I am well pleased."* At this moment, as God looks at you, He sees His son Jesus. You are Christ in Baptism. From the time that you were baptized, God has looked upon you with this great love. You are His beloved son. You are His beloved daughter. With you, He is well pleased.

As you stand there in the bright beaming sun, the Holy Spirit is upon you. The water begins to trickle off your body. Allow yourself to feel that experience of being surrounded by the presence of the Holy Spirit as it comes upon you. Allow yourself to look up into the sky, through the piercing sun and the clouds. Allow yourself to listen to the voice of the Father. Hear His voice. Hear it in your ears, in your heart, and in your soul. Hear His voice say to you, "You are my beloved son. You are my beloved daughter. *With whom I am well pleased."* Spend a few moments in **silence** and imagine yourself standing there in the river. With your arms opened, your head looking up, and the Holy Spirit upon you. With God the Father speaking to you. Realizing your identity in Baptism. You are Christ. You are His beloved one in whom He is well pleased.

Take a moment to **journal** about this experience. What was it like to be Christ in the scene? What was it like to imagine that you were Jesus? What was it like to accept that you are Christ in the world today? What was it like to hear the voice of the Father? Did it have any effect on you? What was it like to see John and have him immerse you into the water? When you came up, did you feel new life? Did you feel like you were born again? Did you experience a glimpse of your identity and how God sees you - "You are my beloved son. You are my beloved daughter. *With whom I am well pleased.*"

PREPARATION FOR TOMORROW:
Read the following Scripture as you prepare for tomorrow:
What will separate us from the love of Christ? Romans 8:35-39.

DAY 14

PRAYING LIKE A PIRATE

PREPARATION:

5 P's of Prayer: Prepare - know your passage ahead of time and meditate on it throughout the day. When you transition into prayer, take time to breathe, relax, slow down, and just rest. Place - go to your prayer place, room or chair. Ninety percent of prayer is just being there. Posture - we pray using our bodies. Try one of the four postures: standing, sitting, kneeling, or prostrating. Presence - make the Sign of the Cross and invite the Father, the Son, and the Holy Spirit into this time of prayer. Invite God the Father to hold you, the Son to be the Good Shepherd to you, and the Holy Spirit to be Christ in you. Passage - hold the Bible in your lap and realize: "The Word of God is alive." The Father will speak to you!

PRAYING LIKE A PIRATE:

ARRR: Acknowledge, Relate, Receive, and Respond to God. Review Praying like a Pirate in the Prayer Exercises section of "Types of Prayer" found in Appendix I.

PRAY NOW:

The exercise that we will do today is Praying like a Pirate - acknowledge, relate, receive, and respond. I encourage you to open your Bible to Romans 8:35-39 and hold it in your lap. Keep it close to you and have your journal ready as well. Today's Scripture passage is based on Romans 8:35-39, *What will separate us from the love of Christ?* Read the passage through one time and then take a moment to acknowledge whatever it is that you are feeling.

What will separate us from the love of Christ? Will anguish, or distress, or persecution, or famine, or nakedness, or peril, or the sword? As it is written: / "For your sake we are being slain all the day; / we are looked upon as sheep to be slaughtered." / No, in all these things we conquer overwhelmingly through him who loved us. For I am convinced that neither death, nor life, nor angels, nor principalities, nor present things, nor future things, nor powers, nor height, nor depth, nor any other creature will be able to separate us from the love of God in Christ Jesus our Lord. (Romans 8:35-39)

Acknowledge What are you feeling right now as you read this passage? What are some of the emotions, thoughts, or feelings that arise in your heart? Maybe there is something in your life that you feel is separating you from the love of Christ. Maybe right now you are struggling with anxiety, depression, anger, sadness, or frustration. Maybe you are grateful, joyful, at peace. Whatever it is that you are feeling, it is acceptable. The important thing to know about feelings is that they are not to be judged as good or bad, but rather, they are indicators of something deeper. So take a moment in **silence** to acknowledge how you are feeling, and when you are ready, **journal** whatever it is that you are feeling. What is going on in your heart, your mind, and your soul?

Relate Now that you have journaled, let's take a moment to read the passage once more. You have acknowledged your feelings, but now try to think how you want to articulate those feelings to God.

What will separate us from the love of Christ? Will anguish, or distress, or persecution, or famine, or nakedness, or peril, or the sword? As it is written: / "For your sake we are being slain all the day; / we are looked upon as sheep to be slaughtered." / No, in all these things we conquer overwhelmingly through him who loved us. For I am convinced that neither death, nor life, nor angels, nor principalities, nor present things, nor future things, nor powers, nor height, nor depth, nor any other creature will be able to separate us from the love of God in Christ Jesus our Lord.

Take a moment of silence now to relate your feelings to God. Tell Him what you are going through. Speak to Him. If you have any questions, ask Him. In some way, relate your interior life to God. Because when we relate to God, we open ourselves up to Him; we reveal ourselves to Him. When we reveal ourselves to Him, He will reveal Himself to us. Spend some time in **silence**. Whatever you are feeling, going through, experiencing, troubled by or enjoying, relate it to God. **Journal** your experience when you are ready.

Receive This is the hardest part because we have to be open to hearing what God wants to say to us. God's ways are so far beyond us. Sometimes it is hard for us to comprehend what He is saying. But God does desire to reveal Himself to you. He wants to give you something right now. He wants to speak something to you right this moment. Read the passage once more and as you do, try to receive whatever He wants to say to you. Maybe there is a Word or a phrase that comes through Scripture. Or maybe, it is just a thought that comes into your mind that brings you consolation.

What will separate us from the love of Christ? Will anguish, or distress, or persecution, or famine, or nakedness, or peril, or the sword? As it is written: / "For your sake we are being slain all the day; / we are looked upon as sheep to be slaughtered." / No, in all these things we conquer overwhelmingly through him who loved us. For I am convinced that neither death, nor life, nor angels, nor principalities, nor present things, nor future things, nor powers, nor height, nor depth, nor any other creature will be able to separate us from the love of God in Christ Jesus our Lord.

Spend some time reflecting on this Scripture passage and give yourself some **silence**. Some solitude. Because God will speak to you. He will respond to whatever it is that you have related to Him. You just have to receive. To receive means that we do nothing. What we do is wait in silence for God to speak his Word to us. Take some time now to be in silence. To receive. When you are ready, **journal** your experience.

Respond Hopefully, God has spoken to you. In some way, you will desire to respond back to Him. Your response might be another question. Your response might be asking Him to speak louder because you are not hearing Him. Your response might be gratitude. Your response might be to ask Him to be with you. Let's read the passage one more time. Try to articulate a response to God in this experience.

What will separate us from the love of Christ? Will anguish, or distress, or persecution, or famine, or nakedness, or peril, or the sword? As it is written: / "For your sake we are being slain all the day; / we are looked upon as sheep to be slaughtered." / No, in all these things we conquer overwhelmingly through him who loved us. For I am convinced that neither death, nor life, nor angels, nor principalities, nor present things, nor future things, nor powers, nor height, nor depth, nor any other creature will be able to separate us from the love of God in Christ Jesus our Lord.

Take a moment in **silence** to respond to Him. Respond to whatever He has said to you. Tell Him what is in your heart. When you are ready, **journal** the experience.

PREPARATION FOR TOMORROW:
Read the following Scripture as you prepare for tomorrow:
Dependence on God, Luke 12:22-34.

DAY 15

PRAYING WITH LECTIO DIVINA

PREPARATION:

5 P's of Prayer: Prepare - know your passage ahead of time and meditate on it throughout the day. When you transition into prayer, take time to breathe, relax, slow down, and just rest. Place - go to your prayer place, room or chair. Ninety percent of prayer is just being there. Posture - we pray using our bodies. Try one of the four postures: standing, sitting, kneeling, or prostrating. Presence - make the Sign of the Cross and invite the Father, the Son, and the Holy Spirit into this time of prayer. Invite God the Father to hold you, the Son to be the Good Shepherd to you, and the Holy Spirit to be Christ in you. Passage - hold the Bible in your lap and realize: "The Word of God is alive." The Father will speak to you!

LECTIO DIVINA:

A type of prayer in which one is reading Scripture, meditating or pondering Scripture, praying vocally with God, and contemplating in silence. Review Lectio Divina in the Prayer Exercises section of "Types of Prayer" in Appendix I.

PRAY NOW:

This prayer experience is based on Dependence on God, Luke 12:22-34. I encourage you to have your Bible and journal ready and on your lap. Today we will be using the exercise of *Lectio Divina*. Remember, the four steps are *Lectio* which means to read, *meditatio* which means meditate, *oratio* which means pray, and *contemplatio* which means contemplate. We will be going through each of these four steps. We will begin by reading the passage. I would like you to focus on one Word or phrase as you read through it.

He said to [his] disciples, "Therefore I tell you, do not worry about your life and what you will eat, or about your body and what you will wear. For life is more than food and the body more than clothing. Notice the ravens: they do not sow or reap; they have neither storehouse nor barn, yet God feeds them. How much more important are you than birds! Can any of you by worrying add a moment to your life-span? If even the smallest things are beyond your control, why are you anxious about the rest? Notice how the flowers grow. They do not toil or spin. But I tell you, not even Solomon in all his splendor was dressed like one of them. If God so clothes the grass in the field that grows today and is thrown into the oven tomorrow, will he not much more provide for you, O you of little faith? As for you, do not seek what you are to eat and what you are to drink, and do not worry anymore. All the nations of the world seek for these things, and your Father knows that you need them. Instead, seek his kingdom, and these other things will be given to you besides. Do not be afraid any longer, little flock, for your Father is pleased to give you the kingdom. Sell your belongings and give alms. Provide money bags for yourselves that do not wear out, an inexhaustible treasure in heaven that no thief can reach nor moth destroy. For where your treasure is, there also will your heart be." (Luke 12:22-34)

What was your Word or phrase? Mine was: *"if even the smallest things are beyond your control, why are you anxious about the rest?"*

Read it one more time. Try to pick out another Word or phrase.

He said to [his] disciples, "Therefore I tell you, do not worry about your life and what you will eat, or about your body and what you will wear. For life is more than food and the body more than clothing. Notice the ravens: they do not sow or reap; they have neither storehouse nor barn, yet God feeds them. How much more important are you than birds! Can any of you by worrying add a moment to your life-span? If even the smallest things are beyond your control, why are you anxious about the rest? Notice how the flowers grow. They do not toil or spin. But I tell you, not even Solomon in all his splendor was dressed like one of them. If God so clothes the grass in the field that grows today and is thrown into the oven tomorrow, will he not much more provide for you, O you of little faith? As for you, do not seek what you are to eat and what you are to drink, and do not worry anymore. All the nations of the world seek for these things, and your Father knows that you need them. Instead, seek his kingdom, and these other things will be given to you besides. Do not be afraid any longer, little flock, for your Father is pleased to give you the kingdom. Sell your belongings and give alms. Provide money bags for yourselves that do not wear out, an inexhaustible treasure in heaven that no thief can reach nor moth destroy. For where your treasure is, there also will your heart be."

Did you have another Word or phrase that struck you? God's Word is alive. He speaks to us every time we read it. Mine was: *Can any of you by worrying add a moment to your life-span?* Now, read it a third time, slower. Once more, try to hold onto a Word or a phrase.

He said to [his] disciples; "Therefore I tell you, do not worry about your life and what you will eat, or about your body and what you will wear. For life is more than food and the body more than clothing. Notice the ravens: they do not sow or reap; they have neither storehouse nor barn, yet God feeds them. How much more important are you than birds! Can any of you by worrying add a moment to your life-span? If even the smallest things are beyond your control, why are you anxious about the rest? Notice how the flowers grow. They do not toil or spin. But I tell you, not even Solomon in all his splendor was dressed like one of them. If God so clothes the grass in the field that grows today and is thrown into the oven tomorrow, will he not much more provide for you, O you of little faith? As for you, do not seek what you are to eat and what you are to drink, and do not worry anymore. All the nations of the world seek for these things, and your Father knows that you need them. Instead, seek his kingdom, and these other things will be given to you besides. Do not be afraid any longer, little flock, for your Father is pleased to give you the kingdom. Sell your belongings and give alms. Provide money bags for yourselves that do not wear out, an inexhaustible treasure in heaven that no thief can reach nor moth destroy. For where your treasure is, there also will your heart be."

What was your Word or phrase this time? Mine was: *"do not worry any more."* If it is fitting for you, do this a fourth time and go even slower until you have a Word or a phrase.

We will move on to the next step which is *meditatio* (meditation). I will lead you through this part of the meditation. At some point, as you read through Scripture, you can use your own thoughts, feelings, and emotions to try to meditate on the passage.

He said to [his] disciples; "Therefore I tell you, do not worry about your life and what you will eat, or about your body and what you will wear." Think about that. For me, it is pretty easy as a priest to not worry about what I am going to wear; pretty much black every day. But for you, do you worry about it? Do you worry about what you are going to wear the next day? Do you worry about what you are going to eat? But Jesus says, *"For life is more than food and the body more than clothing. Notice the ravens: they do not sow or reap; they have neither storehouse nor barn, yet God feeds them. How much more important are you than birds!"* He is trying to show us how absurd it is to think that God is not going to take care of us.

But we worry. We worry that we have to provide for ourselves or for our family. So God says: *"Can any of you by worrying add a moment to your life-span?"* Worrying doesn't do anything for us. It doesn't add to our life-span, it doesn't help us in any way. If anything, it takes away from our life-span. *"If even the smallest things are beyond your control, why are you anxious about the rest?"* Here we realize that we really don't control even the small things in life. If we can't control the small things, how can we control the big things?

"Notice how the flowers grow. They do not toil or spin. But I tell you, not even Solomon and all his splendor was dressed like one of them." God is saying to us: "I take care of the flowers, I am the one that does the growing." The flowers do no work on their own. He raises them from the earth. The same is true for us. He will clothe us and help us grow. Let God be your Father. *"If God so clothes the grass on the field that grows today and is thrown into the oven tomorrow, will he not much more provide for you, O you of little faith?"* Jesus is saying how little is our faith. If we do worry or are anxious, maybe we need to ask Him for an increase of faith.

"As for you [He is talking to you right now; the Word of God is speaking to you] *do not seek what you are to eat or what you are to drink, and do not worry any more."* Do you hear that? That is for you. Do NOT worry any more. You don't ever have to worry again. It is not going to help you. He doesn't want you to worry. So stop it. Do not worry any more.

"All the nations of the world seek for these things, and your Father knows that you need them." God knows what you need. Everybody seeks all of these things. But if we allow God to provide for us, it takes away the worry and anxiety. He will provide. *"Instead, seek his kingdom, and these other things will be given you besides."* He says, if we seek first His kingdom, if we put our hearts, our minds, and our souls on being in heaven with Him, everything else is going to fall into place. Everything in your life that you need will be given to you.

"Do not be afraid any longer, little flock, for your Father is pleased to give you the kingdom." He cares for you so tenderly. *"Do not be afraid any longer."* He doesn't want you to be afraid, *"for your Father is pleased to give you the kingdom."* Right now, right at this moment, God is pleased to give you the kingdom. He wants you to have it.

"Sell your belongings and give alms. Provide money bags for yourselves that do not wear out, an inexhaustible treasure in heaven that no thief can reach nor moth destroy." That is what happens when we save things and try to hold them. They end up getting destroyed, lost, or eaten, and we end up having nothing in the end. *"For where your treasure is, there also will your heart be."* If our treasure is in heaven, and not here on Earth, then that is where our hearts will be and we will get to dwell in heaven with Him.

The third step is *oratio*, which is pray. Right now, try to articulate some prayer to God. It could be a prayer of petition. It could be asking Him for the things that you need. It could be a prayer of gratitude, thanking Him that He provides everything for you. It could be just talking to Him, telling Him it is pretty wonderful that you don't have to worry anymore. He is going to provide everything for you. It almost seems too good to be true! God has this. Go ahead, you can ask Him. Spend some time talking to Him about what you have just experienced.

Finally, *contemplatio* or contemplate. *"Do not be afraid"* to be with Him after this whole journey with all this mix of emotions, hearing His Word over and over, and finally discovering this peace that you don't have to worry anymore. Your Father knows that you need Him. Right now, just rest with whatever Word, phrase, or image that brings you peace, consolation, hope, faith, or love.

Spend some time in **silence**, contemplating. When you are ready, **journal** your experience.

PREPARATION FOR TOMORROW:
Read the following Scripture as you prepare for tomorrow:
The Lord's Supper, Matthew 26:26-30.

DAY 16

PRAYING WITH YOUR SENSES

PREPARATION:

5 P's of Prayer: Prepare - know your passage ahead of time and meditate on it throughout the day. When you transition into prayer, take time to breathe, relax, slow down, and just rest. Place - go to your prayer place, room or chair. Ninety percent of prayer is just being there. Posture - we pray using our bodies. Try one of the four postures: standing, sitting, kneeling, or prostrating. Presence - make the Sign of the Cross and invite the Father, the Son, and the Holy Spirit into this time of prayer. Invite God the Father to hold you, the Son to be the Good Shepherd to you, and the Holy Spirit to be Christ in you. Passage - hold the Bible in your lap and realize: "The Word of God is alive." The Father will speak to you!

PRAYING WITH YOUR FIVE SENSES:

This type of prayer uses your senses, physically and imaginatively (seeing, hearing, smelling, tasting, and touching). Review Praying with Your Senses in the Prayer Exercises section of "Types of Prayer" in Appendix I.

PRAY NOW:

Today we will be praying with our senses using The Lord's Supper, Matthew 26:26-30. Have your Bible and journal on your lap. We will be praying with our senses or the application of the senses as St. Ignatius said. There is no right or wrong way to do this. However, for the purposes of teaching, we are going to go through the passage five times - once for each sense. The first sense that we will begin with is sight. As we pray with this passage, try to see with your own eyes. Use your imagination; place yourself in the scene and see what happens.

While they were eating, Jesus took bread, said the blessing, broke it, and giving it to his disciples said, "Take and eat; this is my body." Then he took a cup, gave thanks, and gave it to them, saying, "Drink from it, all of you, for this is my blood of the covenant, which will be shed on behalf of many for the forgiveness of sins. I tell you, from now on I shall not drink this fruit of the vine until the day when I drink it with you new in the kingdom of my Father." Then, after singing a hymn, they went out to the Mount of Olives. (Matthew 26:26-30)

Imagine the upper room where Jesus was. *While they were eating, Jesus took bread.* Try to picture Jesus. What does He look like to you? Notice His hands as He takes the bread. Watch as He looks up to His Father. With the bread in His hand, He says the blessing, breaks it and *giving it to his disciples said, "Take and eat; this is my body.*" Look into His eyes. He really means this.

Now watch as He takes a cup. How do you picture the cup? Is it gold, silver, glass, or clay? Picture His hands taking the cup, giving thanks and giving it to them saying, "*Drink from it, all of you.*" Look at His eyes and His mouth as He says, "*Drink from it, all of you*." Now watch His lips closely. "*For this is my blood of the covenant*." Notice His lips tremble and quiver. *"Which will be shed on behalf of many for the forgiveness of sins."* Then, He gets a look almost of terror in His eyes. "*I tell you, from now on I shall not drink this fruit of the vine until the day when I drink it with you new in the kingdom of my Father."* Then you see His disposition change to wonderful joy. He imagines His Father, being with Him again. Being with all of us one day.

Take a moment in **silence** and, when you are ready, **journal** whatever was most vivid for you, whatever you could see most clearly. If you are an artist, feel free to draw a picture. But try to really get into the visual of the scene.

The second sense that we will use as we reread this passage is to hear. So try to use your spiritual ears to actually hear the scene. Not only what is said and spoken, but the sounds that are made. Hear what God may be speaking to you. *While they were eating, Jesus took bread, said the blessing, broke it ...* Try to hear the sound of the bread being broken and torn; *and giving it to his disciples said,* [listen to His voice] "*Take this and eat; this is my body*."

Then, *He took a cup*. You can hear the rattle of the cup as He picks it up. *Gave thanks, and gave it to them, saying* [listen to His voice again], "*Drink from it, all of you, for this is my blood of the covenant, which will be shed on behalf of many for the forgiveness of sins. I tell you, from now on I shall not drink this fruit of the vine until the day when I drink it with you new in the kingdom of my Father*." Let His voice resonate within you. Could you hear His voice? Did He speak to you? What did it sound like to hear Jesus say these words about His own body and blood? What was it like to hear Him offer Himself to you? Take a moment in **silence** and **journal** whatever you heard.

The third sense is smell. Try to get the scent of the room. All that we know is that the last supper was held in the upper room. Maybe it is an upper room made of wood. Can you smell the wood? *Jesus took bread.* What does that smell like? *He said the blessing, broke it* [you smell it more as He breaks it open] *and giving it to his disciples said, "Take and eat; this is my body."* Then *he took a cup, gave thanks, and gave it to them, saying "Drink from it, all of you, for this is my blood."* Can you smell the wine? Can you smell the blood? "*Which will be shed on behalf of many for the forgiveness of sins. I tell you, from now on I shall not drink this fruit of the vine*." Can you smell the fruit of the vine? Have you ever smelled an open vineyard?

"*Until the day when I drink it with you new."* What does the newness smell like? *"In the kingdom of my Father*." What does God's Kingdom smell like? We can smell it with our spiritual sense. What does it smell like to you? Take a moment in **silence** and when you are ready, **journal** or meditate further on whatever was most strong or vivid for you.

The next sense is taste. So imagine yourself eating a meal with the disciples and Jesus. It is the last supper. He has probably prepared this wonderful meal for you. What are you eating? Can you taste it? The best food you have ever eaten. The best company you have ever had. But He wants to give you something more.

Jesus took bread, said the blessing, broke it and giving it to his disciples said, "Take and eat; this is my body." You take the bread that has now become His body. You place it in your mouth and you eat it. What do you taste?

Then he took a cup, gave thanks, and gave it to them, saying, "Drink from it, all of you, for this is my blood of the covenant, which will be shed on behalf of many for the forgiveness of sins." Now take the cup of His blood. Pour it into your mouth. As you taste the wine that was made into Jesus' blood, is it sweet or dry? Is it bitter? With that bitterness, there is also joy. Wine often brings a sense of joy, goodness, and gladness. "*I tell you, from now on I shall not drink this fruit of the vine until the day when I drink it with you new in the kingdom of my Father*." Can you taste that, the choicest wine? You notice your saliva begin to well up as you drink this cup, *new in the kingdom of my Father.*

Take a moment in **silence** and meditate. Just allow yourself to dwell on whatever really most got your taste buds going, try to savor that, relish it, dwell in it. When you are ready, **journal** your experience.

The last sense is touch. You are all probably sitting very close around the table. Often times, the disciples would lounge almost laying down on their elbows. Feel the bodies around you. There is a closeness. There is an affection. There is a warmth. You feel very comfortable.

Jesus took bread, said the blessing, broke it, and giving it to his disciples said, "Take and eat; this is my body." Imagine Jesus, with His own hands, handing you the Body of Christ. Hold out your hands. Watch as He places it into your hands. Can you feel the touch of His hand on yours? The Body of Christ in your hands? That sense, that electrical charge of life that you hold in your hands. What does it feel like to have the Body of Christ in your hands?

Then he took a cup, gave thanks, and gave it to them, saying, "Drink from it, all of you, for this is my blood of the covenant, which will be shed on behalf of many for the forgiveness of sins." Now, He hands you the cup. He embraces your hands in His. You feel so loved by Him. You feel that He really wants to give you this cup of His blood. As He is holding your hands and looking into your eyes, He says, "*I tell you, from now on I shall not drink this fruit of the vine until the day when I drink it with you new.*" As He says this to you, He squeezes your hands to let you know He wants to do this with you personally. To drink this cup *with you new in the kingdom of my Father*. What is it like to have your hands in His? To realize that He wants to have you in heaven, ultimately with Him in a completely new way? Not only with Him, but in the kingdom of His Father. He is holding your hands, giving you His precious blood and making this promise, this covenant with you.

Take a moment in **silence** to meditate upon this experience. When you are ready, **journal** your experience.

PREPARATION FOR TOMORROW:
We will pray with Sunday Mass.

PRAYING WITH SUNDAY MASS

Today's prayer will be celebrating the Sunday Mass and experiencing God the Father in the Eucharist and Liturgy. Prepare before Mass with the following and then journal your experience after Mass.

PREPARATION BEFORE SUNDAY MASS:

One of the best ways to prepare for Mass is to pray with the Sunday readings beforehand. Just like we prepare for prayer every day, the Church also expects that we prepare for Mass. When you go to Mass on Sunday, that should not be the first time that you hear the readings. You should actually pray with it all week long so that when you are at Mass you have already had this wonderful, rich dialogue and prayer encounter with God. Or, get to Mass a little bit early and read the readings before Mass. As the Word is proclaimed, it can all come back to life again. But sometimes we don't do that. We rush into Mass, maybe we are even coming in during the opening song, or trying to get our kids in the pew. You sit down, and before you know it, you are already through the readings and the priest starts the Gospel and you have no idea what the Word of God even was. You have missed out on the Word.

What I would like you to do in preparation today is almost like what we do in Lectio Divina. Pray with the readings before Mass. Read them over at least once, maybe twice or three times, slowly. I would like you to find and hold on to one Word. Also, during Mass, listen intently to the Liturgy of the Word. Try to take away one Word or phrase. You have a lot of opportunities: the First Reading, the Responsorial Psalm, the Second Reading, the Gospel, and the Gospel Acclamation. It is at any one of these points that the Word of God is speaking to you, right then and there. I know it is a lot. I know there are a lot of words, but all you need is just one. All you have to hear is one Word from Him. That is your takeaway. You might receive more, but you just need enough attention and focus to receive one Word or phrase. Your preparation for today is to be ready to listen and receive that Word or phrase.

AFTER SUNDAY MASS:

How was Mass today? Did you receive a Word or phrase? Did God speak to you in the readings? What was that Word or phrase that He spoke to you? Do you remember it? Hopefully, you were paying attention. Hopefully, you were listening with all your mind, your heart, and your soul for what God had to say to you. Because at every Mass, He speaks to us. But so often we are not listening. So often, we are preoccupied or running in late. But if we come to Mass early, if we spend time with the readings, if we listen when they are proclaimed and at least try to take away one Word, that Word will transform us. That is God speaking to your heart. Do you have a Word today that was spoken to you? Spend some time and **journal** it.

PREPARATION FOR TOMORROW:
There will not be a Scripture reading for tomorrow.
We will pray with our hands! Get your hands ready.

DAY 17

PRAYING WITH CONTEMPLATIVE PRAYER

PREPARATION:

5 P's of Prayer: Prepare - know your passage ahead of time and meditate on it throughout the day. When you transition into prayer, take time to breathe, relax, slow down, and just rest. Place - go to your prayer place, room or chair. Ninety percent of prayer is just being there. Posture - we pray using our bodies. Try one of the four postures: standing, sitting, kneeling, or prostrating. Presence - make the Sign of the Cross and invite the Father, the Son, and the Holy Spirit into this time of prayer. Invite God the Father to hold you, the Son to be the Good Shepherd to you, and the Holy Spirit to be Christ in you. Passage - hold the Bible in your lap and realize: "The Word of God is alive." The Father will speak to you!

CONTEMPLATIVE PRAYER:

Contemplative prayer is a type of prayer that involves silence and simply being in the presence of God. Review Contemplative Prayer and praying with Nature (Prayer Exercises) in "Types of Prayer" in Appendix I.

PRAY NOW:

Today's exercise is contemplative prayer - contemplating God and nature. St. Bonaventure said that man was made fit for the quiet of contemplation (Cousins, 1978). When we contemplate with nature, we can use any nature. One of the things that we always have with us is our bodies. It is a wonderful experience to spend time contemplating our body. For this prayer, we will contemplate with our hands.

It is important to clarify again the three stages of prayer: vocal prayer, meditative prayer, and contemplative prayer. Vocal prayer is when we talk to God or pray some kind of rote prayer. Meditation is when we use our imagination or we use a thought. We may even use our minds to figure things out or to gain insight. Contemplation is a much simpler form of prayer. It is a much deeper form of prayer. Though it is simple, it can be the most difficult because we are not doing anything. We are simply delighting in God's creation.

Let us, then, contemplate our hands. Again, we are not doing vocal prayer. So there is not going to be any Scripture reading or dialogue. We are not even doing meditative prayer. So try not to use your imagination, your intellect, or your reason. When you look at your hands, don't judge them. Just accept them and look at them with love.

As preparation, take a moment to look at the back of your hands. Just sense them. Notice how all your fingers are formed. Maybe a little crooked depending on how old you are or if you have broken any bones. Notice some of the veins that go through your hands. Maybe your skin is soft and very smooth or maybe it is wrinkly. Just like a feeling, we don't judge it, we just acknowledge it. We accept it, and we look lovingly upon these hands that are such a gift that God gave you. Think about how much good God is doing with your hands, has done with your hands throughout all your life, and will continue to do so.

Now flip them over and see the inside of your hands. Look at the palms of your hands. These hands have held the Body of Christ. That alone makes them sacred. I would like you to now hold your hands together. Embrace them like you would be receiving Communion. Again, without blame or judgment, simply gaze upon them. Delight in them. Look at them as if you have never seen them before. As if you are seeing them for the first time ever. This is a wonderful gift that God gave to you. This gift of your hands.

Spend time now in silent contemplation. If you begin to get distracted and look around, simply return your gaze to your hands. Try to keep your hands and body still. As you bring stillness to your body, your mind will become still, your soul will become still, and before you know it, you will simply be resting; gazing at your hands. Treasure these beautiful hands that God has given to you to do so much good.

Continue your silent contemplation. Remember, if you get distracted, it is okay. Gently return your mind back to your hands. Let your hands be the focal point. Let this nature, this vestige, this creation of God be what leads you back to God. Anytime you get distracted, just return to them. Be gentle with yourself. Be loving to yourself and be grateful for these hands that God has given to you.

Spend the rest of the time in **silence** gazing at your hands. When you are ready, **journal** your experience.

PREPARATION FOR TOMORROW:
Read the following Scripture as you prepare for tomorrow:
The Calming of a Storm at Sea, Mark 4:35-41.

DAY 18

PRAYING WITH SCRIPTURAL RELAXATION

PREPARATION:

5 P's of Prayer: Prepare - know your passage ahead of time and meditate on it throughout the day. When you transition into prayer, take time to breathe, relax, slow down, and just rest. Place - go to your prayer place, room or chair. Ninety percent of prayer is just being there. Posture - we pray using our bodies. Try one of the four postures: standing, sitting, kneeling, or prostrating. Presence - make the Sign of the Cross and invite the Father, the Son, and the Holy Spirit into this time of prayer. Invite God the Father to hold you, the Son to be the Good Shepherd to you, and the Holy Spirit to be Christ in you. Passage - hold the Bible in your lap and realize: "The Word of God is alive." The Father will speak to you!

SCRIPTURE RELAXATION:

The focus of this exercise is Christ healing us and the Word of God helping us to change our thinking patterns. Review Scriptural Relaxation in the Prayer Exercises section of "Types of Prayer" in Appendix I. You can also find the audio version of Scriptural Relaxation at TheProdigalFather.org/Pray40Days.

PRAY NOW:

Today's prayer will use scriptural relaxation with The Calming of a Storm at Sea based on Mark 4:35-41. Have your Bible and journal ready. Begin by reading the passage.

On that day, as evening drew on, he said to them, "Let us cross to the other side." Leaving the crowd, they took him with them in the boat just as he was. And other boats were with him. A violent squall came up and waves were breaking over the boat, so that it was already filling up. Jesus was in the stern, asleep on a cushion. They woke him and said to him, "Teacher, do you not care that we are perishing?" He woke up, rebuked the wind, and said to the sea, "Quiet! Be still!" The wind ceased and there was great calm. Then he asked them, "Why are you terrified? Do you not yet have faith?" They were filled with great awe and said to one another, "Who then is this whom even wind and sea obey?" (Mark 4:35-41)

We will begin the relaxation exercise with some breathing exercises. As we breathe, we will use the phrase *"Quiet! Be still!"* from the Scripture passage. Anytime we pray with the Word of God and we repeat it to ourselves, He speaks to us, He is present to us and His Word has an effect on us. So this now becomes an experience of God's Word bringing us calm. God's Word bringing us peace. Rather than us simply doing it ourselves. *Quiet! Be still!* [Pause for a moment of silence.]

Take a moment now to breathe.... Breathe slowly and gently, all the way in as deep as you can.... Hold it there for a moment.... Repeat these words in your mind. *Quiet! Be still!* Then let out your breath.... Breathe out any anxieties, worries, or frustrations that you may have.... [Pause for a moment of silence.]

Quiet! Be still! Breathe in once more, all the way in as deep as you can.... Hold it there.... Breathe out. Release all your worries, anxieties, or fears.... *Quiet! Be still!* [Pause for a moment of silence.]

One last time, breathe in through your nose as deep as you can.... All the way in.... Hold it there for a moment.... *Quiet! Be still!* Finally, release.... *Quiet! Be still!* [Pause for a moment of silence.]

Imagine you are in the boat.... Whatever is going on in your life right now, Jesus has power over.... He is able to calm the storms.... No matter how violent the squall.... Even if it seems your boat is filling up and about to capsize.... *He* [Jesus] *woke up, rebuked the wind, and said to the sea, "Quiet! Be still!" The wind ceased and there was great calm....* Experience this calmness now.... Imagine you are on the boat, the sea is calm, the rocking has stopped, and there is stillness.... *Quiet! Be still!* [Pause for a moment of silence.]

The next part of this relaxation will focus on heaviness. Imagine your whole body is heavy and pressing into the cushion of the boat.... Just listen to these words and say them to yourself. *Quiet! Be still!* [Pause for a moment of silence.]

My right arm is heavy.... Feel the heaviness.... Sink down into the cushion.... My right arm is heavy.... My right arm is heavy.... My right arm is heavy.... Feel your arm completely rest.... *Quiet! Be still!* [Pause for a moment of silence.]

Now move to your left arm.... Your left arm is heavy and it rests on the cushion.... You release all your anxieties and tension.... My left arm is heavy.... *Quiet! Be still!* My left arm is heavy.... My left arm is heavy.... *Quiet! Be still!* Feel your arm completely rest.... [Pause for a moment of silence.]

Now move to your legs. My right leg is heavy.... Feel your right leg release and sink into the cushion.... My right leg is heavy.... Releasing any tension.... *Quiet! Be still!* My right leg is heavy.... *Quiet! Be still!* [Pause for a moment of silence.]

Imagine you are in the boat.... The storm is calm as you focus your attention to your left leg.... My left leg is heavy.... My left leg is heavy.... *Quiet! Be still!* My left leg is heavy.... Feel your leg sink deeply into the cushion.... [Pause for a moment of silence.]

Focus now on warmth.... The disciples *were filled with great awe and said to one another, "Who then is this whom even the wind and sea obey?"* Focus on the warmth of the sun beating upon you.... [Pause for a moment of silence.]

Start with your right arm... My right arm is warm.... Just feel the warmth radiate throughout your arm.... *Quiet! Be still!* My right arm is warm.... My right arm is so warm.... My right arm is warm.... Feel your right arm warm and heavy.... *Quiet! Be still!* My left arm is warm.... Feel the warmth in your arm.... Feel the warmth coming from the sun.... My left arm is warm.... *Quiet! Be still!* My left arm is warm and heavy.... Feel the comfort of the warmth and the relaxation as your left arm sinks into the cushion.... [Pause for a moment of silence.]

My right leg is heavy and warm.... Feel the warmth of the sun on your leg.... My right leg is heavy and warm.... My right leg is heavy and warm.... My right leg is warm.... *Quiet! Be still!* My right leg is warm and heavy as it sinks into the cushion.... *Quiet! Be still!* Feel the boat gently rocking.... As you focus your attention on your left leg.... My left leg is warm.... Feel the sun and the warmth on your left leg.... My left leg is warm.... *Quiet! Be still!* My left leg is warm.... My left leg is warm and heavy.... *Quiet! Be still!* [Pause for a moment of silence.]

Jesus then asked them, "*Why are you terrified? Do you not yet have faith?" They were filled with great awe and said to one another, "Who then is this who even the wind and sea obey?"* [Pause for a moment of silence.]

We will focus now on a feeling of calm.... My right arm is calm and relaxed.... *Quiet! Be still!* My right arm is calm and relaxed.... Heavy and warm.... *Quiet! Be still!* My left arm is calm.... My left arm is relaxed.... *Quiet! Be still!* My left arm is calm and relaxed.... My left arm is calm, warm, and heavy.... *Quiet! Be still!* [Pause for a moment of silence.]

Imagine you are on the boat in the sun, gently rocking in the sea.... My right leg is calm and relaxed.... *Quiet! Be still!* My right leg is calm.... My right leg is calm and heavy.... My right leg is warm and sinks into the cushion.... *Quiet! Be still!* My left leg is calm and relaxed.... *Quiet! Be still!* My left leg is calm and relaxed.... There is no tension any more.... My left leg is calm, warm and heavy.... *Quiet! Be still!* [Pause for a moment of silence.]

Imagine yourself in the boat with Jesus, and your whole body is calm.... *Quiet! Be still!* He says to you over and over, *"Quiet! Be still!"* Your whole body feels warm in the sun.... *Quiet! Be still!* Your whole body feels heavy and completely relaxed.... Your whole body is warm and calm as you sink into the cushion.... *Quiet! Be still!* [Pause for a moment of silence.]

Spend some time in **silence**, just resting and repeating to yourself: *Quiet. Be still.* When you are ready, **journal** your experience.

PREPARATION FOR TOMORROW:
Read the following Scripture as you prepare for tomorrow:
The Pardon of the Sinful Woman, Luke 7: 36-50.

DAY 19

PRAYING WITH GUIDED MEDITATION

PREPARATION:

5 P's of Prayer: Prepare - know your passage ahead of time and meditate on it throughout the day. When you transition into prayer, take time to breathe, relax, slow down, and just rest. Place - go to your prayer place, room or chair. Ninety percent of prayer is just being there. Posture - we pray using our bodies. Try one of the four postures: standing, sitting, kneeling, or prostrating. Presence - make the Sign of the Cross and invite the Father, the Son, and the Holy Spirit into this time of prayer. Invite God the Father to hold you, the Son to be the Good Shepherd to you, and the Holy Spirit to be Christ in you. Passage - hold the Bible in your lap and realize: "The Word of God is alive." The Father will speak to you!

GUIDED MEDITATION:

Find a quiet room, settle into a spot that will be comfortable, and place your body in a relaxed position, usually without crossed arms or legs. Allow your imagination, fueled by your senses, to enter into the story. Close your eyes as you meditate; at the end of the meditation, do not rush to open your eyes. Let your body tell you when you are ready. Review Guided Meditation under the Prayer Exercises section of "Types of Prayer" in Appendix I.

PRAY NOW:

The following Scripture meditation is based on The Pardon of the Sinful Woman, Luke 7: 36-50.

A Pharisee invited him to dine with him, and he entered the Pharisee's house and reclined at table. Now there was a sinful woman in the city who learned that he was at table in the house of the Pharisee. Bringing an alabaster flask of ointment, she stood behind him at his feet weeping and began to bathe his feet with her tears. Then she wiped them with her hair, kissed them, and anointed them with the ointment. When the Pharisee who had invited him saw this he said to himself, "If this man were a prophet, he would know who and what sort of woman this is who is touching him, that she is a sinner." Jesus said to him in reply, "Simon, I have something to say to you." "Tell me teacher," he said. "Two people were in debt to a certain creditor; one owed five hundred days' wages and the other owed fifty. Since they were unable to repay the debt, he forgave it for both. Which of them will love him more?" Simon said in reply, "The one, I suppose, whose larger debt was forgiven." He said to him, "You have judged rightly." Then he turned to the woman and said to Simon,

"Do you see this woman? When I entered your house, you did not give me water for my feet, but she has bathed them with her tears and wiped them with their hair. You did not give me a kiss, but she has not ceased kissing my feet since the time I entered. You did not anoint my head with oil, but she anointed my feet with ointment. So I tell you, her many sins have been forgiven; hence, she has shown great love. But the one to whom little is forgiven, loves little." He said to her, "Your sins are forgiven." The others at table said to themselves, "Who is this who even forgives sins?" But he said to the woman, "Your faith has saved you; go in peace." (Luke 7:36-50)

Imagine that you are at the Pharisee's house. You are the sinful woman. You are so excited to be with Jesus that you bring Him an alabaster flask of aromatic ointment, the most expensive ointment you could find and buy. As you stand behind Him, at His feet, you find yourself breaking down into tears, weeping. The tears are just streaming down your face at the realization of the cycle of sin that you have been in. The many times you have tried to get out of it. Yet, you are caught. It is so frustrating.

The tears run down your eyes and face. They drip off your face and land on the feet of Jesus. You notice them mix with the dirt on His heels. The more you weep, the more the tears drop on to His feet. The dirt is distilled and you start to see the clean skin of His feet. You begin to bathe them with your tears and to wipe them with your hair. You take your long hair and scrub His feet. As you scrub with your hair and tears, His feet become clean. You gently and reverently kiss each one of them. Then, you take the fragrant ointment and you begin to bless and anoint His feet. As you tenderly rub the oil into His feet, they begin to soften.

When one of the Pharisees *who had invited him saw this he said to himself, "If this man were prophet, he would know who and what sort of woman this is who is touching him, that she is a sinner."* You hear this and feel it to the core of your heart; you are a sinner.

But you notice something. Jesus responds in your defense. *"Simon, I have something to say to you." "Tell me teacher," he says.* Then, Jesus goes on to explain the parable of the two debtors that owed much money. One of them owed an especially great deal and was forgiven. Both of them were forgiven. He says to him; "*Which of them will love him more?" Simon said in reply, "The one, I suppose, whose larger debt was forgiven."* Jesus says to him, *"You have judged rightly*."

Then he turned to the woman and said to Simon; "Do you see this woman?" This is when you notice Jesus is looking at you with great love. He is so proud of you. He is so delighted with you. He is so happy that you are the one that took the time to greet Him. That you are the one that cleaned His feet. That you are the one that was able to even admit and emotionally express sadness for sin. His response is complete mercy and love. He looks at you with such great delight. In that look, you realize that He wants to forgive any sin you have ever committed.

You look around the room. You see that all the disciples are no longer looking at you with disdain, but are looking at you with great joy. They see your face is now transformed. Your tears have stopped. You realize that in that moment, *"Your faith has saved you;* [you can] *go in peace."*

Allow yourself to rest for a moment with Jesus. Allow yourself to experience Him defending you. Allow yourself the experience of touching His feet. Imagine your tears flowing out from you and on to Him. Imagine your hair scrubbing the dirt off of His feet and they become clean. Then imagine Him looking at you. Try to see His face. His eyes. The way that He sees you with great love. In that moment He says, "*Your faith has saved you; go in peace.*" Take a few moments in **silence** to meditate on this. Go deeper into whatever image, scene, scent, smell, touch, or feeling was strongest for you. Let your imagination totally enter into that scene in meditation.

Now that you have spent time in meditation and silence, **journal** your experience. Try to write out in your journal what seemed most real to you. What emotions were strongest for you? What did it feel like to cry and let it all out? How did it feel to wash His feet? What was it like to actually touch the feet of Jesus and to wipe them clean with your hair? What did He look like? Did you see Him? Did you hear His voice? Take another moment now and journal once more because to experience the mercy of Jesus is a very profound moment.

PREPARATION FOR TOMORROW:
Read the following Scripture as you prepare for tomorrow:
The Rich Official, Luke 18:18-23.

DAY 20

PRAYING LIKE A PIRATE

PREPARATION:

5 P's of Prayer: Prepare - know your passage ahead of time and meditate on it throughout the day. When you transition into prayer, take time to breathe, relax, slow down, and just rest. Place - go to your prayer place, room or chair. Ninety percent of prayer is just being there. Posture - we pray using our bodies. Try one of the four postures: standing, sitting, kneeling, or prostrating. Presence - make the Sign of the Cross and invite the Father, the Son, and the Holy Spirit into this time of prayer. Invite God the Father to hold you, the Son to be the Good Shepherd to you, and the Holy Spirit to be Christ in you. Passage - hold the Bible in your lap and realize: "The Word of God is alive." The Father will speak to you!

PRAYING LIKE A PIRATE:

ARRR: Acknowledge, Relate, Receive, and Respond to God. Review Praying like a Pirate in the Prayer Exercises section of "Types of Prayer" found in Appendix I.

PRAY NOW:

This prayer experience is based on The Rich Official: Luke 18:18-23 and we will pray like a pirate: acknowledge, relate, receive, and respond. Have your Bible and journal ready and on your lap. First, read the entire Scripture passage. We will reflect on how the rich official acknowledged, related, received, and responded to Jesus.

An official asked him this question, "Good teacher, what must I do to inherit eternal life?" Jesus answered him, "Why do you call me good? No one is good but God alone. You know the commandments, 'You shall not commit adultery; you shall not kill; you shall not steal; you shall not bear false witness; honor your father and your mother.'" And he replied, "All these I have observed from my youth." When Jesus heard this he said to him, "There is still one thing left for you: sell all that you have and distribute it to the poor, and you will have treasure in heaven. Then come, follow me." But when he heard this he became quite sad, for he was very rich. (Luke 18:18-23)

Acknowledge As we follow the official's encounter with Jesus in this passage, let's try to acknowledge our own feelings. The first thing you notice is that the official asks Jesus a question: *"Good teacher, what must I do to inherit eternal life?"* Jesus responds to him by citing the commandments. The official replies, *"All these I have observed from my youth."* But Jesus tells him that there is still one thing left for him to do: *"Sell all that you have and distribute it to the poor and you will have treasure in heaven. Then come, follow me."* But he became sad because he was very rich. That is all that we know. It ends with an acknowledgement - the acknowledgement that he is sad.

Take a moment and acknowledge what you are feeling now as you pray with this passage. What do you feel in your heart as you ask Jesus, "What must I do to inherit eternal life?" How would you feel if Jesus gave you the response that the official received? What is going through your mind or in your soul? Just acknowledge those feelings.

Before we do anything else, it is good to just be honest. It is important for us to be aware of ourselves. It is also important to be aware of the interior movements going on in us, aware of the spiritual movements, and of some emotional movements as well. What are you feeling right now in your heart? Spend some time in **silence**, then **journal** your experience and acknowledge your feelings.

Relate We hear in this gospel passage how the official relates to Jesus a couple of times. The first time, he asks, *"Good teacher, what must I do to inherit eternal life?"* The second time, he relates to Jesus by saying, *"All these things I have observed from my youth."* Let's take a moment now - you have already acknowledged your feelings to God but now try relating these feelings to God. Try to find a way to speak to Him. Be open and honest like you would be with a good friend or a mentor. Reflect with these questions: What must I do to inherit eternal life? Have I not observed all these things from my youth? You have spent time acknowledging what you are feeling, now try to relate to Jesus what it is that you are desiring or asking for.

One of the very disturbing things about this passage is that when the official hears Jesus say: *"... sell all that you have ... Then come, follow me,"* he becomes very sad because he is very rich. Then, the passage ends there. The official doesn't go back to Jesus to relate his feelings to Him. Right now, however, you have an opportunity to relate the way you are feeling to Jesus. Maybe, when you hear this call to sell everything you have and follow Him, it leaves you sad. Or maybe it leaves you exhilarated. Or it may leave you with more questions. Whatever it does to you, your feelings are perfectly legitimate. The important thing is that you are honest, that you don't stay with those feelings walking away sad, but that you continue to dialogue with Jesus.

Close your eyes now and imagine you are standing there with Him. Tell Him whatever is on your heart. It might be a question, it might be a concern, it might be joy. Whatever it is, relate to Him in **silence**. When you are ready, **journal** your experience.

Receive In this passage, Jesus actually speaks to the official. The official has the opportunity to receive what Jesus says to him. He speaks to Jesus. He acknowledges what he is feeling and he relates it. Then, he receives what Jesus says. First, Jesus says, *"Why do you call me good? No one is good but God alone. You know the commandments ..."* As the official receives this, it does something in him. The first time he receives, he is aware that he has observed all the commandments from his youth and relates this to Jesus. Then, the second thing Jesus says is: *"There is still one thing left for you: sell all that you have and distribute it to the poor, and you will have treasure in heaven."* Again, Jesus speaks and the official listens.

Imagine Jesus speaking these words to you and receive whatever He wants to say to you. Maybe, He is saying a reminder to you to follow the commandments: Honor your father and your mother. You shall not commit adultery. You shall not kill. You shall not steal. You shall not bear false witness. Maybe you are receiving from Him this notion that there is still one thing left for you - sell all that you have and distribute it to the poor and you will have treasure in heaven.

Take a moment now and receive whatever you feel God is speaking to you. You have already acknowledged your feelings and related them to God. Now receive. This is wonderful because, at this point, you don't have to do anything - just wait and listen. This can be difficult for us because we are impatient and we want the answer right away, but the answer will come. God loves you so much and He is going to speak to you. So receive now whatever He wants to say to you or do in you. Sometimes, it may be hard to hear His voice so try to be in silence. If you don't hear anything, simply go back and read the Scripture passage over again and pray with it once more. Spend time with Scripture because often times He will speak the very words that we need to hear. Remember that the Word of God is alive. Spend some time now receiving the Word in **silence**. Just receive whatever He wants to speak to you. When you are ready, **journal** the experience.

Respond There are two wonderful examples of the official responding to Jesus. In the first dialogue with Jesus, the official has this question on his heart: *"Good teacher what must I do to inherit eternal life?"* Though we don't hear the official's acknowledgement, we do hear him relating it to Jesus. Then, we also hear a response from Jesus, where the official receives what he wants him to say. "*You know the commandments, 'You shall not commit adultery; you shall not kill; you shall not steal; you shall not bear false witness; honor your father and your mother.'*" There is a continued dialogue where he relates back to Jesus, *"All these I have observed from my youth."* Again, after he relates, Jesus responds back and he receives. The official receives this, *"There is still one thing left for you: sell all that you have and distribute it to the poor, and you will have treasure in heaven. Then come, follow me."* After he receives this, we see that there is no response back from the official. Instead, he acknowledges his feelings. He went away sad. I wonder what would have happened if he would have expressed his feelings to Jesus. If he had related them back to Him, if he had responded to Jesus rather than just walk away.

Now that you have received something from God, take a moment to respond to Him. Your response can be anything but be honest with your response. This is a good time to journal. When we journal, often times words come out of us that we don't intend or even think about. So, again, when you respond to God, be honest. He just gave you something beautiful. He just spoke to you. As you have received it, respond. Your response could be gratitude for what He has spoken to you. Your response may be sadness. Maybe you feel that you can't do what He is asking you to do. Maybe He is asking something great of you and you are sad about what you have to leave behind. Maybe your response is excitement and enthusiasm. These are perfectly honest responses; it is a wonderful way of praying.

Whatever your response is - whatever your honest response is - He can work with it. He can work with anything that you bring to Him. The important thing is that we don't walk away, that we don't walk away sad, but that we actually respond to Him. That we actually respond in some way to what He has spoken to us. That we let Him know what we are feeling inside. That we let Him know what our response is. Maybe it's a resolute YES. Maybe, we are unsure or maybe it is: "Lord, I don't know if I can do that."

Take some time in **silence** and try to articulate your response. Try saying it out loud or in your mind or your heart. Spend some time responding to Him. You might find that after this exercise there is some other feeling in your heart. You can go through the whole process again of acknowledging, relating, receiving and responding. Do this until you feel like you have completely communicated with the Lord and He with you. Again, take some time now to respond in silence and then **journal** your experience.

PREPARATION FOR TOMORROW:
Read the following Scripture as you prepare for tomorrow:
Psalm 46.

DAY 21

PRAYING WITH LECTIO DIVINA

PREPARATION:

5 P's of Prayer: Prepare - know your passage ahead of time and meditate on it throughout the day. When you transition into prayer, take time to breathe, relax, slow down, and just rest. Place - go to your prayer place, room or chair. Ninety percent of prayer is just being there. Posture - we pray using our bodies. Try one of the four postures: standing, sitting, kneeling, or prostrating. Presence - make the Sign of the Cross and invite the Father, the Son, and the Holy Spirit into this time of prayer. Invite God the Father to hold you, the Son to be the Good Shepherd to you, and the Holy Spirit to be Christ in you. Passage - hold the Bible in your lap and realize: "The Word of God is alive." The Father will speak to you!

LECTIO DIVINA:

A type of prayer in which one is reading Scripture, meditating or pondering Scripture, praying vocally with God, and contemplating in silence. Review Lectio Divina in the Prayer Exercises section of "Types of Prayer" in Appendix I.

PRAY NOW:

For this experience, we will be praying with Lectio Divina using Psalm 46. Open your Bible now to Psalm 46 and place it on your lap. The first step is *Lectio,* which means to read. So let's do that now. Read the passage once very slowly, then a second time slower, then a third and fourth time, even slower.

God is our refuge and our strength,
an ever-present help in distress.
Thus we do not fear, though earth be shaken
and mountains quake to the depths of the sea,
Though its waters rage and foam
and mountains totter at its surging.

Streams of the river gladden the city of God,
the holy dwelling of the Most High.
God is in its midst; it shall not be shaken;
God will help it at break of day.
Though nations rage and kingdoms totter,
he utters his voice and the earth melts.
The LORD of hosts is with us;

our stronghold is the God of Jacob.

Come and see the works of the LORD,
who has done fearsome deeds on earth;
Who stops wars to the ends of the earth,
breaks the bow, splinters the spear,
and burns the shields with fire;
"Be still and know that I am God!
I am exalted among the nations,
exalted on the earth."
The LORD of hosts is with us;
our stronghold is the God of Jacob.
(Psalm 46)

Now that you are acquainted with the passage, read it again. Try to hold on to a Word or a phrase that strikes you. What was the Word or phrase that you heard? Mine was: *the LORD of hosts is with us*.

Now read it one more time. Try to hold on to one Word or phrase. What was your Word or phrase this time? Mine was: *Be still and know that I am God!*

Read it one final time. Again, try to hold on to a Word or phrase. Just meditate on that for a moment in **silence** and then **journal** the Word or phrase you heard God say to you.

Meditatio or meditation is the second step of *Lectio Divina*. So let's spend some time now meditating on the Scripture passage. Like the other experiences of meditation, feel free to use your imagination, intellect, thoughts, reasoning, or your questioning.

God is our refuge and our strength. What is it like to have a refuge? If you think about being out on the water in a boat, a place of refuge is where you can dock and pull in so that you are away from the storm. Maybe you think of a refuge as being a home away from home. Somewhere where you can go when you need to escape. Maybe you are a mother of five or six kids, and your refuge is your bathroom. I don't know. Whatever your refuge is, try to think about that. *And our strength.* God is our strength. *An ever present help in distress*. He is an ever present help. Not only is He ever present, but He is an ever present help, especially in distress. He can be your strength and your refuge. No matter what you are going through.

We do not fear, though the earth be shaken / and mountains quake to the depths of the sea. Imagine the whole earth shaking and the mountains and everything crumbling into the sea. *Though its waters rage and foam and mountains totter at its surging. / Streams of river gladden the city of God, the holy dwelling of the Most High. / God is in its midst.* Right now, God is in your midst. You shall not be shaken. God will help you at the break of day. So think about it: tomorrow morning when you wake up and the sun rises, it is a new day. God will help you.

Though nations rage and kingdoms totter. We can certainly relate to this in our day. *He utters his voice and the earth melts.* The entire earth, at the utterance of God's voice melts before Him. There is no one stronger than He is. There is no one more powerful. All He needs to do is speak a single word and the whole earth melts. *The LORD of Hosts is with us; / our stronghold is the God of Jacob.*

Think about the good things that God has done in your life. If you just look around the world right now, you can probably see something good that God is doing. So *come and see the works of the LORD, / who has done fearsome deeds on the earth; / Who stops wars to the ends of the earth, / breaks the bow, splinters the spear, / and burns the shields with fire.* God can put an end to all of our wars. God can put an end to terrorism. God can put an end to injustice. God can put an end to any kind of oppression you are experiencing. God can bring it all to an end and He does it with such strength.

"*Be still and know that I am God!*" You don't have to fight the battle; He is fighting it for you. "*Be still and know that I am God! / I am exalted among all the nations, / exalted on the earth." / The LORD of Hosts is with us; / our stronghold is the God of Jacob.* The Lord of Hosts is with you. Your stronghold is the God of Jacob.

Take a moment in **silence**. Whatever was strongest for you in the meditation, wherever you felt the greatest surge of emotions, spend some time with that. When you are ready, **journal** your experience.

Now we move to the third step of *Lectio Divina*, which is *oratio* or pray. Try to articulate some kind of prayer to God through all this experience that you have just had. Through the repetition of the reading of the Word of God. Through the meditation. Through everything that has stirred up or has arisen in you. What do you want to say to God? What do you want to ask of God? It could be a question. It could be a petition. It could be asking Him for peace. It could be asking Him to put an end to war on our earth, or in our home. Ask Him for anything. There is nothing too small or too great to ask God.

Also, listen. In *oratio*, we not only speak to God and realize that He does listen to us, but God will speak to us as well. So spend some time in **silence** speaking to God about the experience that you have just had. It can be very informal where you just talk to Him, or it can be a formal prayer that you express to Him. When you are ready, **journal** your experience.

The final step of *Lectio Divina* is *contemplatio*, which is contemplation. You have just had a profound encounter with God. You have read His Word over and over, you have meditated upon it, you prayed with it, you prayed with Him. Hopefully, you have experienced His Word in some way. Hopefully, you felt some presence of God. Now take some time to rest with it. In this time of contemplation, there is nothing that you need to do. *"Be still and know that I am God!"*

Find a posture that is comfortable for you. You are going to spend the next period of time in complete **silence**. All you have to do is be still. If you find yourself getting distracted, just go back to whatever that Word, phrase, or image was and repeat it in your heart, over and over. *"Be still and know that I am God!" "Be still and know that I am God!" "Be still and know that I am God!"* When you are ready, **journal** your experience.

PREPARATION FOR TOMORROW:

Read the following Scripture as you prepare for tomorrow:
The Appearance to the Seven Disciples, John 21:1-14.

DAY 22

PRAYING WITH YOUR SENSES

PREPARATION:

5 P's of Prayer: Prepare - know your passage ahead of time and meditate on it throughout the day. When you transition into prayer, take time to breathe, relax, slow down, and just rest. Place - go to your prayer place, room or chair. Ninety percent of prayer is just being there. Posture - we pray using our bodies. Try one of the four postures: standing, sitting, kneeling, or prostrating. Presence - make the Sign of the Cross and invite the Father, the Son, and the Holy Spirit into this time of prayer. Invite God the Father to hold you, the Son to be the Good Shepherd to you, and the Holy Spirit to be Christ in you. Passage - hold the Bible in your lap and realize: "The Word of God is alive." The Father will speak to you!

PRAYING WITH YOUR FIVE SENSES:

This type of prayer uses your senses, physically and imaginatively (seeing, hearing, smelling, tasting, and touching). Review Praying with Your Senses in the Prayer Exercises section of "Types of Prayer" in Appendix I.

PRAY NOW:

For this prayer experience, we will be praying with our senses - see, hear, smell, taste, and touch. Open your Bible to The Appearance to the Seven Disciples, John 21:1-14, and have your journal ready. Let's read the passage.

After this, Jesus revealed himself again to his disciples at the Sea of Tiberias. He revealed himself in this way. Together were Simon Peter, Thomas called Didymus, Nathanael from Cana in Galilee, Zebedee's sons, and two others of his disciples. Simon Peter said to them, "I am going fishing." They said to him, "We also will come with you." So they went out and got into the boat, but that night they caught nothing. When it was already dawn, Jesus was standing on the shore; but the disciples did not realize that it was Jesus. Jesus said to them, "Children, have you caught anything to eat?" They answered him, "No." So he said to them, "Cast the net over the right side of the boat and you will find something." So they cast it, and were not able to pull it in because of the number of fish. So the disciple whom Jesus loved said to Peter, "It is the Lord." When Simon Peter heard that it was the Lord, he tucked in his garment, for he was lightly clad, and jumped into the sea. The other disciples came in the boat, for they were not far from shore, only about a hundred yards, dragging the net with the fish. When they climbed out on shore, they saw a charcoal fire with fish on it and bread. Jesus said to them, "Bring some of the fish you just caught." So Simon Peter went over and dragged the net ashore full of one hundred fifty-three large fish. Even though there were so many, the net was not torn. Jesus said to them, "Come, have breakfast." And none of the disciples dared to ask him, "Who are you?" because they realized it was the Lord. Jesus came over and took the bread and gave it to them, and in like manner the fish. This was now the third time Jesus was revealed to his disciples after being raised from the dead. (John 21:1-14)

The first sense we will use is sight as we go through the Scripture passage. Try to visualize the events and focus solely on your sense of sight as you see everything happening before you.

After this, Jesus revealed himself again to his disciples at the Sea of Tiberias. He revealed himself in this way. [You are about to experience how Jesus revealed Himself to His disciples in the Resurrection.] *Together were Simon Peter, Thomas called Didymus, Nathanael from Cana in Galilee, Zebedee's sons, and two others of his disciples. Simon Peter said to them, "I am going fishing." They said to him, "We also will come with you." So they went out and got into the boat, but that night they caught nothing.* [Now, here is what I really want you to see.] *When it was already dawn, Jesus was standing on the shore; but the disciples did not realize that it was Jesus.* The sun is just rising, so the darkness is coming to an end. You are in the morning twilight. You can just begin to see. As you look on to the shore, you see a man standing there but you don't know who he is; it is too dark and too blurry.

Jesus said to them, "Children, have you caught anything to eat?" They answered him, "No." So he said to them, "Cast the net over the right side of the boat and you will find something." You look around now at all the disciples' faces. Some of them look tired. Some of them look frustrated. Some of them look confused. You watch as together they cast the net over the right side of the boat. As they do, they *were not able to pull it in because of the number of fish.* Try to see this net being pulled in and all these fish being pulled out of the dark water into that morning light. You see the shimmering as their tails and fins flap through the water.

Then you see the disciple whom Jesus loved. You look at his face as he says to Peter: *"It is the Lord."* You can see in his eyes that he knows it is Jesus. You can see in his face the excitement, joy, and the anticipation that his Lord is here. *When Simon Peter heard that it was the Lord,* [now watch this!] *he tucked in his garment, for he was lightly clad, and jumped into the sea.* You watch him jump over the edge into the dark water and begin swimming to the shore.

The other disciples came in the boat, for they were not far from shore, only about one hundred yards, dragging the net with fish. When they climbed out on shore they saw a charcoal fire with fish on it and bread. Imagine seeing that fire in the morning light on the beach; the embers, the flame, the fish, and the bread. *Jesus said to them, "Bring some of the fish you just caught." So Simon Peter went over and dragged the net ashore full of one hundred fifty-three large fish. Even though there were so many, the net was not torn. Jesus said to them, "Come, have breakfast." And none of the disciples dared to ask him, "Who are you?" because they realized it was the Lord. Jesus came over and took the bread and gave it to them, and in like manner the fish. This was now the third time Jesus was revealed to his disciples after being raised from the dead.* Take a moment in **silence** and then **journal** whatever you saw.

Next, we will apply our sense of hearing. Try to hear the scene, hear the rocking of the boat at night, in the dark, in the quiet. Hear the disciples sleeping; maybe some of them are snoring. Hear what it sounds like when this voice comes from the land: *"Children have you caught anything to eat?"* The disciples all rumble together, *"No." "Cast the net over the right side of the boat and you will find something." So they cast it, and were not able to pull it in because of the number of fish. So the disciple whom Jesus loved said to Peter, "It is the Lord." When Simon Peter heard that it was the Lord, he tucked in his garment, for he was lightly clad, and jumped into the sea.* [Listen as his body crashes into the water.]

The other disciples came in the boat, for they were not far from shore, only about a hundred yards, dragging the net with fish. When they climbed out on shore, they saw a charcoal fire with fish on it and bread. [Try to hear the crackling of the fire and the embers.] *"Bring some of the fish you just caught." So Simon Peter went over and dragged the net ashore full of one hundred fifty-three large fish.* [Try to hear the sound of that net with all the fish splashing around. Hear the dragging of the fish on the shore, through the sand.]

Even though there were so many, the net was not torn. Jesus said to them, "Come, have breakfast." And none of the disciples dared to ask him, "Who are you?" because they realized it was the Lord. Jesus came over and took the bread and gave it to them, and in like manner the fish. This was now the third time Jesus was revealed to his disciples after being raised from the dead. What did you hear in the scene? Which part of it was most real for you? Spend some time in **silence** and **journal** your experience.

The third sense is smell. So again, use your imagination and try to smell what it would be like to be on the Sea of Galilee. Try to smell the fish that are being caught. Try to smell the fresh air at dawn. Imagine now that you are on the shore and you see the fire. You can smell the campfire. There is nothing like a fire, on a beach, by the water. You can smell the soot and the embers. As you get closer, you see that He is cooking the fish and the bread. Try to smell the warm baked bread and fish. Spend some time in **silence** with your sense of smell. When you are ready, **journal** your experience.

Now use your sense of taste. First, let's focus on The Sea of Galilee. It is a body of fresh water. Imagine you are Peter jumping into the sea. He is probably swimming so excitedly that water gets into his mouth. What does it taste like to you?

Second, let's focus on the scene when you get to shore and see that Jesus has prepared a loaf of bread and fish. He invites you to *"Come, have breakfast." And none of the disciples dared to ask him, "Who are you?" because they realized that it was the Lord. Jesus came over and took the bread and gave it to them, and in like manner the fish.* Try first to imagine tasting this warm bread that was just baked on a bonfire, on the beach of the Sea of Galilee. There is nothing like food that is baked on a campfire. It just has that taste to it. Try to taste the bread. It is so good. The same with the fish. It is fresh fish, the freshest fish you have ever had. It is a white fish, baked just to the right amount of crispiness on the outside and tenderness on the inside. You can taste it.

Spend some time now just with your sense of taste. Focus on either the water or the bread and fish. Allow your sense of taste to help you enter into this scene and be there with Jesus. Take some time in **silence** and when you are ready, **journal** your experience.

Finally, touch. Imagine you are out there on the sea at night. You are tired and you are asked to cast this net over the right side of the boat. Imagine what that must have felt like to grab the wet net with your hands. To begin pulling on it, realizing that it is tight. That it is heavy. You can't even pull it in. Try pulling on it. Can you feel that? There are so many fish in there, you don't have the strength to pull it in.

As Jesus calls, the beloved disciple reveals, *"It is the Lord."* Imagine you are Simon Peter lightly clad; so you tuck in your garments and jump into the sea. What does it feel like to jump off the edge of the boat? Almost like you are a child in the air for a moment. Then the splash of the cold water in the morning. You feel the water skimming along your body as you swim to the shore. Now as you get to the shore, you feel the dry land, the rocks, the stones, the coarseness of the earth, and you are cold. But as you approach the fire where Jesus is, you begin to feel warm. You feel the heat of the fire on your skin.

When *Jesus said to them, "Bring some of the fish you just caught,"* imagine you are Simon Peter who goes over and drags *the net ashore full of one hundred fifty-three large fish.* It is implied that Simon Peter is doing this by himself. Imagine you are pulling this net ashore, from the water to the dry land, with all these fish flapping against you. *Even though there were so many, the net was not torn.*

Jesus says to them, "Come have breakfast." And none of his Disciples dared to ask him, "Who are you?" because they realized it was the Lord. Jesus came over and took the bread and gave it to them. Imagine Him handing you a piece of fresh baked bread right off the fire. You are still a little bit cold from the water. But you can feel the warmth from the fire. Now you have a warm piece of bread in your hand. As you put it into your mouth, it feels so good because it is so fresh and warm. You begin to chew on it and then He offers you the fish in a like manner. You take the fresh fish that is cooked. You try a piece of it and it is so tender.

This was now the third time Jesus was revealed to his disciples after being raised from the dead. Read the Scripture passage now once more to yourself and try to apply all of your senses. Then spend some time in silence, meditating with whatever is most powerful for you. Most strong for you. Whatever sense was really the most vivid for you. It helps us to realize that this moment is real for us. That we can enter into it. Spend some time in **silence**; when you are ready, **journal** your experience.

PREPARATION FOR TOMORROW:
We will pray with Sunday Mass.

PRAYING WITH SUNDAY MASS

Today's prayer will be celebrating the Sunday Mass and experiencing God the Father in the Eucharist and Liturgy. Prepare before Mass with the following and then journal your experience after Mass.

PREPARATION BEFORE SUNDAY MASS:

Today, as preparation, we are going to focus on the Liturgy of the Eucharist. An important part of the Liturgy of the Eucharist is the offering of the gifts - when the bread and wine are brought forward. But, it is not only bread and wine that are brought forward. The offering of the gifts is symbolic of bringing forward the gifts of the people. The greatest gift that God has is you. You are His greatest gift. So it is a wonderful thing to be able to offer ourselves with the bread and wine. At Mass today, I would like you to try to do just that.

Go a little bit early to Mass and find where the gifts of bread and wine have been placed. Usually, they are about halfway down the aisle or they might be in the back of the church. Take a few moments to go up to where those gifts are and spend a moment in prayer by them. Those gifts of bread and wine will soon be carried up by the hands of the people of faith.

What I would like you to do is place yourself with those gifts. Imagine that you are there on that gold plate (which is called the ciborium). Imagine that you are there in the chalice. Imagine that you are offering your life, your body, your soul, and your spirit to God. Place yourself with the gifts of bread and wine. Then during Mass, as the gifts are brought forward, I want you to watch who carries them. Those people are carrying you. You are offered up with the gifts of bread and wine. You have laid your life there. You have laid your body down. It is so wonderful to see yourself being carried up by the people of faith.

The gifts that are brought to the altar of God are then handed to the priest and to the servers. You are one of the gifts. Then, as the priest takes the bread and blesses it, you are right there. As the priest takes the wine and blesses it, you are right there. You are the gift. Imagine yourself being picked up by the priest in his hands. Like a little child and offered to God the Father. I think of that moment of Abraham offering his son Isaac. This is your chance to offer your life to God, to give your whole self to Him, to give everything. Whatever you are grateful for, whatever your joys are, whatever your sadness is, whatever your difficulties are, whatever your anxieties are, whatever your worries are, whatever your frustrations are; give yourself to Him. Give your life to Him. Let the priest hold you up and offer you to God: bless you, break you, and share you. That you may become one with Christ at the moment of consecration. That you may be offered with the gifts of bread and wine. Taken, blessed, and offered to the Father.

AFTER SUNDAY MASS:

How was Mass? What was it like to experience praying over the gifts before Mass? Who were the ones who carried you up? Who were the ones who carried the bread and the wine? If you offered yourself, they carried you as well! What was it like to be held in the hands of the priest and offered to God the Father, with the gifts of bread and wine? What was it like to be transformed into the Body of Christ? How does it feel to offer yourself to God in this way? Take a moment and **journal** your experience, especially of offering yourself with the gifts of bread and wine.

PREPARATION FOR TOMORROW:

Read the following Scripture as you prepare for tomorrow: Last Supper Discourses and The Advocate, John 14:1-31.

DAY 23

PRAYING WITH CONTEMPLATIVE PRAYER

PREPARATION:

5 P's of Prayer: Prepare - know your passage ahead of time and meditate on it throughout the day. When you transition into prayer, take time to breathe, relax, slow down, and just rest. Place - go to your prayer place, room or chair. Ninety percent of prayer is just being there. Posture - we pray using our bodies. Try one of the four postures: standing, sitting, kneeling, or prostrating. Presence - make the Sign of the Cross and invite the Father, the Son, and the Holy Spirit into this time of prayer. Invite God the Father to hold you, the Son to be the Good Shepherd to you, and the Holy Spirit to be Christ in you. Passage - hold the Bible in your lap and realize: "The Word of God is alive." The Father will speak to you!

CONTEMPLATIVE PRAYER:

Contemplative prayer is a type of prayer that involves silence and simply being in the presence of God. Review Contemplative Prayer and praying with the Word (Prayer Exercises) in "Types of Prayer" in Appendix I.

PRAY NOW:

Today's experience will be praying with the Word contemplatively using John 14:1-31, Last Supper Discourses and The Advocate. Open your Bible and find the passage. We will pray with the entire chapter.

Read the passage in silence once very slowly. Then read it again slower, until you find a Word or a phrase that you feel God is speaking to you. Remain in silence repeating this Word over and over in your heart. If you get distracted, remember the virtue is returning back to the Word. Continue repeating the phrase over and over again until you come to a place of rest in the Word. Remain in silence, peace, and stillness for as long as the moment lasts. If there is fruit, remain with that Word or phrase. However, if you find the Word or phrase is no longer "working" for you, continue on until God speaks to you in another Word or phrase. It may help to speak it out loud if you are especially distracted. Repeat it over and over again until you become settled and remain in silence.

Contemplative prayer is an intense focused time on the Word. If you notice yourself moving back into vocal prayer or meditative prayer, gently try and let that go so that you can remain in this heightened state of contemplative prayer. Remember, as long as you remain in prayer, "all is grace." God will use it all to bring you closer to Him. The Holy Spirit will be your guide into this deep and abiding prayer with Christ and the Father.

"Do not let your hearts be troubled. You have faith in God; have faith also in me. In my Father's house there are many dwelling places. If there were not, would I have told you that I am going to prepare a place for you? And if I go and prepare a place for you, I will come back again and take you to myself, so that where I am you also may be. Where [I] am going you know the way." Thomas said to him, "Master, we do not know where you are going; how can we know the way?" Jesus said to him, "I am the way and the truth and the life. No one comes to the Father except through me. If you know me, then you will also know my Father. From now on you do know him and have seen him." Philip said to him, "Master, show us the Father, and that will be enough for us." Jesus said to him, "Have I been with you for so long a time and you still do not know me, Philip? Whoever has seen me has seen the Father. How can you say, 'Show us the Father'? Do you not believe that I am in the Father and the Father is in me? The words that I speak to you I do not speak on my own. The Father who dwells in me is doing his works. Believe me that I am in the Father and the Father is in me, or else, believe because of the works themselves. Amen, amen, I say to you, whoever believes in me will do the works that I do, and will do greater ones than these, because I am going to the Father. And whatever you ask in my name, I will do, so that the Father may be glorified in the Son. If you ask anything of me in my name, I will do it.

"If you love me, you will keep my commandments. And I will ask the Father, and he will give you another Advocate to be with you always, the Spirit of truth, which the world cannot accept, because it neither sees nor knows it. But you know it, because it remains with you, and will be in you. I will not leave you orphans; I will come to you. In a little while the world will no longer see me, but you will see me, because I live and you will live. On that day you will realize that I am in my Father and you are in me and I in you. Whoever has my commandments and observes them is the one who loves me. And whoever loves me will be loved by my Father, and I will love him and reveal myself to him." Judas, not the Iscariot, said to him, "Master, [then] what happened that you will reveal yourself to us and not to the world?" Jesus answered and said to him, "Whoever loves me will keep my word, and my Father will love him, and we will come to him and make our dwelling with him. Whoever does not love me does not keep my words; yet the word you hear is not mine but that of the Father who sent me.

"I have told you this while I am with you. The Advocate, the holy Spirit that the Father will send in my name—he will teach you everything and remind you of all that [I] told you. Peace I leave with you; my peace I give to you. Not as the world gives do I give it to you. Do not let your hearts

be troubled or afraid. You heard me tell you, 'I am going away and I will come back to you.' If you loved me, you would rejoice that I am going to the Father; for the Father is greater than I. And now I have told you this before it happens, so that when it happens you may believe. I will no longer speak much with you, for the ruler of the world is coming. He has no power over me, but the world must know that I love the Father and that I do just as the Father has commanded me. Get up, let us go. (John 14:1-31)

Spend the rest of your time in **silent** contemplation. When you are ready, **journal** your experience.

PREPARATION FOR TOMORROW:
Read the following Scripture as you prepare for tomorrow:
Psalm 63.

DAY 24

PRAYING WITH SCRIPTURAL RELAXATION

PREPARATION:

5 P's of Prayer: Prepare - know your passage ahead of time and meditate on it throughout the day. When you transition into prayer, take time to breathe, relax, slow down, and just rest. Place - go to your prayer place, room or chair. Ninety percent of prayer is just being there. Posture - we pray using our bodies. Try one of the four postures: standing, sitting, kneeling, or prostrating. Presence - make the Sign of the Cross and invite the Father, the Son, and the Holy Spirit into this time of prayer. Invite God the Father to hold you, the Son to be the Good Shepherd to you, and the Holy Spirit to be Christ in you. Passage - hold the Bible in your lap and realize: "The Word of God is alive." The Father will speak to you!

SCRIPTURE RELAXATION:

The focus of this exercise is allowing the Word of God to help us relax in the sanctuary of God's love. Review Scriptural Relaxation in the Prayer Exercises section of "Types of Prayer" in Appendix I. You can also find the audio version of Scriptural Relaxation at TheProdigalFather.org/Pray-40Days.

PRAY NOW:

Today, we will relax with Psalm 63:2-9, Ardent Longing for God. Before we begin, take a moment to find a posture that is comfortable and in which you feel relaxed. Either sit or lie down in a comfortable place. Read the entire passage once before starting the relaxation exercise.

O God, you are my God –
it is you I seek!
For you my body yearns;
for you my soul thirsts,
In a land parched, lifeless,
And without water.
I look to you in the sanctuary
to see your power and glory.
For your love is better than life;
my lips shall ever praise you!

I will bless you as long as I live;
I will lift up my hands, calling on your name.
My soul shall be sated as with choice food,

with joyous lips my mouth shall praise you!
I think of you upon my bed,
I remember you through the watches of the night.
You indeed are my savior,
and in the shadow of your wings I shout for joy.
My soul clings fast to you;
your right hand upholds me.
(Psalm 63:2-9)

O God, you are my God – / it is you I seek! / For you my body yearns; / for you my soul thirsts. Allow your body to rest right now. Close your eyes or allow them to gaze unfocused. We are going to spend a few moments merely breathing. The phrase I want you to meditate on is *O God, you are my God.* [Pause for a moment of silence.]

As we begin, take a long, slow, deep breath in through your nose.... *O God, you are my God....* Hold it there for a moment then, through your mouth, release as you breathe out.... Breathe out any worries or anxiety.... [Pause for a moment of silence.]

As you take second long, slow, deep breath through your nose, breath in the Holy Spirit.... *O God, you are my God....* Hold it there for a moment and release.... Breathe out anything that you may be pre-occupied with.... Just breathe it out and give it to God.... [Pause for a moment of silence.]

Take one final long, slow, deep breath in through your nose... As long as you can.... Fill your lungs completely inviting the Holy Spirit to come into you.... *O God, you are my God....* Hold it for a moment, then slowly release and breathe out through your mouth.... Offer anything to God that may be causing you worry or anxiety.... All you have to do is rest and continue to breathe gently.... [Pause for a moment of silence.]

As I reflect with you on the *Ardent Longing for God*, you are going to focus on your body. Resting, feeling heavy and warm. Let's begin with your head.... Just feel your head sink into your cushion or your pillow.... As it sinks down, meditate upon these words - *O God, you are my God – / it is you I seek!* As your mind comes to rest, your head sinks deeper into the pillow and feels heavy and warm.... [Pause for a moment of silence.]

For you my body yearns.... Imagine this heaviness moving down to your neck.... Your shoulders begin to release any tension.... You feel that warmth radiate down from the tip of your head to your shoulders.... Your neck and shoulders feel heavy and warm as they sink into the cushion.... *O God, you are my God – / it is you I seek!* [Pause for a moment of silence.]

For you my soul thirsts.... You have this yearning and this thirst for God.... Right now, all you can do is surrender.... You can't fulfill that yearning or fill that thirst or that void without God.... Just allow your body to relax.... Imagine your chest loosening up.... Breathe out.... You feel the warmth radiate through your chest and in your heart, your soul and your mind .... Your head, your shoulders, and your chest sink deeply into the cushion. [Pause for a moment of silence.]

In a land parched, lifeless, / and without water.... Imagine your face and your mouth.... Whatever tension is there begins to release.... Your whole face feels heavy and warm.... Your head, your shoulders, your face and your chest sink deeper into the cushion.... You begin to rest.... *O God, you are my God – / it is you I seek!* [Pause for a moment of silence.]

I look to you in the sanctuary / to see your power and glory.... Now feel as your entire torso.... your stomach.... your back.... and your spine begins to release.... Relax.... You feel the warmth radiate down from your shoulders.... To your chest.... Through your back.... Into your stomach.... The body begins to rest.... It feels heavy and warm as you sink into the cushion.... [Pause for a moment of silence.]

For your love is better than life; Continue down your body and allow the heaviness and the warmth to spread down through your torso.... To your legs.... Beginning to relax.... Release.... *O God, you are my God – / it is you I seek!* If there is any pain or discomfort, it begins to subside.... The entire upper half of your body feels heavy and warm and relaxed....

... my lips shall ever praise you! / I will bless you as long as I live; Your face continues to relax.... Your lips relax.... All of your body relaxes right now in praise to God.... *O God, you are my God – / it is you I seek!* [Pause for a moment of silence.]

I will lift up my hands, calling on your name.... Feel your hands now, all the tension and stress releasing as they relax.... You feel the warmth radiate in your shoulders.... to your arms.... to your hands. They feel heavy and warm.... and sink deeply into the cushion.... [Pause for a moment of silence.]

I will lift up my hands, calling on your name. / My soul shall be sated as with choice food.... Imagine now your entire body being filled with the Holy Spirit.... *O God, you are my God – / it is you I seek!* [Pause for a moment of silence.]

... with joyous lips my mouth shall praise you! Once more, your lips begin to rest and the warmth travels through your entire body.... From your

head.... to your legs... to your feet... Your legs and feet feel heavy and warm as they sink into the cushion.... Release any tension.... *O God, you are my God – / it is you I seek!* Begin to feel relaxed, heavy, and warm as they sink into the cushion.... [Pause for a moment of silence.]

I think of you upon my bed.... Your entire body now is relaxed.... You feel the warmth of God's presence radiate through your whole body.... Your body feels warm and heavy.... as you sink into the cushion.... *I think of you upon my bed....* Just ponder all the good things of God.... all that He does for you.... [Pause for a moment of silence.]

I remember you through the watches of the night. / You indeed are my savior, / and in the shadow of your wings I shout for joy.... Right now, you are safe.... You are protected in the shadow of God's wings surrounded by the angels.... [Pause for a moment of silence.]

My soul clings fast to you; / your right hand upholds me.... Right now, at this moment, your soul is joined to God and clings to Him.... Not only does your soul experience this safety, this closeness, but your entire body feels close to God.... safe.... held.... warm.... resting.... sinking gently into the cushion.... *O God, you are my God – / it is you I seek!* [Pause for a moment of silence.]

I think of you upon my bed, / I remember you through the watches of the night.... Spend a few moments now and just repeat that phrase over and over.... *I think of you upon my bed, / I remember you through the watches of the night....* Right now, as you lay and rest in this time of scriptural relaxation, all you have to do is rest with God.... All you have to do is to allow your soul to cling to Him.... Allow yourself to be held in the palm of His hands surrounded by the angels.... Your entire body now is resting.... Your body is at peace.... Your mind is at peace.... Your soul is at peace.... You feel heavy, warm, safe and relaxed.... *I think of you upon my bed....* [Pause for a moment of silence.]

I think of you upon my bed.... / I think of you upon my bed, / I remember you through the watches of the night. Rest now in **silence**. *I think of you upon my bed.... O God, you are my God.* When you are finished, **journal** your experience.

PREPARATION FOR TOMORROW:
Read the following Scripture as you prepare for tomorrow:
The Blind Bartimaeus, Mark 10:46-52.

DAY 25

PRAYING WITH GUIDED MEDITATION

PREPARATION:

5 P's of Prayer: Prepare - know your passage ahead of time and meditate on it throughout the day. When you transition into prayer, take time to breathe, relax, slow down, and just rest. Place - go to your prayer place, room or chair. Ninety percent of prayer is just being there. Posture - we pray using our bodies. Try one of the four postures: standing, sitting, kneeling, or prostrating. Presence - make the Sign of the Cross and invite the Father, the Son, and the Holy Spirit into this time of prayer. Invite God the Father to hold you, the Son to be the Good Shepherd to you, and the Holy Spirit to be Christ in you. Passage - hold the Bible in your lap and realize: "The Word of God is alive." The Father will speak to you!

GUIDED MEDITATION:

Find a quiet room, settle into a spot that will be comfortable, and place your body in a relaxed position, usually without crossed arms or legs. Allow your imagination, fueled by your senses, to enter into the story. Close your eyes as you meditate; at the end of the meditation, do not rush to open your eyes. Let your body tell you when you are ready. Review Guided Meditation under the Prayer Exercises section of "Types of Prayer" in Appendix I.

PRAY NOW:

This meditation is based on The Blind Bartimaeus, Mark 10:46-52.

They came to Jericho. And as he was leaving Jericho with his disciples and a sizable crowd, Bartimaeus, a blind man, the son of Timaeus, sat by the roadside begging. On hearing that it was Jesus of Nazareth, he began to cry out and say, "Jesus, son of David, have pity on me." And many rebuked him, telling him to be silent. But he kept calling out all the more, "Son of David, have pity on me." Jesus stopped and said, "Call him." So they called the blind man, saying to him, "Take courage; get up, he is calling you." He threw aside his cloak, sprang up, and came to Jesus. Jesus said to him in reply, "What do you want me to do for you?" The blind man replied to him, "Master, I want to see." Jesus told him, "Go your way; your faith has saved you." Immediately he received his sight and followed him on the way. (Mark 10:46-52)

Imagine yourself in Jericho. You are the blind man sitting by the roadside begging. You hear the crowds going by, the noise of the people. You can't see. You are just sitting there begging, completely impoverished. Waiting for someone to help you.

Maybe there is something right now in your life that you find yourself unable to do or complete. Maybe it is your faith. Maybe you are unable to see Jesus. Maybe you are unable to really experience Him or feel Him in prayer. You are like the blind man, just sitting there. You have the opportunity right now to call out to Him. To ask Him to help you to see.

Imagine yourself there, sitting on the side of the road. You hear a rumbling in the crowd and you hear someone say that it is Jesus of Nazareth. So you begin to cry out; without even thinking about it, you cry out and you scream: "*Jesus, son of David, have pity on me.*" But then the crowd begins to make fun of you and rebuke you. They are telling you to be silent, to shut up. You get this feeling of rejection. But still all the more you keep calling out. *"Jesus, son of David, have pity on me."* You want so much to see.

You hear the crowd act rather strangely. They start to talk. Then the noises begin to subside. You get the feeling that somebody is walking right up to you. You hear the sound of His footsteps. His leather sandals hitting the ground, step... step... step. You smell the scene. You smell the dust.

Then you hear the voice of Jesus say, *"Call him." "Call him."* So, they call you, saying, *"Take courage; get up, he is calling you."* Without even thinking about it, you stand up. You throw your cloak aside and go to Jesus. When you throw your cloak aside, you are throwing aside all of your own protection. All of the ways that you have been trying to live this life by yourself. Control this life by yourself. Survive by yourself. You are throwing it all aside. Trusting that He can heal you.

As you walk up to where you think Jesus is, you hear His voice right in front of you: "*What do you want me to do for you?*" Notice that He realizes you are blind; He can see it. He sees the crowd. He is taking in the whole experience. But He wants to give you the freedom to ask for it. So He says, "*What do you want me to do for you?*" Right now in your prayer, you can ask Him for anything. What do you want Jesus to do for you? Right now in your heart, in your mind, or even out loud, ask Him.

"Master, I want to see." These are good words, because sometimes we can't even see what we want. Sometimes we are blind to what we need Jesus to give to us. But if we say, "*Master; I want to see*", and we really have faith, He will give us sight.

Imagine yourself saying that to Jesus, just say it: "*Master, I want to see.*" Then notice Jesus say to you, "*Go your way; your faith has saved you.*" As He says that, immediately you can see. Your eyes are completely opened. Jesus is standing before you. Looking at you with great intensity. Realizing that your faith in Him is what opened your eyes and allowed you to see. You want nothing more than to follow Him.

Take a moment in **silence** and just meditate upon this passage. Meditate upon what it is like to now be able to see Him. To hear His voice say to you: "*Go your way; your faith has saved you.*" As you see Him, look at Him; see the way that He looks at you. You desire to follow Him *on the way.*

As you come to the end of this meditation, **journal** your experience. What was it like to feel blind? What was it like to be sitting there on the side of the road completely incapable of doing anything for yourself? Then, what was it like to feel the rejection of the crowd of people, making fun of you because you wanted to see Jesus? Experiencing, not rejection from Jesus, but acceptance. He calls you to Him. You go to Him. You throw off your cloak. As you go to Him, He says, *"What do you want me to do for you?"*

Because desire is so important in prayer, we express our desire to Jesus. What is your desire? Because He gives us freedom, He will never make us do anything. He will not act on us without us asking. So ask Him for sight. Ask Him for whatever is your heart's greatest desire. Ask Him with great faith and He will answer it. Spend some time and **journal** your experience.

PREPARATION FOR TOMORROW:
Read the following Scripture as you prepare for tomorrow:
The Call of Simon the Fisherman, Luke 5:1-11.

DAY 26

PRAYING LIKE A PIRATE

PREPARATION:

5 P's of Prayer: Prepare - know your passage ahead of time and meditate on it throughout the day. When you transition into prayer, take time to breathe, relax, slow down, and just rest. Place - go to your prayer place, room or chair. Ninety percent of prayer is just being there. Posture - we pray using our bodies. Try one of the four postures: standing, sitting, kneeling, or prostrating. Presence - make the Sign of the Cross and invite the Father, the Son, and the Holy Spirit into this time of prayer. Invite God the Father to hold you, the Son to be the Good Shepherd to you, and the Holy Spirit to be Christ in you. Passage - hold the Bible in your lap and realize: "The Word of God is alive." The Father will speak to you!

PRAYING LIKE A PIRATE:

ARRR: Acknowledge, Relate, Receive, and Respond to God. Review Praying like a Pirate in the Prayer Exercises section of "Types of Prayer" found in Appendix I.

PRAY NOW:

Today's prayer experience is based on The Call of Simon the Fisherman, Luke 5:1-11. We will be using the exercise of Praying like a Pirate: ARRR (acknowledge, relate, receive and respond). Read the passage one time straight through and acknowledge your feelings. Try to be aware of them and get in touch with what is going on in your mind, in your heart, and in your soul.

While the crowd was pressing in on Jesus and listening to the word of God, he was standing by the Lake of Gennesaret. He saw two boats there alongside the lake; the fishermen had disembarked and were washing their nets. Getting into one of the boats, the one belonging to Simon, he asked him to put out a short distance from the shore. Then he sat down and taught the crowds from the boat. After he had finished speaking, he said to Simon, "Put out into deep water and lower your nets for a catch." Simon said in reply, "Master, we have worked hard all night and have caught nothing, but at your command I will lower the nets." When they had done this, they caught a great number of fish and their nets were tearing. They signaled to their partners in the other boat to come to help them. They came and filled both boats so that they were in danger of sinking. When Simon Peter saw this, he fell at the knees of Jesus and said, "Depart from me, Lord, for I am a sinful man." For astonishment at the catch of fish they had made seized him and all those with him, and likewise James and John, the sons of Zebedee, who were partners of Simon. Jesus said to Simon, "Do not be afraid; from now on you will be catching men." When they brought their boats to the shore, they left everything and followed him. (Luke 5:1-11)

Acknowledge What was going on in Simon's heart? Imagine you are Simon after a long night's work. How would you feel after Jesus' request? Take a moment now to acknowledge your feelings. Be honest. What is going on in your heart, in your mind, in your soul? Try to get in touch with yourself; know thyself. Realize what it is you are experiencing. Some days we are going about so busy that we have no idea what our internal disposition is. What we are really feeling deep down inside. So take a moment in **silence.** Acknowledge to yourself what you are feeling. When you are ready, **journal** the experience.

Relate *After he had finished speaking, he said to Simon, "Put out into deep water and lower your nets for a catch."* Simon must have been feeling tired, confused, and a little perplexed by why Jesus would want them to do that. So he relates to Jesus. He tells Him what he is feeling. He says, "*Master, we have worked hard all night and have caught nothing, but at your command I will lower the nets.*" So he relates what he is feeling to Jesus. He is not afraid to tell Jesus what is going on inside of him. He is not afraid to question Him or to even tell Him - "Hey, if you didn't realize it, we have been up all night, we are tired. We have worked hard all night and have caught nothing. Can't you see that?" "*But at your command I will lower the nets.*" So he relates his feelings to Jesus. He tells Him he is tired. He is frustrated. He has been trying all night. But he will listen to Jesus. If Jesus commands him to do it, he will lower the net.

Take a moment in **silence** to relate your feelings to Jesus, or to the Father, or to the Holy Spirit, or to the blessed mother Mary. What are you feeling right now? What do you need to tell God? Take some time now and try to articulate that. Either speak it out loud, in your heart, or in your soul. When you are ready, **journal** your experience.

Receive After acknowledging your feelings and relating them to God the Father, the Son, the Holy Spirit, or to Mary, take some time to receive whatever God wants to give to you. It is difficult for us to receive because we can't make it happen. But we can ask. We can ask God to speak to us. He does desire to have this communion with you. If you have been so generous to give this time to Him, He is going to bless you and speak to you. Whatever it is that you acknowledged, whatever was going on in your heart, whatever you related to Him, He is going to give to you in some way. With either an answer, a sense of peace, consolation, or an experience of closeness to Him. You may be as surprised and filled with wonder just as the disciples; *for astonishment at the catch of fish they had made seized him and all those with him.*

Receive whatever He wants to give to you. In order to receive, we need to empty ourselves. We need to open our hands, hearts, and our minds. The best way to do that is to be in **silence** and receive whatever He wants to give to you. If you find yourself distracted or frustrated by that, pray with the Word. Read the Scripture until He does speak something to you and remain in silence. Maybe He will say something to you like this, "*Do not be afraid; from now on you will be catching men.*" Take time to receive. When you are ready, **journal** your experience.

Respond In the Gospel of Luke, the disciples responded to Jesus when He said to them, "*Do not be afraid; from now on you'll be catching men.*" They responded when they brought their boats to the shore. They left everything and followed Him.

Now, having acknowledged your own feelings, related them to God and received something, there is probably some natural response. Maybe your response is to leave everything and follow Him. Maybe it is a little bit more subtle. But in some way respond back to Him; finish this dialogue. Allow Him to know that you heard what He said. Respond back in some way. Or repeat back what He said to you. Or ask Him if it was really Him who said it to you. Sometimes He says things to us that are hard to believe. Sometimes we have to test what is said to us. That can be your response. Take time to respond in some way. You can do that out loud. You can do it spontaneously. You can do it as a prayer. You can speak it in your heart, in your mind, or in your soul. Try to imagine saying it back to the Father, the Son, the Holy Spirit, or to Mary.

Whatever you have received, take a moment in **silence** to respond. When you are ready, **journal** your experience.

PREPARATION FOR TOMORROW:

Read the following Scripture as you prepare for tomorrow:
The Parable of the Lost Sheep, Luke 15:1-7.

DAY 27

PRAYING WITH LECTIO DIVINA

PREPARATION:

5 P's of Prayer: Prepare - know your passage ahead of time and meditate on it throughout the day. When you transition into prayer, take time to breathe, relax, slow down, and just rest. Place - go to your prayer place, room or chair. Ninety percent of prayer is just being there. Posture - we pray using our bodies. Try one of the four postures: standing, sitting, kneeling, or prostrating. Presence - make the Sign of the Cross and invite the Father, the Son, and the Holy Spirit into this time of prayer. Invite God the Father to hold you, the Son to be the Good Shepherd to you, and the Holy Spirit to be Christ in you. Passage - hold the Bible in your lap and realize: "The Word of God is alive." The Father will speak to you!

LECTIO DIVINA:

A type of prayer in which one is reading Scripture, meditating or pondering Scripture, praying vocally with God, and contemplating in silence. Review Lectio Divina in the Prayer Exercises section of "Types of Prayer" in Appendix I.

PRAY NOW:

Today's prayer uses *Lectio Divina* as we pray with The Parable of the Lost Sheep, Luke 15:1-7. I encourage you to open your Bible, find the passage and refer to it whenever you need to. This is a good experience to journal with as well. The first step is *Lectio* (reading).

The tax collectors and sinners were all drawing near to listen to him, but the Pharisees and scribes began to complain, saying, "This man welcomes sinners and eats with them." So to them he addressed this parable. "What man among you having a hundred sheep and losing one of them would not leave the ninety-nine in the desert and go after the lost one until he finds it? And when he does find it, he sets it on his shoulders with great joy and, upon his arrival home, he calls together his friends and neighbors and says to them, 'Rejoice with me because I have found my lost sheep.' I tell you, in just the same way there will be more joy in heaven over one sinner who repents than over ninety-nine righteous people who have no need of repentance." (Luke 15:1-7)

Now that you are introduced to it, read it again and try to hold on to a Word or phrase that captures your attention. Read it a little slower this time.

The tax collectors and sinners were all drawing near to listen to him, but the Pharisees and scribes began to complain, saying, "This man welcomes sinners and eats with them." So to them he addressed this parable. "What man among you having a hundred sheep and losing one of them would not leave the ninety-nine in the desert and go after the lost one until he finds it? And when he does find it, he sets it on his shoulders with great joy and, upon his arrival home, he calls together his friends and neighbors and says to them, 'Rejoice with me because I have found my lost sheep.' I tell you, in just the same way there will be more joy in heaven over one sinner who repents than over ninety-nine righteous people who have no need of repentance."

What was the Word or phrase that you heard God speak to you? Mine was "*drawing near to listen to him.*" Read it once more slowly.

The tax collectors and sinners were all drawing near to listen to him, but the Pharisees and scribes began to complain, saying, "This man welcomes sinners and eats with them." So to them he addressed this parable. "What man among you having a hundred sheep and losing one of them would not leave the ninety-nine in the desert and go after the lost one until he finds it? And when he does find it, he sets it on his shoulders with great joy and, upon his arrival home, he calls together his friends and neighbors and says to them, 'Rejoice with me because I have found my lost sheep.' I tell you, in just the same way there will be more joy in heaven over one sinner who repents than over ninety-nine righteous people who have no need of repentance."

What was your Word or phrase that time? Mine was "*with great joy.*" A final time, read it very slowly and rest with it in **silence** for a while. When you are ready, **journal** whatever that Word or phrase was that came to you.

The second step of *Lectio Divina* is *meditatio* or meditation. We will go through this passage line by line and just meditate upon it. This is a wonderful time for you to use all the things that we have learned: your imagination, your senses, meditating, wondering, pondering, questioning, relating your life to it, and dialoguing. That is all part of meditation.

The tax collectors and sinners were all drawing near to listen to him. Think about that. They were attracted to Him, these tax collectors and sinners. They were not afraid of Him. They were drawing near to Him to listen to Him. But it was the Pharisees and scribes who began to complain saying, "*This man welcomes sinners and eats with them.*" That is amazing - Jesus welcomes the sinners and eats with them. One of the most intimate things He does with his disciples is He eats with them.

So to them he addressed this parable. [Imagine Jesus saying this to the Pharisees] "*What man among you having a hundred sheep and losing one of them would not leave the ninety-nine in the desert and go after the lost one until he finds it? And when he does find it, he sets it on his shoulders with great joy.*" Try to imagine this man with one hundred sheep in the desert. One of them is lost, so he leaves the ninety-nine knowing that they are together. He goes after the lost one and he searches. He doesn't give up; he searches until he finds it. When he does, he sets it on his shoulders.

Imagine Jesus setting that lost sheep on His shoulders. He is talking about the tax collectors and sinners. They are the ones who are lost. When He finds them, He picks them up. When they come to Him, He doesn't reject them. They draw near to Him to listen to Him. He welcomes them and eats with them. He places them right on His shoulders with great joy. He has so much joy finding the lost sheep.

And, upon his arrival home, he calls together his friends and neighbors and says to them, 'Rejoice with me because I have found my lost sheep.' Just imagine the excitement of Jesus finding the lost sheep. In finding the sinner who has been away. "*I tell you, in just the same way there will be more joy in heaven over one sinner who repents than over ninety-nine righteous people who have no need of repentance.*" Maybe you are a sinner. We are all sinners. There is more joy over our repenting then there is over us trying to be righteous. There is more joy in being the lost sheep that is found.

Meditate upon this experience for a moment in **silence**. When you are ready, **journal** your experience.

The third step is *oratio* which means pray. This step could be a formal prayer that you offer to God or it could be very spontaneous. It could be a dialogue with you just talking to God.

Imagine as you pray with this passage that your prayer is something like seeking the lost sheep. Maybe you know someone who is away from the faith or away from the church and you want God to find them. Or maybe it is you. Maybe you are listening to this right now and you are the lost sheep. You are the one that has been away.

Maybe there is some sin that you have and you have felt rejected by people. As the sinners all draw near to Jesus, you feel attracted to draw close to Him, too. As you draw close to Him, pray with Him, talk to Him, tell Him what is on your heart. Rejoice with Him. Imagine Him placing you on His shoulders with great joy. Maybe your prayer is to ask Him for forgiveness. Maybe your prayer is repentance, telling Him you are sorry for however or whatever you may have sinned. Or maybe it is gratitude. Maybe you are found. Maybe you were once lost and you have been found. Take some time in **silence** to pray with Him. When you are ready, **journal** your experience.

The final step is *contemplatio*, which is contemplation. Now that you have been reading, meditating, and praying with Him, it is time to just rest. To rest with Him. To enjoy what it is like to be with Him. Perhaps during this time of contemplation, you realize with great joy that you are on His shoulders. Maybe you allow yourself to rest on His shoulders. Maybe you contemplate on a Word or phrase in the passage. It might be that you contemplate by drawing near to listen to Him. That is what contemplation is - drawing near to listen to Him.

So right now in this final moment of **silence**, draw near and listen to Him. Let Him hold you on His shoulders and experience the great joy of contemplative prayer. When you are ready, **journal** your experience.

PREPARATION FOR TOMORROW:
Read the following Scripture as you prepare for tomorrow:
Mark 2:1-12, The Healing of the Paralytic.

DAY 28

PRAYING WITH YOUR SENSES

PREPARATION:

5 P's of Prayer: Prepare - know your passage ahead of time and meditate on it throughout the day. When you transition into prayer, take time to breathe, relax, slow down, and just rest. Place - go to your prayer place, room or chair. Ninety percent of prayer is just being there. Posture - we pray using our bodies. Try one of the four postures: standing, sitting, kneeling, or prostrating. Presence - make the Sign of the Cross and invite the Father, the Son, and the Holy Spirit into this time of prayer. Invite God the Father to hold you, the Son to be the Good Shepherd to you, and the Holy Spirit to be Christ in you. Passage - hold the Bible in your lap and realize: "The Word of God is alive." The Father will speak to you!

PRAYING WITH YOUR FIVE SENSES:

This type of prayer uses your senses, physically and imaginatively (seeing, hearing, smelling, tasting, and touching). Review Praying with Your Senses in the Prayer Exercises section of "Types of Prayer" in Appendix I.

PRAY NOW:

Today's prayer experience will be praying with your senses in Mark 2:1-12, The Healing of the Paralytic. Let's read the Scripture passage through once and try to see everything that is going on. See it like a movie that is playing before you. Realize that when we use our sense of sight with our imagination in Scripture, we actually enter into the scene. As you read this scripture, ask the Holy Spirit to help you see physically and spiritually what God wants you to see.

When Jesus returned to Capernaum after some days, it became know that he was at home. Many gathered together so that there was no longer room for them, not even around the door, and he preached the word to them. They came bringing to him a paralytic carried by four men. Unable to get near Jesus because of the crowd, they opened up the roof above him. After they had broken through, they let down the mat on which the paralytic was lying. When Jesus saw their faith, he said to the paralytic, "Child, your sins are forgiven." Now some of the scribes were sitting there asking themselves. "Why does this man speak that way? He is blaspheming. Who but God alone can forgive sins?" Jesus immediately knew in his mind what they were thinking to themselves, so he said, "Why are you thinking such things in your hearts? Which is easier, to say to the paralytic, 'Your sins are forgiven,' or to say, 'Rise, pick up your mat, and walk'? But that you may know that the Son of Man has authority to forgive sins on earth" - he said to the paralytic, "I say to you, rise, pick up your mat, and go home." He rose, picked up his mat at once, and went away in the sight of everyone. They were all astounded and glorified God, saying, "We have never seen anything like this." (Mark 2:1-12)

When Jesus returned to Capernaum after some days, it became known that he was at home. Try to imagine Capernaum. Capernaum is a small town by the Sea of Galilee. *Many gathered together so that there was no longer room for them, not even around the door.* Try to see the home where everyone is gathered together; where Jesus is preaching the Word to them. There are so many people that they spill out the front door.

They came bringing to him a paralytic carried by four men. Try to imagine that you are the paralytic. You are laying on the mat down on the ground and as you look up, you see four faces. Imagine yourself being carried. Who are the people that carry you in life? If you need to be carried to Jesus, who are the ones that will do it? Try to actually see their faces, whoever they may be. Try to see all four people looking down at you with great love, great determination, great care, and great concern. They lift you up off the ground and begin to carry you.

You begin to see the crowd as you near the home. Unable to get near to Jesus because of the crowd, the four begin to carry you up over the crowd onto the roof of the home because they want to get you to Him so desperately. They want to get you near to Jesus and so they begin to open up the roof above Him.

Watch as they tear it open until there is a big enough hole. Then *they let down the mat* gently and you see Jesus for the first time. He is looking up at you through the sun light breaking through the dust from the broken roof. He looks at the four people that have carried you, broken through the roof, and lowered you down to Him. When He sees their faces, He says to you, "Child, your sins are forgiven."

Try to picture Jesus' face as He says this to you. Look at His face as He looks around at the faces of the four who have carried you. Then, see how He looks at you and He calls you "child."

Now some of the scribes were sitting there asking themselves, "Why does this man speak that way, He is blaspheming. Who but God alone can forgive sins?" You look around at the people there who are in disbelief. Jesus knew immediately what was in their minds; you can see it on His face. *So he said, "Why are you thinking such things in your hearts? Which is easier to say to the paralytic? 'Your sins are forgiven' or to say, 'Rise, pick up your mat and walk?' But that you may know that the Son of Man has authority to forgive sins on earth..."* He pauses, looks at you, and He says, *"I say to you, rise, pick up your mat and go home."*

Now try to look down at your feet and your legs. You see, all of a sudden, that they are able to move. At once, you rise. You stand up and everybody looks with great awe at what Jesus has just done. *They were all astounded and glorified God, saying, "We have never seen anything like this."*

Look around at their faces, at the wonder and awe. Look at the four who carried you to Jesus. How joyful they are. How happy they are. Take some time in **silence** with whatever was most vivid. When you are ready, **journal** the experience of sight.

Now try to apply your sense of hearing. Not only hearing the people, places and things, but what God may be saying to you. Try to take in the noise of the crowd. You can hear Jesus preaching from inside the house. You hear the four who gathered around you to pick you up off of the ground. You hear the sound of the parting crowd as you begin the climb up the roof. Then you hear the noise as *they opened up the roof above him;* breaking through the roof. Listen to the intensity of that sound and the breaking, so determined are they to get you to Jesus. You hear a hush come upon the crowd as you are lowered down.

Then, you hear Jesus' voice speak directly to you, *"Child, your sins are forgiven."* Let His voice penetrate your ears, *"Child, your sins are forgiven."*

Then, immediately, you hear rumbling in the crowd as the scribes and Pharisees ask themselves, *"Why does this man speak that way? He is blaspheming. Who but God alone can forgive sins?"* You hear Jesus say, *"Why are you thinking such things in your hearts? Which is easier, to say to the paralytic, 'Your sins are forgiven,' or to say, 'Rise, pick up your mat, and walk'? But that you may know that the Son of Man has authority to forgive sins on earth ..."* He says to you, *"I say to you, rise, pick up your mat, and go home."* You hear this. His voice has power. So much power that His voice causes you to rise, pick up your mat and go home.

Listen to the joy and wonder in their voices when you hear them saying, *"We have never seen anything like this,"* and glorifying God. Listen to them tremble now with awe. Listen to the sound of the crowd begin to fade in the distance as you walk away carrying your mat. Continue to hold on to the voice of Jesus that you heard: *"Child, your sins are forgiven."*

Take a moment now to just allow the voice of Jesus to echo in your ears. Spend some time in **silence** and hear whatever God wants to speak to you right now and then **journal** your experience.

Now use your sense of smell. The sense of smell will be a bit more difficult in this scene, but try to imagine what it smells like. Ask the Holy Spirit to give you a spiritual sense of smell. What I mean by that is that we have the ability to take things in through what is called our spiritual senses. Maybe you smell something that is not even in the scene. Allow this to happen and ask God to use your sense of smell - your spiritual sense.

Replay the entire scene in your head. Maybe you smell the sea. Maybe it is flowers growing near the home. Perhaps it is the smell of the crowd. Or it could be the smell of wood as the roof is torn open. What smell does Jesus exude? Try to linger with whatever sense of smell God is inviting you into right now. Spend some time in **silence** and just try to smell, in a spiritual sense, whatever was most fragrant for you. Then **journal** your experience.

Taste - this may also be a little difficult. There's not much here that we would explicitly taste, but again, we can use our spiritual sense of taste. Ask the Holy Spirit now to give you some sense, on a spiritual level, of taste in this scene. It could be the taste of the sea water that lingers in the air. It could be the taste of the dust as the roof is broken open. It could be some other taste that forms in your mouth right now. Read the passage once more and try to taste this scene on a spiritual level. Spend some time in **silence** just to linger with whatever sense of taste you had and then **journal** your experience.

Focus on your sense of touch in this Scripture passage. Begin with getting in touch with what you need healing. Maybe there is an ache or a pain. Maybe there is something more serious that needs to be healed.

Try to feel your body laying on the ground paralyzed. It can't move. As the four come to help you, feel the sensation of your body being lifted up off the ground. Your body begins to feel loose while it is supported and carried by the four people that love you so much. You feel an uneasiness as they begin to part the crowd and make the climb to the top of the roof.

You feel the sun on your face and you sense the change of temperature as they lower your body down into the crowded home. You feel relief as they gently place you before Jesus. As He speaks the healing words to you, feel

Jesus' words vibrate through your entire body. The power of these words: *"Rise, pick up your mat, and go home."* At that moment, you feel the Holy Spirit surge through your entire body. You feel healed.

Try to feel now as you stand up with strength. You pick up your mat, put it on your shoulders, and you walk home. Spend some time in **silence** and then **journal** your experience.

PREPARATION FOR TOMORROW:
We will pray with Sunday Mass.

PRAYING WITH SUNDAY MASS

Today's prayer will be celebrating the Sunday Mass and experiencing God the Father in the Eucharist and Liturgy. Prepare before Mass with the following and then journal your experience after Mass.

PREPARATION BEFORE SUNDAY MASS:

Receiving the Body and Blood of Christ is to be in union with Him. The reception of the Eucharist is the source and summit of our faith. At that moment, you receive God. As preparation before Mass, you will focus on that moment when you receive the Body of Christ, and if you have the chance, the Blood of Christ. Oftentimes, as we are receiving Communion, we can be distracted. Sometimes there is a line of people or it goes so fast that it is over before we know it. In preparation before Mass, we should spend some time and think about how we are going to go up to the altar. Think about the way that we will bow with reverence. Think about the moment that we will receive Him. Think about what it is going to be like to hold open our hands and receive Him in our hands. Or to open our mouth and receive Him in our mouth. What it will be like to go to the chalice and receive His precious blood. Prepare yourself to receive Him. Actually open yourself up. Ask God that you may truly receive Him into your life. Let this be your special focus as you prepare for Mass today so that, when this part of the Liturgy happens, you can be so aware that you will take in every moment of it. Hopefully, you will experience a profound reception of the Body of Christ. Becoming one with Christ at that moment.

AFTER SUNDAY MASS:

How was Mass? What was it like to actually pay attention when you went up to Communion? Did you feel more reverent? Did you more fully receive Him? Did you feel a union with Him? Was there any time afterwards where there was silence and you got to sit there holding the Body of Christ? Knowing that He was in you and you were in Him? What an amazing experience we get to have. Take some time and **journal** this experience.

PREPARATION FOR TOMORROW:

There will not be a Scripture reading for tomorrow.
Rather, we will be praying with an icon - the San Damiano Cross.

DAY 29

PRAYING WITH CONTEMPLATIVE PRAYER

PREPARATION:

5 P's of Prayer: Prepare - know your passage ahead of time and meditate on it throughout the day. When you transition into prayer, take time to breathe, relax, slow down, and just rest. Place - go to your prayer place, room or chair. Ninety percent of prayer is just being there. Posture - we pray using our bodies. Try one of the four postures: standing, sitting, kneeling, or prostrating. Presence - make the Sign of the Cross and invite the Father, the Son, and the Holy Spirit into this time of prayer. Invite God the Father to hold you, the Son to be the Good Shepherd to you, and the Holy Spirit to be Christ in you. Passage - hold the Bible in your lap and realize: "The Word of God is alive." The Father will speak to you!

CONTEMPLATIVE PRAYER:

Contemplative prayer is a type of prayer that involves silence and simply being in the presence of God. Review Contemplative Prayer and praying with Icons (Prayer Exercises) in "Types of Prayer" in Appendix I.

PRAY NOW:

Today, we will be using the icon of the San Damiano Cross (see Figure 2 in this chapter). As with all icons, there is no need to really know its background in order to contemplate with it because it is the visual Word of God represented to us. But, sometimes, it does help to have the background in order to prepare to pray with it.

The San Damiano Cross is the actual icon that St. Francis was praying with when he received his commission to go forth and rebuild the church. It is known as the icon of the Transfigured Christ. It contains the story of Christ's death, Resurrection and Ascension into glory - the entire Paschal Mystery. In the Eastern Church, the icon always represents the image of the living God. By gazing upon this icon, we actually get the experience of gazing upon Christ, of coming into His presence, and of having a personal encounter with the sacred image of Him through the grace of the Holy Spirit.

Note that the central figure on the San Damiano Cross is Christ on the cross. Notice that it is the brightest part. He is the light that comes into the world. We hear in John 8:12; "*I am the light of the world. Whoever follows me will not walk in darkness, but will have the light of life.*" Notice, also, that Christ stands upright; he is not nailed to the cross. His eyes are open. He looks out at you, into the world. He is very much alive.

Look at the red circle above Christ. You will see that Christ is portrayed as breaking out of that circle. He is dressed not in loincloth, but in fine robes of gold; these wonderful garments are the portrayal of the Ascension.

Look at the hand at the very top of the icon. This hand looks like it is blessing the entire image. Notice again how the fingers are laid out; there are two fingers pointed forward and three tucked under. The two fingers symbolize that Jesus is fully human and fully divine, while the three tucked under symbolize the three Persons of God: the Father, the Son, and the Holy Spirit. This hand can be understood as the Father's hand blessing His Son.

To the left of Christ are Mary and the beloved disciple. They are looking at each other, gazing into each other's eyes. Jesus has said to them: "*Woman, behold, your son*" (John 19:26) and *to the disciple, "Behold, your mother*." (John 19:27). The beloved disciple can represent all of us. You are the beloved disciple. Mary is your mother and she gazes at you.

To the right of Christ, you will notice Mary of Magdala. She is known as the apostle of apostles because she was the first to discover the empty tomb and see the risen Christ. She has her hand towards her face, almost in profound shock, both at the horror of His crucifixion and then at the wonder of His Resurrection. The woman next to her is probably Mary, the wife of Clopas and the mother of James. Then the third figure on the right is the centurion. Notice in his left hand that he holds the piece of wood. You can see in his face that he is transformed as he looks upon Christ. The little boy above his shoulder is believed to be his son who was healed.

At the bottom left is the centurion with the spear, the one who pierced Jesus' side. You can see the blood and water flowing from Christ's side. You will also notice the five wounds of Christ: two in His hands, two in His feet, and one at His side. St. Francis would himself later receive the stigmata and bear these wounds.

Finally, the darkness behind Christ represents the empty tomb. There are also some unknown saints and angels in this icon.

As you pray with this icon, especially in the beginning, allow your eyes to take in the entire image just as you would read over a Scripture passage. At some point, your eyes will probably settle upon one part of the image. Maybe it is directly on the eyes of Christ. Perhaps it is on Mary and the beloved disciple. Or maybe it is on the blood gushing from His side. Perhaps you are drawn to the Father's hand in blessing. Allow your eyes to gaze to wherever they are drawn and spend time contemplatively with the icon.

This contemplation time is not about trying to figure it out or even understand it, but to simply be with Christ. If you find yourself distracted, allow your eyes to move to another part of the icon until they rest again on another image. Remain with that image. Just gaze upon it and be with the Lord in this wonderful icon of San Damiano - a glimpse of heaven, an image of the visible Christ.

Spend the rest of the time in **silence** contemplating and gazing upon the icon on the following page. When you are ready, **journal** your experience.

REX IVDEORV
MARIA
IOANNES

REXIVDEORV
IOANNES

PREPARATION FOR TOMORROW:
Read the following Scripture as you prepare for tomorrow:
The Gentle Mastery of Christ, Matthew 11:28-30.

Figure 2: San Damiano Cross - The Transfigured Christ. (Wikipedia, 2016)

DAY 30

PRAYING WITH SCRIPTURAL RELAXATION

PREPARATION:

5 P's of Prayer: Prepare - know your passage ahead of time and meditate on it throughout the day. When you transition into prayer, take time to breathe, relax, slow down, and just rest. Place - go to your prayer place, room or chair. Ninety percent of prayer is just being there. Posture - we pray using our bodies. Try one of the four postures: standing, sitting, kneeling, or prostrating. Presence - make the Sign of the Cross and invite the Father, the Son, and the Holy Spirit into this time of prayer. Invite God the Father to hold you, the Son to be the Good Shepherd to you, and the Holy Spirit to be Christ in you. Passage - hold the Bible in your lap and realize: "The Word of God is alive." The Father will speak to you!

SCRIPTURE RELAXATION:

The focus of this exercise is allowing the Word of God to help us relax in the sanctuary of God's love. Review Scriptural Relaxation in the Prayer Exercises section of "Types of Prayer" in Appendix I. You can also find the audio version of Scriptural Relaxation at TheProdigalFather.org/Pray-40Days.

PRAY NOW:

In this prayer experience, we will be using The Gentle Mastery of Christ, Matthew 11:28-30 with Scriptural Relaxation. Find a posture that you are comfortable with. I recommend either sitting or lying down prostrate for this one (or whatever you are physically capable of doing.) Read the Scripture first and then we will enter into the process of relaxation.

"Come to me, all you who labor and are burdened, and I will give you rest. Take my yoke upon you and learn from me, for I am meek and humble of heart; and you will find rest for yourselves. For my yoke is easy, and my burden light." (Matthew 11:28-30)

Take a moment now to breathe in deeply through your nose.... As you breathe in, think of the words *"Come to me"* and hold it there for a moment.... Breathe out.... *"all you who labor and are burdened."* [Pause for a moment of silence.]

One more time, take a long, slow deep breath in through your nose.... *"Come to me."* Hold it there.... Release.... *"all you who labor and are burdened."* [Pause for a moment of silence.]

One more time, take a long, slow, deep breath in through your nose.... Invite the Holy Spirit to come into you.... *"Come to me."* Slowly breathe it all out.... *"all you who labor and are burdened.*" Breathe out as deep as you can.... *"and I will give you rest."* All you have to do right now is rest.... Jesus is inviting you to come to Him with your burdens, and rest.... [Pause for a moment of silence.]

"Come to me, all you who labor and are burdened, and I will give you rest. Take my yoke upon you and learn from me, for I am meek and humble of heart; and you will find rest for yourselves. For my yoke is easy, and my burden light." [Pause for a moment of silence.]

The first part of this relaxation is to focus on heaviness. Feel the weight of your body as Jesus invites you to come to Him with all your burdens.... *"Take my yoke upon you and learn from me. For my yoke is easy, and my burden light.*" Your whole body feels heavy now.... You can feel your body sink into the chair, into the ground, or into the bed.... [Pause for a moment of silence.]

Your right hand feels heavy.... *"Come to me, all you who labor and are burdened.*" Your right hand feels heavy.... *"Come to me, all you who labor and are burdened.*" Your right hand sinks deeply into the ground.... *"Come to me, all you who labor and are burdened."* Your right hand feels heavy.... Your left arm feels heavy.... *"Come to me, all you who labor and are burdened, and I will give you rest."* [Pause for a moment of silence.]

Your left arm completely rests.... Your left arm feels heavy.... You will find rest for yourselves.... Your left arm feels heavy and sinks down.... Your left arm feels heavy.... *"Come to me, all you who labor and are burdened.*" [Pause for a moment in silence.]

Now focus your attention on your right leg.... Your right leg feels heavy and it sinks into the ground.... *"Come to me, all you who labor and are burdened."* Your right leg feels heavy.... *"Come to me, all you who labor and are burdened, and I will give you rest.*" Your right leg feels heavy.... *"Come to me, all you who labor and are burdened, and I will give you rest."* [Pause for a moment of silence.]

Your left leg feels heavy.... *"Take my yoke upon you and learn from me, for I am meek and humble of heart; and you will find rest for yourselves."* Your left leg feels heavy.... So heavy you would not even be able to lift it.... As it gently sinks into the ground, your left leg feels heavy.... *"Come to me, all you who labor and are burden."* Your left leg feels heavy.... *"and I will give you rest.*" [Pause for a moment of silence.]

Focus now on warmth.... Your whole body feels warm.... *"For my yoke is easy, and my burden light."* Your whole body feels warm in the presence of Christ.... *"Come to me, all you who labor and are burdened, and I will give you rest."* Your right hand and arm feels warm.... *"I will give you rest."* Your right hand feels warm and heavy.... *"I will give you rest."* Your right hand feels warm.... *"Take my yoke upon you and learn from me.... and you will find rest for yourselves."* [Pause for a moment of silence.]

Your left hand feels warm.... Your left hand and entire arm feels warm and heavy.... *"Come to me, all you who are burdened. Take my yoke upon you and learn from me.... and you will find rest for yourselves."* Your left arm feels warm.... [Pause for a moment of silence.]

Now move to your legs.... *"Come to me, all you who labor and are burdened, and I will give you rest."* Your right leg feels warm.... Your right leg feels warm and heavy.... *"For my yoke is easy and my burden light."* Your right leg feels warm and heavy.... *"For I am meek and humble of heart; and you will find rest for yourselves."* [Pause for a moment of silence.]

Your left leg feels warm.... *"All you who labor and are burdened."* Your left leg feels warm and heavy.... *"Learn from me."* Your left leg feels warm.... [Pause for a moment of silence.]

"For I am meek and humble of heart; and you will find rest for yourselves." Your entire body feels warm and heavy and relaxed.... Your whole body feels relaxed.... This entire burden you have been carrying has been lifted.... [Pause for a moment of silence.]

"Come to me, all you who labor and are burdened, and I will give you rest. Take my yoke upon you and learn from me, for I am meek and humble of heart; and you will find rest for yourselves. For my yoke is easy, and my burden light." Your entire body feels rested and warm and heavy.... Your right arm feels rested and relaxed.... The burden of your shoulders relieved.... Your right arm is relaxed.... *"I will give you rest."* Your right arm is relaxed and warm and heavy.... [Pause for a moment of silence.]

"For my yoke is easy, and my burden light." Your left arm is completely relaxed and loose.... *"For I am meek and humble of heart; and you will find rest for yourselves. Take my yoke upon you and learn from me."* Your left arm feels rested.... Your left arm feels relaxed, rested, and loose.... Your left arm is relaxed, warm and heavy.... *"Come to me, all you who are burdened, and I will give you rest."* [Pause for a moment of silence.]

Your right leg is completely relaxed.... *"For my yoke is easy, and my burden light."* Your right leg is completely relaxed, heavy and warm.... *"I will give you rest....* Your right leg is relaxed....[Pause for a moment of silence.]

Your left leg is relaxed.... Completely loose and unburdened.... *"Take my yoke upon you and learn from me, for I am meek and humble of heart; and you will find rest for yourselves."* Your left leg is relaxed.... Your left leg is relaxed, warm, and heavy.... *"For my yoke is easy, and my burden light."* [Pause for a moment of silence.]

Your entire body is now relaxed.... *"Come to me, all you who labor and are burdened, and I will give you rest."* Your entire body feels heavy.... *"Take my yoke upon you and learn from me, for I am meek and humble of heart; and you will find rest for yourselves."* Your entire body is warm.... *"For my yoke is easy, and my burden light."* [Pause for a moment of silence.]

Let your body rest now in the Word of God. *"Come to me, all you who labor and are burdened, and I will give you rest."* Spend some time in **silence** and **journal** your experience.

PREPARATION FOR TOMORROW:

Read the following Scripture as you prepare for tomorrow:
A Woman Caught in Adultery, John 7:53-8:11.

DAY 31

PRAYING WITH GUIDED MEDITATION

PREPARATION:

5 P's of Prayer: Prepare - know your passage ahead of time and meditate on it throughout the day. When you transition into prayer, take time to breathe, relax, slow down, and just rest. Place - go to your prayer place, room or chair. Ninety percent of prayer is just being there. Posture - we pray using our bodies. Try one of the four postures: standing, sitting, kneeling, or prostrating. Presence - make the Sign of the Cross and invite the Father, the Son, and the Holy Spirit into this time of prayer. Invite God the Father to hold you, the Son to be the Good Shepherd to you, and the Holy Spirit to be Christ in you. Passage - hold the Bible in your lap and realize: "The Word of God is alive." The Father will speak to you!

GUIDED MEDITATION:

Find a quiet room, settle into a spot that will be comfortable, and place your body in a relaxed position, usually without crossed arms or legs. Allow your imagination, fueled by your senses, to enter into the story. Close your eyes as you meditate; at the end of the meditation, do not rush to open your eyes. Let your body tell you when you are ready. Review Guided Meditation under the Prayer Exercises section of "Types of Prayer" in Appendix I.

PRAY NOW:

This meditation is based on A Woman Caught in Adultery, John 7:53-8:11.

Then each went to his own house, while Jesus went to the Mount of Olives. But early in the morning he arrived again in the temple area, and all the people started coming to him, and he sat down and taught them. Then the scribes and the Pharisees brought a woman who had been caught in adultery and made her stand in the middle. They said to him, "Teacher, this woman was caught in the very act of committing adultery. Now in the law, Moses commanded us to stone such women. So what do you say?" They said this to test him, so that they could have some charge to bring against him. Jesus bent down and began to write on the ground with his finger. But when they continued asking him, he straightened up and said to them, "Let the one among you who is without sin be the first to throw a stone at her." Again he bent down and wrote on the ground. And in response, they went away one by one, beginning with the elders. So he was left alone with the woman before him. Then Jesus straightened up and said to her, "Woman, where are they? Has no one condemned you?" She replied, "No one, sir." Then Jesus said, "Neither do I condemn you. Go [and] from now on do not sin any more." (John 7:53-8:11)

Imagine Jesus coming back from the Mount of Olives. *But early in the morning he arrived again in the temple area, and all the people started coming to him, and he sat down and taught them.* Watch as Jesus calmly gathers this crowd around Him. They are looking at Him as one with great authority as He begins to teach them. While He is teaching them, there is a commotion. There is a ruckus coming from one of the homes. You can hear things crashing. You hear a woman scream. Then you see the scribes and Pharisees; this group of men bring a woman before Him. She had been caught literally in the act of adultery. So they made her stand up in the middle. You see her; she is partially naked. She is horrified, embarrassed, and humiliated. She is terrified because she knows that she could possibly be stoned. You see that her hair is disheveled. You can smell the heavy perfume on her. You see the crowd. The tension is building.

One of them says to Him, "*Teacher, this woman was caught in the very act of committing adultery. Now in the Law, Moses commanded us to stone such women. So what do you say?"* You see this man looking at Jesus and he is trying to trap Him. He is trying to find something wrong with Him, some guilt in Jesus that can then condemn Him. *They said this to test him.* You look over to Jesus. He doesn't look upset. He doesn't seem angry at the woman or disgusted with her. Rather, He is angry and disgusted by the crowd. This crowd that He was teaching just a moment ago has now turned on this woman. Jesus realized that they were trying to catch Him into saying something wrong.

Watch as Jesus bends down and begins to write on the ground with His finger. Try to imagine the dry earth. You notice that as He traces on the ground the dust begins to rise. You are not sure what He is tracing, but all His intensity is focused right there on that ground. He doesn't look up at the woman or the crowd. He just traces on to the ground.

Then, He gets this idea and looks up and says, *"Let the one among you who is without sin be the first to throw a stone at her."* Once more, He bends back down and continues to write on the ground. In response, you notice the crowd goes away, one by one, beginning with the elders. Just watch as all these angry people who were ready to kill the woman, condemn her, and entrap Jesus, are now stunned by His mercy. They are stunned by the realization of their own sin. They are ashamed. The first man drops his rock and walks away. Then a second, and a third, and a fourth, until the whole crowd is gone.

Before you know it, just the woman and Jesus are left standing there. She is left alone with Him. You watch as Jesus straightens up and says to her: "*Woman, where are they? Has no one condemned you?*" You look and see in the woman's eyes a sense of wonder, bewilderment, and awe. She says, *"No one, sir."* She realizes that no one is condemning her anymore. Once, she was so afraid, terrified of losing her life, humiliated, ashamed, filled with regret, remorse, and guilt. But, all of a sudden, everything is okay. Jesus looks at her with great love and says to her, "*Neither do I condemn you. Go [and] from now on do not sin any more.*"

Take a few moments in **silence** and meditate upon whatever part of this was most real for you. Whatever was most vivid for you. Whatever you felt deeply. Maybe there is some sin in your life or some experience in your life where you felt like the woman did. Or perhaps, you realize that you have been condemning other people. Or maybe, you just want Jesus to look at you like that and clear the crowd. Clear everybody away who is ready to condemn you. Just look at you with love and hear Him say, "*Neither do I condemn you.*" Spend some time in silence.

After meditating upon this, take a moment to **journal**. Spend some time reflecting on what you felt. What you thought. What was your response to the transformation of the crowd? That crowd that was so angry but, then, just walked away. What must it have been like to be caught in the act? To be publicly humiliated, to be placed before Jesus and then to discover not condemnation, but love? He stood up for her. He helped others to see their own sin. They walked away. What was it like for you to experience the intimacy of the woman before Jesus? Not looking at her as an adulterer, but looking at her with great love. What is it like for you to be loved by Jesus in the midst of your sin?

PREPARATION FOR TOMORROW:
Read the following Scripture as you prepare for tomorrow:
The Wedding at Cana, John 2:1-12.

DAY 32

PRAYING LIKE A PIRATE

PREPARATION:

5 P's of Prayer: Prepare - know your passage ahead of time and meditate on it throughout the day. When you transition into prayer, take time to breathe, relax, slow down, and just rest. Place - go to your prayer place, room or chair. Ninety percent of prayer is just being there. Posture - we pray using our bodies. Try one of the four postures: standing, sitting, kneeling, or prostrating. Presence - make the Sign of the Cross and invite the Father, the Son, and the Holy Spirit into this time of prayer. Invite God the Father to hold you, the Son to be the Good Shepherd to you, and the Holy Spirit to be Christ in you. Passage - hold the Bible in your lap and realize: "The Word of God is alive." The Father will speak to you!

PRAYING LIKE A PIRATE:

ARRR: Acknowledge, Relate, Receive, and Respond to God. Review Praying like a Pirate in the Prayer Exercises section of "Types of Prayer" found in Appendix I.

PRAY NOW:

For this experience, we will be praying like a pirate (acknowledge, relate, receive, and respond) with The Wedding at Cana, John 2:1-12. I encourage you to have your Bible and your journal with you. As we read through this passage the first time, try to get in touch with your feelings. Whatever is going on in your heart, mind, or soul. Be honest right now. Try to be aware of whatever you have been going through during this day. Whatever you might be preoccupied with, whatever you might be experiencing, try to get in touch with that and acknowledge your feelings.

On the third day there was a wedding in Cana in Galilee, and the mother of Jesus was there. Jesus and his disciples were also invited to the wedding. When the wine ran short, the mother of Jesus said to him, "They have no wine." [And] Jesus said to her, "Woman, how does your concern affect me? My hour has not yet come." His mother said to the servers, "Do whatever he tells you." Now there were six stone water jars there for Jewish ceremonial washings, each holding twenty to thirty gallons. Jesus told them, "Fill the jars with water." So they filled them to the brim. Then he told them, "Draw some out now and take it to the headwaiter." So they took it. And when the headwaiter tasted the water that had become wine, without knowing where it came from (although the servers who had drawn the water knew), the headwaiter called the bridegroom and said to him,

"Everyone serves good wine first, and then when people have drunk freely, an inferior one; but you have kept the good wine until now." Jesus did this as the beginning of his signs in Cana in Galilee and so revealed his glory, and his disciples began to believe in him.

After this, he and his mother, [his] brothers, and his disciples went down to Capernaum and stayed there only a few days. (John 2:1-12)

Acknowledge The disciples and Jesus were all invited to a wedding and the wine was running short. Mary must have felt concern, compassion, or desire for this wonderful celebration to continue. Mary must have seen the goodness and the beauty of this wedding event. The joy that wine brings. So after she feels this, whatever she is feeling, she then relates it to Jesus and she says, "*They have no wine*." Notice, she then receives whatever Jesus says. He says to her, *"Woman, how does your concern affect me? My hour has not yet come*." Mary responds, "*Do whatever he tells you."*

We have seen in Prayer Day 2, The Announcement of the Birth of Jesus, how acknowledge, relate, receive, and respond worked in the life of Mary. At this time, in **silence**, speak to Jesus and acknowledge your own feelings. What are you feeling right now? What is going on in your life? What is going on in your heart, in your soul, in your mind? Pause now, acknowledge, and **journal** whatever you would like.

Relate Having acknowledged your feelings, we now relate those feelings just as Mary related to Jesus when she said to Him, "*They have no wine*." You can relate to Jesus whatever you want. Whatever you are experiencing, just tell Him. God is so respectful and reverent of us. He will not do anything in our lives without our permitting it. Without our allowing it. We have to give Him some indication that we want Him present in our lives. That we want Him to interact with what is going on in our world. So now having acknowledged your feelings, take some time to relate them to Jesus. Just like Mary did. Mary simply said, "*They have no wine,*" and she didn't use a lot of explanation. She just simply stated what the reality was. Take a moment now and state your reality to Jesus. What are you feeling? What are you experiencing? Take some time in **silence** and relate it to Him. Either with words, out loud, or in your heart. When you are ready, **journal** what you related.

Receive Sometimes we don't get the answer we are expecting. I am sure Mary was surprised by what she received from Jesus. "*Woman, how does your concern affect me? My hour has not yet come*." We have to receive whatever He gives to us. Whatever He speaks to us. Having acknowledged your feelings and related them to Jesus, take some time now to receive whatever He wants to speak to you. Whatever He wants to say to you. Whatever He wants to do in you. This part is very simple, but for some of us it is very difficult to just receive because we can't do anything. We can't make God tell us anything. All we can do is wait and ask. We have acknowledged our feelings; we have related them to God. Now we allow Jesus to speak to us. To give us what He desires. So now take the time to receive. Spend some time in **silence**. You may want to reread the Scripture passage because He often speaks to us in Words. Receive whatever He wants to tell you. When you are ready, **journal** your experience.

Respond Mary's response was very strong and very simple. She said to the servers, "*Do whatever he tells you.*" Your response now is to respond accordingly to whatever He has told you to do. Maybe your response is to continue dialoguing with Him. To continue asking Him for clarification. Maybe you know very well what He wants you to do; your response is simply to do it. So take some time now and try to realize how you want to respond. He has given you free will so you can respond in any way that you want. You have acknowledged your feelings, you related them to Jesus, you received whatever He has given to you, and now take some time in **silence** to respond. When you are ready, **journal** your response.

PREPARATION FOR TOMORROW:
Read the following Scripture as you prepare for tomorrow:
The Way of Love, 1 Corinthians, 13:1-8.

DAY 33

PRAYING WITH LECTIO DIVINA

PREPARATION:

5 P's of Prayer: Prepare - know your passage ahead of time and meditate on it throughout the day. When you transition into prayer, take time to breathe, relax, slow down, and just rest. Place - go to your prayer place, room or chair. Ninety percent of prayer is just being there. Posture - we pray using our bodies. Try one of the four postures: standing, sitting, kneeling, or prostrating. Presence - make the Sign of the Cross and invite the Father, the Son, and the Holy Spirit into this time of prayer. Invite God the Father to hold you, the Son to be the Good Shepherd to you, and the Holy Spirit to be Christ in you. Passage - hold the Bible in your lap and realize: "The Word of God is alive." The Father will speak to you!

LECTIO DIVINA:

A type of prayer in which one is reading Scripture, meditating or pondering Scripture, praying vocally with God, and contemplating in silence. Review Lectio Divina in the Prayer Exercises section of "Types of Prayer" in Appendix I.

PRAY NOW:

Today's prayer experience will be based on The Way of Love, 1 Corinthians, 13:1-8. Get your Bible, journal, and pen ready. We will be praying using the ancient practice of Lectio Divina. The first part of Lectio Divina is *Lectio* or to read. We will read the Scripture passage four times. The first time, you will read it just to get acquainted with it. The second time, I want you to see if there is a Word or phrase that sticks out to you. The third time, you can read it out loud. Then the fourth time, I would like you to read it at a very slow pace.

If I speak in human and angelic tongues but do not have love, I am a resounding gong or a clashing cymbal. And if I have the gift of prophecy and comprehend all mysteries and all knowledge; if I have all faith so as to move mountains but do not have love, I am nothing. If I give away everything I own, and if I hand my body over so that I may boast but do not have love, I gain nothing.

Love is patient, love is kind. It is not jealous, [love] is not pompous, it is not inflated, it is not rude, it does not seek its own interests, it is not quick-tempered, it does not brood over injury, it does not rejoice over wrongdoing but rejoices with the truth. It bears all things, believes all things, hopes all things, endures all things.

Love never fails. (1 Corinthians, 13:1-8)

Let's read it again. This time try to pick out a Word or phrase that you feel God is speaking to you or that is revealing something to you.

If I speak in human and angelic tongues but do not have love, I am a resounding gong or a clashing cymbal. And if I have the gift of prophecy and comprehend all mysteries and all knowledge; if I have all faith so as to move mountains but do not have love, I am nothing. If I give away everything I own, and if I hand my body over so that I may boast but do not have love, I gain nothing.

Love is patient, love is kind. It is not jealous, [love] is not pompous, it is not inflated, it is not rude, it does not seek its own interests, it is not quick-tempered, it does not brood over injury, it does not rejoice over wrongdoing but rejoices with the truth. It bears all things, believes all things, hopes all things, endures all things.

Love never fails.

What is the Word or phrase that spoke to you? Mine was *comprehend all mysteries.* Let's read it a third time and try to pick out a Word or phrase again. Read it slower this time. You can read it out loud or you can read it silently in your heart.

If I speak in human and angelic tongues but do not have love, I am a resounding gong or a clashing cymbal. And if I have the gift of prophecy and comprehend all mysteries and all knowledge; if I have all faith so as to move mountains but do not have love, I am nothing. If I give away everything I own, and if I hand my body over so that I may boast but do not have love, I gain nothing.

Love is patient, love is kind. It is not jealous, [love] is not pompous, it is not inflated, it is not rude, it does not seek its own interests, it is not quick-tempered, it does not brood over injury, it does not rejoice over wrongdoing but rejoices with the truth. It bears all things, believes all things, hopes all things, endures all things.

Love never fails.

What was your Word or phrase this time? Mine was *I am nothing*. Now read it a fourth time. Read it at a very slow pace so that the Words can really sink in.

If I speak in human and angelic tongues but do not have love, I am a resounding gong or a clashing cymbal. And if I have the gift of prophecy and comprehend all mysteries and all knowledge; if I have all faith so as to move mountains but do not have love, I am nothing. If I give away everything I own, and if I hand my body over so that I may boast but do not have love, I gain nothing.

Love is patient, love is kind. It is not jealous, [love] is not pompous, it is not inflated, it is not rude, it does not seek its own interests, it is not quick-tempered, it does not brood over injury, it does not rejoice over wrongdoing but rejoices with the truth. It bears all things, believes all things, hopes all things, endures all things.

Love never fails.

What was your Word or phrase this time? Mine was *I am nothing*.

The second step of Lectio Divina is *meditatio* or meditation. This can be a wonderful passage to meditate on for two reasons. First, I think it is a wonderful passage with which to examine ourselves and how loving we are. Secondly, I think it reveals something tremendous to us about God the Father. This passage has always been very important for me. I made a retreat and Jesus really revealed to me that this is how the Father loves us. This is ultimately what love is. If God is love, then God the Father could be replaced in this sentence with love. So just for the sake of a meditation, I will do that with you.

First of all, try to apply it to yourself. *If I speak in human and angelic tongues but do not have love, I am a resounding gong or a clashing cymbal.* Have you ever had times or experiences where you were very ineffective? You realized it because you were doing it on your own. Or maybe not even doing it with love or with God.

And if I have the gift of prophecy and comprehend all mysteries and all knowledge; if I have all faith so as to move mountains, [that is wonderful if we have that kind of faith] *but do not have love, I am nothing.* Without love, without God, on our own, we are nothing. We can accomplish nothing. We can do nothing.

If I give away everything I own - I think we are all tempted to do that at some point, either tempted or invited to. But, oftentimes, it is out of pride. If I do this out of pride, *if I hand my body over so that I may boast but do not have love, I gain nothing.* Jesus promises us that if we give Him everything in this life, He will give us one hundred fold here in this world and eternal life to come. But if we don't do it with love, we gain nothing.

Now here is the part that you can really use as a self-examine, especially for Confession. Is your love *patient*? Are you patient with those around you? *Love is kind*. Are you kind and gentle? *It is not jealous*. Do you experience any jealousy? If you do, it is not love; stop doing it. *[Love] is not pompous*. If you notice that you are doing things to be seen, it is not love. *It is not inflated*. It is not all about you. It is not all about me. *It is not rude*. Are you rude to the people that you are with? Are you rude to your family, your parents, your siblings, or your children? Are you rude to the waitress that helps you? Are you rude to the people in traffic? That is not love. *It does not seek its own interests*. Do you seek whatever is best for you in any given situation? *It is not quick-tempered*. Are you quick-tempered? Are you quick to become enraged? *It does not brood over injury*. I love this Word. If you find yourself brooding over injury, over something that someone has done to you, that is not love. Don't do it. Let it go. Forgive. *It does not rejoice over wrongdoing*. Are you critical of others? Do you take delight when you see others fail? That is not love.

But rejoices with the truth. What is the truth? That every human being was created in the image and likeness of God. God delights in them as much as He delights in you. As much as He delights in His Son, Jesus Christ. If we love in this way, as it is laid out before us in Corinthians, this love will bear all things, this love will believe all things, this love will hope all things, this love will endure all things, this love will never fail. Again, this is a wonderful exercise to do a self-examination of conscience with, especially before we go to Confession or before we go to Mass. Even at the end of the night, it could be a beautiful thing to reflect on - how have we been loving or how have we failed to be loving?

The second part of this meditation is going to be based on the notion that God is love. If the Father is love, then we can replace the Father in this passage every time we hear love. So I will start with the litany of *love is patient*. Now think about God the Father. God the Father is love, but maybe you don't have a great image of God the Father. Maybe you didn't have a great father growing up or you have had authority figures in your life that were not fatherly to you. Jesus came to show us who the Father really is and what His love is like. He's been dying to tell you about Him.

The Father is patient. God the Father is so patient with you. The Father is kind. Sometimes we think we have this Father that is just like an authoritarian figure. But He is so kind and He is so gentle as you get to know Him. The Father is so tender. The Father is not jealous. The Father is not pompous. The Father is not inflated. The Father's total focus is on you and all of us. He loves us. He sent His only Son into the world because God desired to give and receive this love with us. The Father is not rude.

The Father does not seek His own interests. Sometimes we think that God wants to use us like pawns for His own game. That is simply a distorted view of God. The Father does not seek His own interests. He has your best interests at heart. He does love you. He will not manipulate you. He wants so much for you to have life and have it in abundance.

The Father is not quick tempered. That means He does not have a temper. He is not quick to do that. This is wonderful because oftentimes we have grown up to think of this fierce angry God. That is not His tendency. His tendency is to be patient with us. Just think about how patient He has been with the human race over all these thousands of years. We sin and we fall and He just keeps trying to bring us back into His love. The Father does not brood over injury. In some translations, this says the Father does not take offense. There is nothing that you do that is going to offend Him. The Father is not going to focus on how He has been injured or hurt by you. The Father just wants to love you and only God can do that so unconditionally. God never rejoices in your wrongdoing. But the Father rejoices with the truth. The truth is: you are precious in His eyes. You are His beloved son. You are His beloved daughter. The truth is: He loves you with love beyond all telling.

Now, this is the great part - the Father bears all things. He can handle everything with you. The Father believes all things. He believes in you. The Father hopes all things. He has hope in you and your salvation. The Father endures all things. There is nothing He will not endure with you. The Father never fails. The Father will not fail you. He will always come through. Spend some time in **silence** just meditating on this passage and what God is speaking to you through it. When you are ready, **journal** your experience.

The third step in Lectio Divina is *oratio* or pray. This passage evokes a prayer of sorrow. If there were times that you have not been loving, tell God. Ask for His forgiveness. Ask for His help. Also, this passage evokes a prayer of gratitude for love. For knowing that we have a Father who loves us like this. For knowing that God the Father is not some distorted image that we have. But truly is a loving, patient, and kind Father who believes in you, hopes in you, endures with you, and will not fail you. How wonderful is that? Take some time now and express your prayer to God. It can be very simple. It can be spontaneous. It can be a petition to grow in love. It can be asking Him to experience His love like this. Whatever your prayer is, whatever your heart desires right now, spend some time in **silence** asking Him for that. When you are ready, **journal** your experience.

Finally, *contemplatio* or contemplation. You are going to spend the next few moments in **silence**. Complete silence. Just delighting in this wonderful passage of love is patient, love is kind, the Father is patient, the Father is kind. Find a Word or phrase somewhere in this passage that speaks to you and just dwell in it. Just let yourself dwell in this reality of love. This love that bears all things, believes all things, hopes all things, and endures all things. This love that will never fail. When you are ready, **journal** your experience.

PREPARATION FOR TOMORROW:
Read the following Scripture as you prepare for tomorrow:
The Crucifixion of Jesus, John 19:17-30.

DAY 34

PRAYING WITH YOUR SENSES

PREPARATION:

5 P's of Prayer: Prepare - know your passage ahead of time and meditate on it throughout the day. When you transition into prayer, take time to breathe, relax, slow down, and just rest. Place - go to your prayer place, room or chair. Ninety percent of prayer is just being there. Posture - we pray using our bodies. Try one of the four postures: standing, sitting, kneeling, or prostrating. Presence - make the Sign of the Cross and invite the Father, the Son, and the Holy Spirit into this time of prayer. Invite God the Father to hold you, the Son to be the Good Shepherd to you, and the Holy Spirit to be Christ in you. Passage - hold the Bible in your lap and realize: "The Word of God is alive." The Father will speak to you!

PRAYING WITH YOUR FIVE SENSES:

This type of prayer uses your senses, physically and imaginatively (seeing, hearing, smelling, tasting, and touching). Review Praying with Your Senses in the Prayer Exercises section of "Types of Prayer" in Appendix I.

PRAY NOW:

This prayer experience will be based on The Crucifixion of Jesus, John 19:17-30. We will be doing what St. Ignatius called the application of the senses or praying with your senses. We will start first with the sense of sight. As you read through this passage, try to allow yourself to see everything that is happening. Try to allow yourself to see this great love, the greatest act of love that ever happened for us - Jesus giving his life.

So they took Jesus, and carrying the cross himself he went out to what is called the Place of the Skull, in Hebrew, Golgotha. There they crucified him, and with him two others, one on either side, with Jesus in the middle. Pilate also had an inscription written and put on the cross. It read, "Jesus the Nazorean, the King of the Jews." Now many of the Jews read this inscription, because the place where Jesus was crucified was near the city; and it was written in Hebrew, Latin, and Greek. So the chief priests of the Jews said to Pilate, "Do not write 'The King of the Jews,' but that he said, 'I am the King of the Jews.'" Pilate answered, "What I have written, I have written."

When the soldiers had crucified Jesus, they took his clothes and divided them into four shares, a share for each soldier. They also took his tunic, but the tunic was seamless, woven in one piece from the top down. So they said to one another, "Let's not tear it, but cast lots for it to see whose it will be," in order that the passage of scripture might be fulfilled [that says]: "They divided my garments among them, / and for my vesture they cast lots." / This is what the soldiers did. Standing by the cross of Jesus were his mother and his mother's sister, Mary the wife of Clopas, and Mary of Magdala. When Jesus saw his mother and the disciple there whom he loved, he said to his mother, "Woman, behold, your son." Then he said to the disciple, "Behold, your mother." And from that hour the disciple took her into his home.

After this, aware that everything was now finished, in order that the scripture might be fulfilled, Jesus said, "I thirst." There was a vessel filled with common wine. So they put a sponge soaked in wine on a sprig of hyssop and put it up to his mouth. When Jesus had taken the wine, he said, "It is finished." And bowing his head, he handed over the spirit. (John 19:17-30)

So they took Jesus, and carrying the cross himself .... Try to imagine Him carrying the cross *out to what is called the Place of the Skull, in Hebrew, Golgotha.* He is carrying it up to the top of Golgotha. See the heaviness of it. See the pain and the anguish He is going through. The humiliation. But also see the great love in His eyes. He is doing it for you. He loves you so much. He loves all of us so much. He loves the world so much. He loves the Father so much that He embraces the cross.

There they crucified him, and with him two others, one on either side, with Jesus in the middle. So imagine Him on the cross with two others by His side. *Pilate also had an inscription written and put on the cross. It read, "Jesus the Nazorean, the King of the Jews."* Try to see this inscription with your own eyes, right above His head. Is it on wood or cloth? What is it written on? Is it painted? *"Jesus the Nazorean, the King of the Jews." Now many of the Jews read this inscription, because the place where Jesus was crucified was near the city; and it was written in Hebrew, Latin, and Greek.* Have you seen any of those languages? Can you picture what they look like? The lettering? The words? *So the chief priests of the Jews said to Pilate, "Do not write 'The King of the Jews,' but that he said, 'I am the King of the Jews.'" Pilate answered, "What I have written, I have written."*

When the soldiers had crucified Jesus, they took his clothes and divided them into four shares, a share for each soldier. Watch as the soldiers laugh and jealously take His clothes. *They also took his tunic, but the tunic was seamless, woven in one piece from the top down. So they said to one another, "Let's not tear it, but cast lots for it to see whose it will be," in order that the passage of scripture might be fulfilled [that says]: "They divided my garments among them, / and for my vesture they cast lots."* Imagine them now kneeling down, casting lots, rolling the dice. *This is what the soldiers did.*

Standing by the cross of Jesus were his mother and his mother's sister, Mary the wife of Clopas, and Mary of Magdala. You see the three women right by the cross. Now you watch as *Jesus saw his mother and the disciple there whom he loved.* Imagine you are the disciple and Jesus looks down at you from the cross. He looks at His mother and says, *"Woman, behold, your son."* Then He looks you deeply in the eyes with great love, giving you the gift of His Mother and He says to you, *"Behold, your mother."* Then you turn your eyes and you look to Mary and she is crying. She looks at you through her tears. Knowing that although she may lose her only son, she now gains you as a son or a daughter.

After this, aware that everything was now finished, in order that the scripture might be fulfilled, Jesus said, "I thirst." There was a vessel filled with common wine. So they put a sponge soaked in wine on a sprig of hyssop and put it up to his mouth. Imagine the sprig of hyssop being lifted all the way to His mouth. *When Jesus had taken the wine, he said, "It is finished." And bowing his head, he handed over the spirit.* Watch now as His lips pronounce these last Words, *"It is finished."* His head drops. He hands over the spirit. Spend some time in **silence**. Try to visualize the whole scene. Try to play it out before you like a movie. Try to see everything in the scene and try to do it all from your visual memory. When you are ready, **journal** your experience.

The next step of praying with the senses is to hear. We will focus on some of the noises, sounds, and voices. Especially pay attention to the voice of Jesus speaking to you. Imagine Him carrying the cross as He goes through the city of Jerusalem, up to Golgotha. The crowds are jeering. They are screaming out. Throwing things at Him. They are humiliating Him. They are persecuting Him. You hear Jesus continue to take steps. As they crucify Him, you hear the hammers strike the nails. You hear Him scream out in pain and agony. You hear the creaking of the wood of the cross as they lift Him up. You hear the voice of Pilate say, *"Jesus the Nazorean, the King of the Jews."* You hear the soldiers taking His clothes and dividing them into four shares, one for each soldier. You hear their voices saying, *"Let's not tear it, but cast lots for it to see whose it will be."*

Then, all is silent as you realize you are standing right there at the foot of the cross. As Jesus is suffering, you hear Him moaning in agonizing pain. You are standing there with the three women: Jesus' Mother Mary,

Mary the wife of Clopas, and Mary of Magdala. You see Jesus look at his mother. Listen to Him say, "*Woman, behold, your son.*" He says it with such joy. That He can give you as a gift to Mary. Then He says to you, "*Behold, your mother.*" The next Words He says in order that Scripture might be fulfilled are, "*I thirst.*" "*I thirst.*" "*I thirst.*" Imagine someone bringing the *vessel filled with common wine*; you can hear the wine swishing around. They soak the *sprig of hyssop and put it up to his mouth.* You can hear His mouth with His dry lips taking some of the wine. He says, *"It is finished."* There is silence. Spend time in **silence** now meditating upon what you have heard. **Journal** your experience when you are ready.

The third step is smell. Smell can often be a difficult sense to imagine, especially in this scene. The smells are not too pleasant. The smell of a crucifixion, the smell of flesh being torn open, the smell of death in the air, of people dying on the cross. You smell the common wine and the wine odor overtakes you. Spend some time allowing yourself to enter into Calvary, to enter into Golgotha, to enter into that smell of death. Meditate upon the sense of smell and spend some time in **silence** with that. When you are ready **journal** your experience.

The fourth step is taste. The part in this passage that is so strong with taste is of Jesus tasting His final thing: the wine. He had just said on the cross: "*I thirst.*" *There was a vessel filled with common wine* (so it wasn't good wine). *So they put a sponge soaked in wine on a sprig of hyssop and put it up to his mouth.* See this final gesture of kindness. Try to picture the man, or imagine someone you know in the scene offering this wine to the Lord. Imagine Jesus' face as *they put a sponge soaked in wine on a sprig of hyssop and put it up to his mouth.* Notice the humanity of Christ as he humbles Himself for us, that the final thing He tastes is common wine. What does it taste like? Spend some time in **silence** meditating upon taste. Try to have the experience of tasting that wine in your mouth. When you are ready, **journal** the experience.

Finally, the fifth step is touch. With the crucifixion, touch will be a painful experience. There are times of pain, but there are also moments of tenderness. Try to imagine as the crucifixion is happening. You can feel His pain. You can feel the nails being driven through your hands and your feet. What is it like to hang there in agony on the cross, just waiting to die? What does it feel like to thirst so bad that you scream out your final words, "*I thirst*"? You feel the warm wine in your mouth. All you feel behind you is the wood of the Cross, the nails, and the cold wind blowing on your body.

Maybe you are the beloved disciple standing at the foot of the cross.

You can feel the closeness and the tenderness of the women that are caring for Him. Especially Mary, the Mother of God, who is now your mother. What does it feel like to embrace her? To take her into your arms? To love her like a mother? To be loved by her like a son or daughter? Spend some time in **silence** with the sense of touch until that final moment when Jesus says, "*It is finished." And bowing his head, he handed over the spirit.* When you are ready, **journal** your experience.

PREPARATION FOR TOMORROW:
We will pray with Sunday Mass.

PRAYING WITH SUNDAY MASS

Today's prayer will be celebrating the Sunday Mass and experiencing God the Father in the Eucharist and Liturgy. Prepare before Mass with the following and then journal your experience after Mass.

PREPARATION BEFORE SUNDAY MASS:

Christ is present in four ways during Mass. First, He is present in the Eucharist which the priest takes, blesses, breaks, and shares. Christ is also present in the minister of the priest. Christ is present in the Word of God and in the Scriptures that we hear. Christ is also present in the assembled people of God, in the general assembly, in the gathered assembly. What I would like you to do today is to try to be aware of those four ways that Christ is present: first in the Eucharist, second in the priest, third in the Word, and finally in the gathered assembly. I would like you to have your eyes, ears, heart, and all of your senses open to experiencing Christ in each of these four ways.

Try to discover one moment of experiencing Him in the Eucharist. You have time during the entire Eucharistic prayer, the whole prayer that the priest says at the altar. Every single word that he says is important and comes from Scripture. As the bread and wine are taken, blessed, broken and shared, they are transformed into the Body and Blood of Jesus. They are no longer bread and wine. They are His Body and Blood. His real presence. He is right there. Try to have one moment where you can glimpse Him or you can experience Him. Where you can truly be with Him.

Try to discover one moment during Mass where you experience Christ through the priest. Maybe it is right there at the altar when he is transforming the bread and wine into the Body and Blood of Christ. Maybe it is when he is doing the prayers. Maybe it is at the sign of peace. One moment where you discover Christ in the priesthood.

The third is the Word of God. As we have talked about before, at every Mass we hear the Scriptures proclaimed. Usually one from the Old Testament, one from the Psalms, one from the New Testament, and one from the Gospel. In all of these, we have a chance to experience Christ speaking His Word to us. Try and focus on that. To really encounter Him in the Liturgy of the Word.

Finally, Christ is present in all the people of the assembly. Everybody that is gathered around you. You are Christ in the person next to you. Every baptized person that is in that church is Christ. Because we were baptized into Christ, we were baptized as priest, prophet, and King. You represent Christ in the gathered assembly. Everyone around you does. So here at Mass, especially during those times where you may be distracted, look around, because He is there in each of the faces around you. Try to see Him in just one face. Try to experience Him in one sign of peace. Try to experience Him during the singing of the songs or in the hymns.

Those are four things to prepare with today. Try to really experience Christ in the Eucharist, in the priest, in the Word of God, and in the gathered assembly. Go now and experience Him.

AFTER SUNDAY MASS:

How was Mass? Did you experience Christ in any of those four ways? Or in all four ways? Did you experience Him more deeply in the Eucharist? How about the priest? Were you able to relate an experience to Christ in the priesthood? Did you hear Him in the Word of God? Did you see Him, feel Him, or touch Him in the gathered assembly? We actually get to touch the Body of Christ, especially when we offer the sign of peace. Take a moment now to journal your experience and try to reflect back on Mass. That is called "mystagogy." It is the mystery of reflecting back on this wonderful experience we have had. In remembering it, we can even more deeply experience Christ in the Eucharist, in the priest, in the Word, and in the gathered assembly. Try to think of one moment for each of those four and **journal** now.

PREPARATION FOR TOMORROW:
Tomorrow we will be praying with nature.

DAY 35

PRAYING WITH CONTEMPLATIVE PRAYER

PREPARATION:

5 P's of Prayer: Prepare - know your passage ahead of time and meditate on it throughout the day. When you transition into prayer, take time to breathe, relax, slow down, and just rest. Place - go to your prayer place, room or chair. Ninety percent of prayer is just being there. Posture - we pray using our bodies. Try one of the four postures: standing, sitting, kneeling, or prostrating. Presence - make the Sign of the Cross and invite the Father, the Son, and the Holy Spirit into this time of prayer. Invite God the Father to hold you, the Son to be the Good Shepherd to you, and the Holy Spirit to be Christ in you. Passage - hold the Bible in your lap and realize: "The Word of God is alive." The Father will speak to you!

CONTEMPLATIVE PRAYER:

Contemplative prayer is a type of prayer that involves silence and simply being in the presence of God with Word, icon, or nature. Praying with nature grants us the ability to glimpse God the Father through creation, infinite beauty, and goodness. Review Contemplative Prayer and praying with Nature (Prayer Exercises) in "Types of Prayer" in Appendix I.

PRAY NOW:

For this prayer experience, we are going to use contemplative prayer with nature. As with contemplating the Word or icons, nature will be the focal point. God has created the wonder of nature, which is like an icon itself. It is not God, but it certainly is a window into the Creator. He has left His thumbprint all over the world.

In contemplating with nature, I recommend that you focus on something that is alive. If you are in your house, you can look out the window. Maybe you have a bird feeder and can watch the birds. Also, if you are inside, you may have a plant, or fish, or a pet (though sometimes they can be a bit feisty) that you can hold or gaze upon. I used to contemplate and pray with my nieces and nephew when they were infants, just holding and gazing upon them. There is nothing more contemplative than holding an infant. If you are married, if you have a good friend, or somebody that you are dating, they could be your contemplation. You can simply gaze into each other's eyes without saying a word. That may seem awkward at first or uncomfortable, but it is a very powerful and beautiful experience. You can also hold each other and feel what it is like to be held. It is a very intimate experience for couples. Do not do anything else; just be held.

If you want to go outside, that is wonderful too. Go out and explore nature. Make a pilgrimage of it. Once you have found your place, make sure that you can be comfortable in one of the prayer postures (sitting, standing, kneeling or prostrating) where you won't have to move. Take some time to do this so that you can be sure that you are comfortable and can remain comfortable for an extended period of time. So if it is cold or if it is hot, you want to make sure that you dress appropriately. You can even stay in your car. The idea is not to be walking around. Although a good walk through an area can be a very good way to prepare and a good walk afterwards can be a wonderful way to reflect and meditate, I would suggest that during the time of contemplation (as with the other times), you try to pick one of the four postures and allow your body to be totally still. With contemplative prayer, we remain still with our bodies. Then, our mind begins to become still and, then, our soul begins to become still. So it helps to remain still. Trying not to move a muscle. Just taking in the experience.

Here are some ideas for outside. You could watch the sun rise or set. Go near a body of water like a lake, river, pond, or a waterfall. You could take a drive or even a day trip to a place where you can be still. Go out and find an open field, farm, forest, beach, top of a mountain or a hill. Places where you have a sense of wonder and awe. If you can't get outdoors, look out your back window. If you have a view of nature from your window, gaze at the beauty of God's creation right in your own backyard. Enjoy your time now, resting with God, while contemplating nature. When He created it, He found it good. When He created us, He found us very good. Remain in complete **silence** and stillness. Take in nature with all your senses as you gaze, dwell, and delight in God's created beauty. When you are ready, **journal** your experience.

PREPARATION FOR TOMORROW:
Read the following Scripture as you prepare for tomorrow:
The Call of Jeremiah, Jeremiah 1:4-9.

DAY 36

PRAYING WITH SCRIPTURAL RELAXATION

PREPARATION:

5 P's of Prayer: Prepare - know your passage ahead of time and meditate on it throughout the day. When you transition into prayer, take time to breathe, relax, slow down, and just rest. Place - go to your prayer place, room or chair. Ninety percent of prayer is just being there. Posture - we pray using our bodies. Try one of the four postures: standing, sitting, kneeling, or prostrating. Presence - make the Sign of the Cross and invite the Father, the Son, and the Holy Spirit into this time of prayer. Invite God the Father to hold you, the Son to be the Good Shepherd to you, and the Holy Spirit to be Christ in you. Passage - hold the Bible in your lap and realize: "The Word of God is alive." The Father will speak to you!

SCRIPTURE RELAXATION:

The focus of this exercise is Christ healing us and the Word of God helping us to change our thinking patterns. Review Scriptural Relaxation in the Prayer Exercises section of "Types of Prayer" in Appendix I. You can also find the audio version of Scriptural Relaxation at TheProdigalFather.org/Pray40Days.

PRAY NOW:

This prayer experience is based on The Call of Jeremiah, Jeremiah 1:4-9. We will be using the exercise of Scriptural Relaxation. The three things that we will focus on are the heaviness, the warmth, and the resting of your body. Doing this with Scripture, it is not you who is bringing yourself to rest; rather you are allowing the Word of God to bring you to rest. Find a position that is comfortable, where you can remain for at least fifteen minutes to an hour, depending on how long you will be doing this exercise. Know that if this is done every day, not only will it bring you closer to God, but it will greatly reduce the stress in your life. Read the passage straight through first and then we will take some time to focus on the relaxation.

The word of the LORD came to me: / Before I formed you in the womb I knew you, / before you were born I dedicated you, / a prophet to the nations I appointed you. / "Ah, Lord GOD!" I said, / "I do not know how to speak. I am too young!" / But the LORD answered me, / Do not say, "I am too young." / To whomever I send you, you shall go; / whatever I command you, you shall speak. / Do not be afraid of them, / for I am with you to deliver you - oracle of the LORD. / Then the LORD extended his hand and touched my mouth, saying to me, / See, I place my words in your mouth! (Jeremiah 1:4-9)

Let's begin with some breathing exercises. We will use this phrase: *Before I formed you in the womb I knew you....* Begin by just allowing your body to rest.... Either sitting or lying down. Take a deep breath in through your nose.... Breathing all the way in.... Opening your chest all the way down through your stomach.... *Before I formed you in the womb I knew you.* Breathe out any worries, anxieties, or frustrations that you may have.... Invite the Holy Spirit to come into you as you breathe in.... Take a long, deep breath in through your nose.... *Before I formed you in the womb I knew you.* Hold it.... Then slowly breathe out through your mouth.... Breathe all the way out.... Letting it all out.... Pushing the air out.... Once more, take a long, slow, deep breath in through your nose.... Breath in deeply, as deep as you can.... *Before I formed you in the womb I knew you.* Hold it for a moment.... Release.... Breathe out.... [Pause for a moment of silence.]

The word of the LORD came to me.... Imagine your whole body is heavy and sinking into the cushion... Focus your attention on your right arm.... Your right arm is heavy.... *The word of the LORD came to me....* Your right arm is heavy.... *The word of the LORD came to me....* Your right arm is heavy.... [Pause for a moment of silence.]

Now focus on your left arm.... *Before you were born I dedicated you.* Your left arm is heavy.... *Before you were born I dedicated you....* Your left arm is heavy and sinks into the cushion.... Your left arm is heavy.... *Before you were born I dedicated you.* [Pause for a moment of silence.]

Your right leg is heavy.... *"Ah, Lord GOD!" I said, / "I do not know how to speak. / I am too young!"* Your right leg is heavy and it sinks into the cushion.... Your right leg is heavy.... *But the LORD answered me, / Do not say, "I am too young."* [Pause for a moment of silence.]

Now focus on your left leg.... Your left leg is heavy.... *To whomever I send you, you shall go.* Your left leg is heavy and sinks into the cushion.... *Whatever I command you, you shall speak.* Your left leg is heavy.... [Pause for a moment of silence.]

You feel the weight of your head sink into the cushion.... *Do not be afraid of them.* Your head sinks into the cushion and it is heavy.... You can't hold it up.... *Do not be afraid of them.* Your head feels heavy and sinks into the cushion.... Your whole body feels heavy.... [Pause for a moment of silence.]

The word of the LORD came to me. Your body feels warm.... *The word of the LORD came to me*. Your head, as it sinks into the cushion feels warm.... *The word of the LORD came to me*. Your head feels heavy and warm.... *The word of the LORD came to me.* Your head sinks into the cushion.... It is heavy and warm.... *The word of the LORD came to me*. [Pause for a moment of silence.]

Your right arm feels heavy and warm.... *Before I formed you in the womb I knew you*. Your arm feels warm.... *Before I formed you in the womb I knew you*. Your right arm feels warm and heavy and sinks into the cushion.... [Pause for a moment of silence.]

Your left arm feels warm.... *Before you were born I dedicated you.* Your left arm feels warm and heavy and sinks into the cushion.... *Before you were born I dedicated you.* Your left arm feels warm and heavy.... *Before you were born I dedicated you.* [Pause for a moment of silence.]

Your right leg feels warm.... *"Ah, Lord GOD!" I said, /"I do not know how to speak. I am too young!"* Your right leg feels warm and heavy.... *"Ah, Lord GOD!" I said, /"I do not know how to speak. I am too young!"* Your right leg feels heavy and warm and sinks into the cushion.... Your right leg is heavy and warm.... *"I do not know how to speak, I am too young."* [Pause for a moment of silence.]

Your left leg feels heavy and warm.... *But the LORD answered me, / Do not say "I am too young."* Your left leg feels warm.... *Do not say, "I am too young."* Your left leg feels warm and heavy and sinks into the cushion.... [Pause for a moment of silence.]

To whomever I send you, you shall go; / *whatever I command you, you shall speak*. Your whole body feels warm and heavy and gently sinks into the cushion.... *Do not be afraid of them, / for I am with you to deliver you.* [Pause for a moment of silence.]

Then the LORD extended his hand and touched my mouth, saying to me, / See I place my words in your mouth! As He does this, your mouth, your face, and your head feel completely relaxed.... As He places His Words in your mouth, your head feels relaxed and heavy and warm.... [Pause for a moment of silence.]

Then the LORD extended his hand and touched my mouth, saying to me, / See I place my words in your mouth! Your whole head and face feel relaxed, warm, heavy, and sink gently into the cushion.... *Then the LORD extended his hand and touched my mouth, saying to me, / See I place my words in your mouth!* [Pause for a moment of silence.]

Your right hand feels relaxed.... Your right arm feels relaxed and heavy and warm.... *The word of the LORD came to me.* Your whole right side is heavy and warm and completely relaxed....[Pause for a moment of silence.]

Before I formed you in the womb I knew you. Your left hand and arm are relaxed.... *Before you were born I dedicated you.* Your left arm relaxes further.... It is heavy and warm and sinks into the cushion.... *A prophet to the nations I appointed you.* Your whole left side relaxes.... It is heavy and warm.... [Pause for a moment of silence.]

Now you feel your feet and your legs completely relax.... *"Ah, Lord GOD!" I said, /"I do not know how to speak. I am too young!"* Your feet and legs completely relax, feel heavy, and are warm.... [Pause for a moment of silence.]

"Ah, Lord GOD!" I said, /"I do not know how to speak. I am too young!" You relax and release even more.... Your feet and your legs feel heavy and warm and completely relaxed as they sink into the cushion.... [Pause for a moment of silence.]

But the LORD answered me, / Do not say, "I am too young." / To whomever I send you, you shall go. Your legs relax even more.... *Whatever I command you, you shall speak.* Your legs relax, your feet relax, you feel heavy and warm.... Your whole body is now relaxed.... *Do not be afraid of them.* Your whole body is relaxed, warm and heavy, as it sinks into the cushion.... [Pause for a moment of silence.]

Do not be afraid of them, / for I am with you to deliver you. Your entire body is relaxed.... Your head.... Your shoulders.... Your arms.... Your back.... Your legs.... Your feet.... Your whole body is relaxed, heavy and warm, as you sink into the cushion.... *Then the LORD extended his hand and touched my mouth, saying to me, / See I place my words in your mouth! Do not be afraid of them, / for I am with you to deliver you.* [Pause for a moment of silence.]

Allow yourself to rest and relax in **silence**. When you are ready, **journal** your experience.

PREPARATION FOR TOMORROW:
Read the following Scripture as you prepare for tomorrow: The Appearance on the Road to Emmaus, Luke 24:13-35.

DAY 37

PRAYING WITH GUIDED MEDITATION

PREPARATION:

5 P's of Prayer: Prepare - know your passage ahead of time and meditate on it throughout the day. When you transition into prayer, take time to breathe, relax, slow down, and just rest. Place - go to your prayer place, room or chair. Ninety percent of prayer is just being there. Posture - we pray using our bodies. Try one of the four postures: standing, sitting, kneeling, or prostrating. Presence - make the Sign of the Cross and invite the Father, the Son, and the Holy Spirit into this time of prayer. Invite God the Father to hold you, the Son to be the Good Shepherd to you, and the Holy Spirit to be Christ in you. Passage - hold the Bible in your lap and realize: "The Word of God is alive." The Father will speak to you!

GUIDED MEDITATION:

Find a quiet room, settle into a spot that will be comfortable, and place your body in a relaxed position, usually without crossed arms or legs. Allow your imagination, fueled by your senses, to enter into the story. Close your eyes as you meditate; at the end of the meditation, do not rush to open your eyes. Let your body tell you when you are ready. Review Guided Meditation under the Prayer Exercises section of "Types of Prayer" in Appendix I.

PRAY NOW:

This is a guided meditation based on The Appearance on the Road to Emmaus, Luke 24:13-35. I encourage you to have your Bible and journal with you.

Now that very day two of them were going to a village seven miles from Jerusalem called Emmaus, and they were conversing about all the things that had occurred. And it happened that while they were conversing and debating, Jesus himself drew near and walked with them, but their eyes were prevented from recognizing him. He asked them, "What are you discussing as you walk along?" They stopped, looking downcast. One of them, named Cleopas, said to him in reply, "Are you the only visitor to Jerusalem who does not know of the things that have taken place there in these days?" And he replied to them, "What sort of things?" They said to him, "The things that happened to Jesus the Nazarene, who was a prophet mighty in deed and word before God and all the people, how our chief priests and rulers both handed him over to a sentence of death and crucified him. But we were hoping that he would be the one to redeem Israel;

and besides all this, it is now the third day since this took place. Some women from our group, however, have astounded us: they were at the tomb early in the morning and did not find his body; they came back and reported that they had indeed seen a vision of angels who announced that he was alive. Then some of those with us went to the tomb and found things just as the women had described, but him they did not see." And he said to them, "Oh, how foolish you are! How slow of heart to believe all that the prophets spoke! Was it not necessary that the Messiah should suffer these things and enter into his glory?" Then beginning with Moses and all the prophets, he interpreted to them what referred to him in all the scriptures. As they approached the village to which they were going, he gave the impression that he was going on farther. But they urged him, "Stay with us, for it is nearly evening and the day is almost over." So he went in to stay with them. And it happened that, while he was with them at table, he took bread, said the blessing, broke it, and gave it to them. With that their eyes were opened and they recognized him, but he vanished from their sight. Then they said to each other, "Were not our hearts burning [within us] while he spoke to us on the way and opened the scriptures to us?" So they set out at once and returned to Jerusalem where they found gathered together the eleven and those with them who were saying, "The Lord has truly been raised and has appeared to Simon!" Then the two recounted what had taken place on the way and how he was made known to them in the breaking of the bread. (Luke 24:13-35)

Now that very day two of them were going to a village seven miles from Jerusalem called Emmaus. What I would like you to do is imagine you are one of the two going to Emmaus. Then think of another person to walk with you. Just allow whoever God brings forth in your mind and in your heart to walk with you. Who is that person? It can be anybody that you desire: living or deceased. But, hopefully, God will place somebody in your heart right now that you are supposed to walk with in this prayer.

Now imagine you are walking with that person. You are on a seven mile walk going to a village from Jerusalem called Emmaus. You are *conversing about all the things that have occurred.* Think about all your prayer experiences. Think about all these encounters you have had with God. Think about your entire life and how you have experienced God. Think about what these disciples experienced. They encountered the miracles of Jesus. The wonderful life of Jesus. The way that He taught them how to pray and encounter God the Father. The way that He gave Mary to be their mother. The way that He carried the cross. The way He endured His passion, suffered, died, and was resurrected. Allow all of these memories to come to mind. All of these things that have occurred in your life, in the life of Scripture, and how you have really encountered God as you prayed with Scripture.

And it happened that while they were conversing and debating, Jesus himself drew near and walked with them. So imagine that the two of you are walking together. All of a sudden, you get the sense that somebody is walking right next to you. *But their eyes were prevented from recognizing him.* You almost don't even acknowledge Him because you are so deep in conversation.

He asks you, *"What are you discussing as you walk along?"* You stop. *Looking downcast*, you are sad because of the crucifixion. Maybe you have yet to have an experience of His Resurrection. Your friend says, *"Are you the only visitor to Jerusalem who does not know of the things that have taken place there in these days?" And he replied to them, "What sort of things?" They said to him, "The things that happened to Jesus the Nazarene, who was a prophet mighty in deed and word before God and all the people, how our chief priests and rulers both handed him over to a sentence of death and crucified him. But we were hoping that he would be the one to redeem Israel; and besides all this, it is now the third day since this took place. Some women from our group, however, have astounded us: they were at the tomb early in the morning and did not find his body; they came back and reported that they had indeed seen a vision of angels who announced that he was alive. Then some of those with us went to the tomb and found things just as the women had described, but him they did not see."*

Maybe there have been times in your life where all you see is an empty tomb. Maybe there have been times when you don't see Jesus. When you don't feel God's presence. When you don't feel like you are living in the Resurrection. Maybe you even felt abandoned by God.

Then Jesus *said to them, "Oh, how foolish you are! How slow of heart to believe all that the prophets spoke! Was it not necessary that the Messiah should suffer these things and enter into his glory?" Then beginning with Moses and all the prophets, he interpreted to them what referred to him in all the scriptures.* I don't know about you, but sometimes Scripture can be overwhelming. Sometimes there are a lot of references that I don't even understand. But during this time, He has been revealing Himself to you through Scripture.

Imagine you continue walking with your friend and with Jesus. As you approach the village, you get the impression that Jesus was going to keep on going further. One of you speaks out. Is it you or is it your friend? *"Stay with us, for it is nearly evening and the day is almost over."* What would you say to Jesus right now to convince Him to stay with you? Go ahead and tell Him whatever is in your heart. What do you want to hear more about?

So he went in to stay with them. And it happened that, while he was with them at table ... they recognized him. Imagine the two of you are with Jesus at the table. Watch right now as the miracle happens. He takes the bread, says the blessing, breaks it, and gives it to you. With that, your eyes are opened and you recognize Him. But, instantly, He vanishes from your sight. For that one brief moment you did see Him. You did recognize His presence. Now it is just you and your friend again. What do you say to each other? What do you share with your best friend? Or the person that God has chosen to allow you to journey with on this meditation?

"Were not our hearts burning [within us] while he spoke to us on the way and opened the Scriptures to us?" At any point during these times of prayer were not your hearts burning within you as He opened the Scripture to you?

So they set out at once and returned to Jerusalem where they found gathered together the eleven and those with them who were saying, "The Lord has truly been raised and has appeared to Simon!" Then the two recounted what had taken place on the way and how he was made known to them in the breaking of the bread. Try to imagine yourself and the other person now joined together with the eleven and the other people that were with them. It is your turn to tell the story of what you have experienced. During all these times of prayer, when did you see Him? When did you hear His voice? When did you touch Him? When did you feel truly present with Him? Tell them your story. Because this story is a real story - it is how God is present right now in the world today for you.

But it is not for you alone. Any time we experience something wonderful, we have this innate desire to share it. Now try to take that desire that you have and share your experience. Spend some time in meditation and share your experience; either talk it out loud like you are there with the disciples or speak it in your mind, in your heart, or journal the experience. This may even be a good time to review all your days of prayer. To see when God was walking with you. When the Father was holding you. When Jesus was right there as your Good Shepherd. When you felt the Holy Spirit present in you. When you encountered Mary as your beloved mother.

Take time now to meditate in **silence** and then **journal** when you are ready.

PREPARATION FOR TOMORROW:
Read the following Scripture as you prepare for tomorrow:
Jesus and Peter, John 21:15-19.

DAY 38

PRAYING LIKE A PIRATE

PREPARATION:

5 P's of Prayer: Prepare - know your passage ahead of time and meditate on it throughout the day. When you transition into prayer, take time to breathe, relax, slow down, and just rest. Place - go to your prayer place, room or chair. Ninety percent of prayer is just being there. Posture - we pray using our bodies. Try one of the four postures: standing, sitting, kneeling, or prostrating. Presence - make the Sign of the Cross and invite the Father, the Son, and the Holy Spirit into this time of prayer. Invite God the Father to hold you, the Son to be the Good Shepherd to you, and the Holy Spirit to be Christ in you. Passage - hold the Bible in your lap and realize: "The Word of God is alive." The Father will speak to you!

PRAYING LIKE A PIRATE:

ARRR: Acknowledge, Relate, Receive, and Respond to God. Review Praying like a Pirate in the Prayer Exercises section of "Types of Prayer" found in Appendix I.

PRAY NOW:

In this prayer experience, we will be praying with Jesus and Peter, John 21:15-19. I encourage you to have your Bible and journal with you for this exercise. We will be praying like a pirate today: ARRR - acknowledge, relate, receive, and respond. Read the passage through once to get familiar with it. Then try to acknowledge what you are feeling.

When they had finished breakfast, Jesus said to Simon Peter, "Simon, son of John, do you love me more than these?" He said to him, "Yes, Lord, you know that I love you." He said to him, "Feed my lambs." He then said to him a second time, "Simon, son of John, do you love me?" He said to him, "Yes, Lord, you know that I love you." He said to him, "Tend my sheep." He said to him the third time, "Simon, son of John, do you love me?" Peter was distressed that he had said to him a third time, "Do you love me?" and he said to him, "Lord, you know everything; you know that I love you." [Jesus] said to him, "Feed my sheep. Amen, amen, I say to you, when you were younger, you used to dress yourself and go where you wanted; but when you grow old, you will stretch out your hands, and someone else will dress you and lead you where you do not want to go." He said this signifying by what kind of death he would glorify God. And when he had said this, he said to him, "Follow me." (John 21:15-19)

Acknowledge What are you feeling right now? What do you feel when Jesus asks you, *"Do you love me?"* We hear very clearly that Peter was distressed the third time he was questioned - Why is Jesus asking me this three times? I have already told Him 'yes' twice. *"Do you love me?"* How do you feel when Jesus asks you that question? Imagine, right now, you are with Him on the beach with a fire, the shore, and the waves. He is cooking the bread and the fish. You get to experience Him in the Resurrection. He asks not only, *"Do you love me?"* but also says: *"Follow me."* Take some time in **silence** to acknowledge your feelings. When you are ready, **journal** what you acknowledged.

Relate Now that you have gotten in touch with your internal emotions and spiritual disposition (whether you are in consolation or desolation, whatever you are feeling), it is wonderful to acknowledge it and accept it. Now we have an opportunity to relate those feelings to Jesus. Peter did this in the Scripture passage today. He related to Jesus each time. When he became distressed, he said, "*Lord, you know everything*; *you know that I love you.*" I love how honest and candid Peter could be with Jesus. Can you be the same way with Him? Can you be that honest, open, and raw with your feelings, whatever you are experiencing? Can you shout it out to Him right now?

Take some time to relate to Jesus. Imagine you are Peter, there on the shore, experiencing the Resurrection of Jesus. You have just swum onto shore from the boat and you are being warmed by the fire. He has fed you with bread and fish. Now it is just you and Him. He asks you three times, *"Do you love me?"* You have acknowledged how you feel and now you have the opportunity to relate it to Him. Just as Simon Peter was very honest and candid when he said, "*Lord, you know everything; you know that I love you.*" You can be just that honest with Him. There is nothing you can say wrong to Him. He just wants you to express yourself to Him. So take a moment of **silence** and relate your feelings to Jesus. When you are ready, **journal** what you related.

Receive Now that you have acknowledged your feelings and related them to Jesus, take some time to receive whatever He wants to say to you. When Simon Peter related his feelings to Jesus, *"Lord, you know everything; you know that I love you,"* Jesus said to him, *"Feed my sheep. Amen, amen, I say to you, when you were younger, you used to dress yourself and go where you wanted; but when you grow old, you will stretch out your hands, and someone else will dress you and lead you where you do not want to go." He said this signifying by what kind of death he would glorify God. And when he had said this, he said to him, "Follow me."*

What is Jesus saying to you right now? Can you hear His voice? What words arise in your heart? What is He speaking to you? If you are not sure, read the passage again and spend some time in silence. Receive whatever He wants to say to you or do in you. You will know that it is Him because He will bring with Him all the gifts of the Holy Spirit; you will experience an increase of faith, an increase of hope, and an increase of love. Spend some time in **silence** and then **journal** your experience.

Respond We do not hear Peter's response, but we know that he did respond affirmatively. Jesus said to him finally, "*Follow me.*" We know that Peter would go on to become the first pope of our church. He would be known as The Rock. Though he denied Jesus three times, this was now his chance to reaffirm his love for Jesus and to say to Him three times: "*I love you. I love you. I love you.*"

Jesus says, "*Feed my sheep. Tend my sheep. Feed my lambs. Follow me.*" What is your response? How do you respond to this invitation to Jesus? How do you respond to this challenge of *when you were younger, you used to dress yourself and go where you wanted; but when you grow old, you will stretch out your hands, and someone else will dress you and lead you where you do not want to go*?

When He says, *"Follow me,"* how do you respond? What did He say to you in the silence? What did He ask of you? What did He speak to you? Take some time in **silence** and respond back to Him. It could be with prayer, it could be with spontaneous dialogue, or it could just be speaking from your heart. It could be: "Yes, Lord, I will follow you." Be sincere in this response and respond out of your free will to His call. When you are ready, **journal** your experience.

PREPARATION FOR TOMORROW:
Read the following Scripture as you prepare for tomorrow:
Thomas, John 20:24-29.

DAY 39

PRAYING WITH LECTIO DIVINA

PREPARATION:

5 P's of Prayer: Prepare - know your passage ahead of time and meditate on it throughout the day. When you transition into prayer, take time to breathe, relax, slow down, and just rest. Place - go to your prayer place, room or chair. Ninety percent of prayer is just being there. Posture - we pray using our bodies. Try one of the four postures: standing, sitting, kneeling, or prostrating. Presence - make the Sign of the Cross and invite the Father, the Son, and the Holy Spirit into this time of prayer. Invite God the Father to hold you, the Son to be the Good Shepherd to you, and the Holy Spirit to be Christ in you. Passage - hold the Bible in your lap and realize: "The Word of God is alive." The Father will speak to you!

LECTIO DIVINA:

A type of prayer in which one is reading Scripture, meditating or pondering Scripture, praying vocally with God, and contemplating in silence. Review Lectio Divina in the Prayer Exercises section of "Types of Prayer" in Appendix I.

PRAY NOW:

This prayer experience will be based on Thomas, John 20:24-29. I encourage you to open your Bible and have your journal ready because today we will be using Lectio Divina. Read the Scripture passage first to get acquainted with it, then a second time where you will hold on to a Word or a phrase. Read it a third time very slowly and the fourth time you will read it even slower. So the first step is *Lectio,* to read.

Thomas, called Didymus, one of the Twelve, was not with them when Jesus came. So the other disciples said to him, "We have seen the Lord." But he said to them, "Unless I see the mark of the nails in his hands and put my finger into the nailmarks and put my hand into his side, I will not believe." Now a week later his disciples were again inside and Thomas was with them. Jesus came, although the doors were locked, and stood in their midst and said, "Peace be with you." Then he said to Thomas, "Put your finger here and see my hands, and bring your hand and put it into my side, and do not be unbelieving, but believe." Thomas answered and said to him, "My Lord and my God!" Jesus said to him, "Have you come to believe because you have seen me? Blessed are those who have not seen and have believed." (John 20:24-29)

Let's read it a second time and try to hold in your heart a Word or phrase that you feel God is speaking to you.

Thomas, called Didymus, one of the Twelve, was not with them when Jesus came. So the other disciples said to him, "We have seen the Lord." But he said to them, "Unless I see the mark of the nails in his hands and put my finger into the nailmarks and put my hand into his side, I will not believe." Now a week later his disciples were again inside and Thomas was with them. Jesus came, although the doors were locked, and stood in their midst and said, "Peace be with you." Then he said to Thomas, "Put your finger here and see my hands, and bring your hand and put it into my side, and do not be unbelieving, but believe." Thomas answered and said to him, "My Lord and my God!" Jesus said to him, "Have you come to believe because you have seen me? Blessed are those who have not seen and have believed."

What is the Word or phrase that you feel God was speaking to you? Mine was, *his disciples were again inside*. Let's read it a third time and try to hold on to another Word or phrase.

Thomas, called Didymus, one of the Twelve, was not with them when Jesus came. So the other disciples said to him, "We have seen the Lord." But he said to them, "Unless I see the mark of the nails in his hands and put my finger into the nailmarks and put my hand into his side, I will not believe." Now a week later his disciples were again inside and Thomas was with them. Jesus came, although the doors were locked, and stood in their midst and said, "Peace be with you." Then he said to Thomas, "Put your finger here and see my hands, and bring your hand and put it into my side, and do not be unbelieving, but believe." Thomas answered and said to him, "My Lord and my God!" Jesus said to him, "Have you come to believe because you have seen me? Blessed are those who have not seen and have believed."

What is the Word or phrase that you have now? Mine was, *believe.* Now, and very slowly, read this a fourth time. You can read it out loud or you can read it **silently** in your own heart. Try to hold onto one Word or phrase. Then **journal** that Word or phrase.

Thomas, called Didymus, one of the Twelve, was not with them when Jesus came. So the other disciples said to him, "We have seen the Lord." But he said to them, "Unless I see the mark of the nails in his hands and put my finger into the nailmarks and put my hand into his side, I will not believe." Now a week later his disciples were again inside and Thomas was with them. Jesus came, although the doors were locked, and stood in their midst and said, "Peace be with you." Then he said to Thomas, "Put your finger here and see my hands, and bring your hand and put it into my side, and do not be unbelieving, but believe." Thomas answered and said to him, "My Lord and my God!" Jesus said to him, "Have you come to believe because you have seen me? Blessed are those who have not seen and have believed."

The next step in Lectio Divina is *meditatio* or meditation. I will lead you line by line through this meditation. Hopefully, at some point, you will be able to do this on your own, using your own imagination, your own wonder, and your own creativity.

Thomas, called Didymus, one of the Twelve, was not with them when Jesus came. Very interesting, he wasn't with them when Jesus came. *So the other disciples said to him, "We have seen the Lord."* What must it have felt like to be Thomas, the one who missed out on seeing Jesus? To hear the disciples say, *"We have seen the Lord."* I can imagine Thomas would be very upset and in denial. *"Unless I see the mark of the nails in his hands and put my finger into the nailmarks and put my hand into his side, I will not believe."* He wants to not only see, but he wants to probe. To put his finger into the nailmarks and put his hand into Jesus' side. Unless I do that, *I will not believe.* That is a pretty strong statement. That is a pretty strong demand of Jesus.

Now this is the interesting part… *A week later his disciples were again inside.* I love that they were all together, inside, gathered closely. *And Thomas was with them.* So this time, they were gathered together and Thomas was with them. Jesus says, "*For where two or three are gathered together in my name, there am I in the midst of them*" (Matthew 18:20). Thomas could not experience Him alone, he needed to be together with all the disciples.

Jesus came, although the doors were locked. This is another amazing part; He came through locked doors. You may be familiar with the painting where Jesus is outside of the door and He is knocking. There is no handle on the outside, the only handles are on the inside. The significance of the door is that only YOU can let Him in. But what I love about this is that He comes through locked doors. Even when we are too paralyzed to get up to the door and let Him in, even when we are hurting, afraid, trapped in sin, trapped in anger, or trapped in denial (as Thomas was), Jesus can come through locked doors. He comes through our locked doors and stands right in our midst and says to us that there is no sin that you have done that can keep Him away from you. Right now, He comes through your locked door, into your locked heart, and He says to you, "*Peace be with you.*"

Now, Jesus knows what Thomas said, *"Unless I see the mark of the nails in his hands and put my finger into the nailmarks, and put my hand into his side, I will not believe."* Jesus says this to Thomas [imagine Jesus saying this to you because He wants you to believe], *"Put your finger here and see my hands."* Try to imagine His hands - look at His hands. He is holding them out for you right now. You can see He is resurrected. You can still see the wounds in His hands. You can still see the marks.

"And bring your hand and put it into my side." Maybe you are a little hesitant at first. He takes your hand, pulls it to Him, and puts it right in His side so that you can feel.

Then, He looks you in the eyes and He says with such great love, with such great hope, with such patience, "*Do not be unbelieving, but believe.*" Thomas answered Him and said [maybe you say this, too], "*My Lord and My God!*" Jesus said to him, "*Have you come to believe because you have seen me? Blessed are those who have not seen me and have believed.*" Who is that? That is you! You are the blessed one who has not seen Him, but believes. We live right now in a more blessed age than the people that actually got to see Jesus physically, than the people that actually got to see Him in the Resurrection, because now we see Him through the grace of the Holy Spirit. Through the gift of Pentecost that He has given to us. We can see Him now and believe in Him in a deeper way than even the Apostles could. *"Do not be unbelieving, but believe."* Take some time in **silence** and meditate on this passage by yourself. When you are ready, **journal** your experience.

Oratio or pray. Imagine you are right there with Jesus. He has just taken your hand and put it into His side. He says to you, *"Do not be unbelieving, but believe."* What are the words that you speak? What do you say at that moment? Thomas answered, "*My Lord and my God*!" What is your answer? What do you speak? What is your prayer? What is your desire? Take a moment in **silence** and express that to Jesus. Say it out loud or say it in your heart. **Journal** the experience when you are ready.

Finally, *contemplatio* or contemplate. You have just had a very real, amazing, powerful, personal, and intimate experience with our Lord Jesus. Spend the rest of your time in silent contemplation with whatever Word, phrase, or image was strongest for you. Allow yourself to dwell in that. Let yourself enter into that moment deeper and into that reality because that really was Christ. That is Christ with you, right now, as you hear the Word proclaimed. As you pray with it. As you read it. As you meditate upon it. Spend some time in wonderful, quiet contemplation. When you are ready, **journal** your experience.

PREPARATION FOR TOMORROW:
Read the following Scripture as you prepare for tomorrow:
The Prayer of Jesus, John 17:1-26.

DAY 40

PRAYING WITH THE CONTEMPLATIVE PRAYER

PREPARATION:

5 P's of Prayer: Prepare - know your passage ahead of time and meditate on it throughout the day. When you transition into prayer, take time to breathe, relax, slow down, and just rest. Place - go to your prayer place, room or chair. Ninety percent of prayer is just being there. Posture - we pray using our bodies. Try one of the four postures: standing, sitting, kneeling, or prostrating. Presence - make the Sign of the Cross and invite the Father, the Son, and the Holy Spirit into this time of prayer. Invite God the Father to hold you, the Son to be the Good Shepherd to you, and the Holy Spirit to be Christ in you. Passage - hold the Bible in your lap and realize: "The Word of God is alive." The Father will speak to you!

PRAYING WITH CONTEMPLATIVE PRAYER:

Contemplative prayer is a type of prayer that involves silence and simply being in the presence of God with Word, icon, or nature. Praying with Word is a way to concentrate on Christ through Scripture. The Word is God alive. Review Contemplative Prayer and praying with Word (Prayer Exercises) in "Types of Prayer" in Appendix I.

PRAY NOW:

Today, I encourage you to read the Word from your Bible as we contemplate on The Prayer of Jesus, John 17:1-26. Hopefully, at this point, you will be able to do this prayer exercise on your own, to experience contemplation on your own. I encourage you to read the Word slowly, to spend time with Scripture contemplating whatever God speaks to you, and to spend more time resting in silence. Let yourself truly dwell with Him and just be in His presence.

Read the passage in silence once very slowly. Then read it again slower until you find a Word or a phrase that you feel God is speaking to you. Remain in silence repeating this Word over and over in your heart. If you get distracted, and you will, remember the virtue is returning back to the Word. Continue repeating the phrase over and over until you come to a place of rest in the Word. Remain in silence, peace, and stillness for as long as the moment lasts. If there is fruit, remain with that Word or phrase. However, if you find the Word or phrase is no longer "working" for you, continue on until God speaks to you in another Word or phrase. It may help to speak it out loud if you are especially distracted. Repeat it over and over until you become settled and remain in silence. Contemplative prayer is an intense focused time on the Word. If you notice yourself moving into vocal or meditative prayer, gently try and let that go so that you can remain in this heightened state of contemplative prayer. Remember, as long as you remain in prayer, "all is grace." God will use it all to bring you closer to Him. The Holy Spirit will guide you into this deep and abiding prayer with Christ and the Father.

When Jesus had said this, he raised his eyes to heaven and said, "Father, the hour has come. Give glory to your son, so that your son may glorify you, just as you gave him authority over all people, so that he may give eternal life to all you gave him. Now this is eternal life, that they should know you, the only true God, and the one whom you sent, Jesus Christ. I glorified you on earth by accomplishing the work that you gave me to do. Now glorify me, Father, with you, with the glory that I had with you before the world began.

"I revealed your name to those whom you gave me out of the world. They belonged to you, and you gave them to me, and they have kept your word. Now they know that everything you gave me is from you, because the words you gave to me I have given to them, and they accepted them and truly understood that I came from you, and they have believed that you sent me. I pray for them. I do not pray for the world but for the ones you have given me, because they are yours, and everything of mine is yours and everything of yours is mine, and I have been glorified in them. And now I will no longer be in the world, but they are in the world, while I am coming to you. Holy Father, keep them in your name that you have given me, so that they may be one just as we are. When I was with them I protected them in your name that you gave me, and I guarded them, and none of them was lost except the son of destruction, in order that the scripture might be fulfilled. But now I am coming to you. I speak this in the world so that they may share my joy completely. I gave them your word, and the world hated them, because they do not belong to the world any more than I belong to the world. I do not ask that you take them out of the world but that you keep them from the evil one. They do not belong to the world any more than I belong to the world. Consecrate them in the truth. Your word is truth. As you sent me into the world, so I sent them into the world. And I consecrate myself for them, so that they also may be consecrated in truth.

"I pray not only for them, but also for those who will believe in me through their word, so that they may all be one, as you, Father, are in me and I in you, that they also may be in us, that the world may believe that you sent me. And I have given them the glory you gave me, so that they may be one, as we are one, I in them and you in me, that they may be brought to perfection as one, that the world may know that you sent me, and that you loved them even as you loved me. Father, they are your gift

to me. I wish that where I am they also may be with me, that they may see my glory that you gave me, because you loved me before the foundation of the world. Righteous Father, the world also does not know you, but I know you, and they know that you sent me. I made known to them your name and I will make it known, that the love with which you loved me may be in them and I in them." (John 17:1-26)

I leave you, my dear reader, with these final words of Jesus, a priestly prayer for His disciples. My hope is that you hear Him speak these words to you. Spend time in **silent** contemplation. When you are ready, **journal** your experience.

PREPARATION FOR TOMORROW:
Tomorrow, we conclude *Pray40Days* by praying with Sunday Mass.

PRAYING WITH SUNDAY MASS

Today's prayer will be celebrating the Sunday Mass and experiencing God the Father in the Eucharist and Liturgy.

PREPARATION BEFORE SUNDAY MASS:

Go in peace glorifying the Lord by your life. At every Mass, we are supposed to be transformed. As you prepare for Mass today, I want you to think about that. You are supposed to walk out a different person than when you walked in. There is supposed to be a transformation in your life. By preparing for it, we can really enter more deeply into the Eucharist. The more deeply we enter into the Eucharist, the more deeply we are going to be transformed. How would you like to be transformed? Listen during Mass to what God is calling you to because at every Mass there is a sending forth. At the end of every Mass, the priest or the deacon sends you forth into the world saying, "Go in peace glorifying the Lord by your life." At the end of Mass, you should be in such a place of peace that, when you leave there, people are going to see Christ in you. You are going to transform the world. You become a light to those in darkness. Think about that today as you go to Mass. How will you be transformed? What will your life be like when you walk out of Mass today? Ask God for that transformation and ask Him for some direction. You have a calling in every Mass. At every Mass, He is calling you to serve more. He is calling you deeper. At every Mass, He is sending you out on a mission. Ask Him to give you guidance in your life so that when you go forth from Mass you have a mission, you have a purpose. What will your mission be today? Try and experience that during Mass.

AFTER SUNDAY MASS:

How was Mass? Did you experience a transformation? Do you find yourself more peaceful now than when you entered? Are you transformed? Are you different? Will you go forth now and glorify the Lord by your life? Have you been given any sense of purpose, mission, or call? Did God give you some notion of what He wants you to do in the world or with your life? At every Mass, He commissions you and sends you out. Take some time to reflect and **journal** what God is calling you to do. Go in peace glorifying the Lord by your life.

CONCLUSION

Wow, this has been an exhilarating 40 days of prayer! I have no doubt that you have grown in your prayer life and encountered God in a way that you never have before through: Guided Meditation, Praying like a Pirate, *Lectio Divina*, Praying with Your Senses, Contemplative Prayer, and Scriptural Relaxation. I hope that your newfound prayer life will continue well after you have finished this book. I desire for you to continue to feel the love of God in your heart, to sense His presence, to feel His touch, to know that you are so loved that He will always guide you, protect you, and never leave you. You can ALWAYS go to the Father as you are and experience His unconditional love, mercy and forgiveness no matter what you have done or whatever situation you have gotten yourself into. You never have to fear anything, ever again. God has you. He will never leave you. He loves you so very much. The Prodigal Father will continue to lavish you with His grace as you continue on this great adventure of prayer.

As you come to the end of *Pray40Days*, my hope is that you have discovered a deeper, more intimate, more personal experience with God the Father, the Son, the Holy Spirit and your mother, Mary. Now you are ready to meditate and contemplate on your own! You will always have these guided meditations to go back to, but I hope and pray that you will find your own way, guided by the Holy Spirit, to go even deeper into prayer and continue to know, love and serve Jesus with all of your heart, your mind, and your soul.

I hope that *Pray40Days* has set you on fire! My deepest desire for writing this book was that each person who read it would, as Karl Rahner once said, become a mystic (one who has experienced God for real). You have experienced and encountered God in a very real way through these various forms of meditation and contemplation. Maybe you have even experienced prayer in such a wonderful way that you will love spending time with God, the Father. If you continue to pray in this way, you will come to know the Father. Jesus will make His home in you and you in Him. The Holy Spirit will be your guide whenever you pray. Always remember that we have a desire to pray and God wants that for you even more. Hopefully, you have integrated these different types of praying into your prayer life and feel comfortable praying with Scripture. I encourage you to pray everyday, to spend some time with the Lord either praying with the upcoming Sunday readings or praying with any scripture passage that appeals to you. You now have the tools that you need to pray with Scripture. You have the tools to kindle the fire through different prayer types - now continue to use them. You can continue to experience God for real and always have that personal relationship with God that you have always wanted! Whenever you feel like you need to refuel or refresh your prayer life, you will always be able to challenge yourself again with *Pray40Days*.

I would love to hear from you! Share with me your favorite day! How have you grown in your prayer life? What did God reveal to you? Which prayer type did you like best? How have you continued to grow in your prayer life since finishing *Pray40Days*? If you are registered for the program, you will receive a survey by e-mail. Your feedback is essential as I continue to develop prayer resources. You can also send an e-mail to FrMichael@TheProdigalFather.org or complete the survey at TheProdigalFather.org/Pray40Days.

KEEP ON PRAYING!!!!

ACKNOWLEDGMENTS AND GRATITUDE

My Bishop, The Most Reverend Richard G. Lennon (retired), Bishop of Cleveland, for ordaining me, assigning me to three wonderful parishes, and helping me see the importance of authorship, teaching, and evangelization.

Rev. Fred Pausche, my Pastor at St. Gabriel Parish in Concord, Ohio and the people of St. Gabriel for welcoming me with open arms to your parish.

Rev. Lawrence N. Martello and Rev. Timothy J. O'Connor, my Pastors at St. Joseph Parish in Amherst, Ohio, for encouraging me to use my gifts and talents, and for entrusting me to participate in their leadership of our Parish - especially with regards to the renewals and spiritual life.

The people of St. Joseph Parish, Amherst, Ohio, whom I had the privilege and pleasure of serving, and for permitting me the opportunity to pray for and minister to them; also for praying for me.

Each and all of the priests and religious who have inspired me – who have walked with me, taught me, and directed me in my spiritual life – not too numerous to mention but too precious to overlook even one, so I shall leave you unnamed, but *cor meum in vobis nominantur*.

The people of St. Barnabas Parish in Northfield, Ohio, and of St. John Vianney in Mentor, Ohio, and their priests, religious, and lay ministers, all of whom graced me with their support in my seminarian internship and my assignment as parochial vicar.

Those whose charity and talent contributed to this book and who aided in developing the *Pray40Days* program, especially: Rev. Robert L. McCreary OFM Capuchin, for writing the book's Foreword; Dr. Michelle Bussard, for her hours of work transcribing and editing; my sister Christie (Denk) Cereshko for layout and cover design; and a special thanks to Rev. Thomas Rosica CSB, Rev. Norm Douglas, Rev. Patrick Anderson, and Dr. Eugene Gan, for their kind endorsements and encouragement along the way.

To the amazingly talented Olivia Sliman from the YouTube Show, *Olivia's Got Talent Tuesday*. Thank you for being the 'guinea pig' for the *Pray40Days* program with your "Video Journals" – Olivia, you are a true joy, an inspiration, and open to any adventure! What's next?

A whole host of witnesses, each of which I wish to thank for their help in the *Pray40Days* program, this book, and my ministry:

Andy Flynn
Linda Rourke
Matt Smith
Everyone at Diocesan Publications, especially Art, Dan, and Mike
Everyone at Salt & Light Catholic Media Foundation
Susan Moore, Stephanie Sierra, Kathy Flynn, Cathy Camp, and Joanne Green
Tom Benstein of Art of Technology, and Ryan Ksenich
Keith Gutierrez and our friends at Modgility
Mark Wilhelm, Brian Houlahan, Missy Hayes, and Tom Theado
Kathryn Perales
Debbie May
Tim Champion

I received a wonderful formation from priests in the seminary, brother priests, and other religious whom God has providentially placed into my life. To all of these people, including those who directed me in my dissertation or on retreat, your influence has ultimately led to the formation of this book: Fr. John Loya, Fr. Jim Ols, Fr. John G. Vrana, Fr. Tom Johns, Fr. Mike Woost, Fr. Bob McCreary OFM Cap., Fr. Bob Welsh SJ, and Msgr. John Esseff.

To Fr. Timothy Gallagher OMV, whose *Discernment of Spirits* has greatly influenced the prayer Apps that I am developing; having not traveled down that road, this book may not have ever been written.

And to my mom and dad, and each of my sisters and brothers: Julie, Bobby, Jimmy, Christie and Sheri…and my adorable and beloved nieces and nephew. You have been my "primary church" where I first learned to pray, and thankfully you still let me go off and pray in peace! "I love you!" - Mike

APPENDIX I

TYPES OF PRAYER

Pray40Days will guide you through different types of prayer that will immerse you in the life of Christ, fill you with the Holy Spirit, and allow you to be held and loved by the Father. By the end of *Pray40Days,* you will come to love spending time with God and look forward to the wonder that awaits you every time you enter into this quality time with God. You will come to not only a "head knowledge" but a felt "heart knowledge" of God. Through these experiences of prayer, you will grow to love God with all of your heart, all of your mind, and all of your soul. This love will impact you and touch everyone that comes into contact with you.

In the Christian tradition, there have been three levels or expressions of prayer: vocal prayer, meditative prayer, and contemplative prayer. Hopefully, at different points in our lives, we experience and pray in these different ways. There is a progression in prayer. As was mentioned earlier, if we are not growing in prayer, we are dying.

In addition to the three levels of prayer, you will encounter six types of prayer exercises in this book: Guided Meditation, Praying like a Pirate, Lectio Divina, Praying with Your Senses, Contemplative Prayer, and Scriptural Relaxation. I will describe each of the types for you in this section of the book. **However, if you find it too overwhelming to read about all of them at once, you can instead read about them before each day's prayer experience.** You may also want to occasionally come back to this section and refresh your memory about the types of prayer.

VOCAL PRAYER: Vocal prayer is the most basic and beginner prayer. Vocal prayer can be spontaneous talking to God or it can be something that we have memorized or read from a devotional book. "Prayer is the raising of one's mind and heart to God or the requesting of good things from God" (CCC, 2590).

The Catechism relays the importance of these types of prayer: Blessing and Adoration, Prayer of Petition, Prayer of Intercession, Prayer of Thanksgiving, and Prayer of Praise. "These formulations are developed in the great liturgical and spiritual traditions. The *forms of prayer* revealed in the apostolic and canonical Scriptures remain normative for Christian prayer" (CCC, 2625).

Vocal prayer includes the traditional way that God speaks to us through His Word, and we can speak to God by using our words. Throughout the entire Scriptures, we have experiences of people praying vocally. It is an essential part of the Christian life. The first prayer that Jesus teaches to His disciples is "The Lord's Prayer" (the Our Father). When His disciples ask Him how to pray, Jesus starts with vocal prayer. However, He gently reminds them that it is not about the words themselves but what is behind the words. Vocal prayer is really about trying to express and articulate what is inside of us. Jesus teaches us that the purpose of vocal prayer is not to just recite something mindlessly, but to pray it with our whole heart, mind, body, and soul. *"In praying, do not babble like the pagans, who think that they will be heard because of their many words. Do not be like them. Your Father knows what you need before you ask him"* (Matthew 6:7-8). He then goes on to teach the disciples the vocal prayer of the Our Father, *The Lord's Prayer: "This is how you are to pray..."* (Matthew 6:9).

MEDITATIVE PRAYER: The next stage of prayer beyond vocal prayer is meditative prayer. The Catechism describes meditation as a great adventure! "Meditation is, above all, a quest. The mind seeks to understand the why and how of the Christian life, in order to adhere and respond to what the Lord is asking. The required attentiveness is difficult to sustain. We are usually helped by books, and Christians do not want for them: the Sacred Scriptures, particularly the Gospels, holy icons, liturgical texts of the day or season, writings of the spiritual fathers, works of spirituality, the great book of creation, and that of history - the page on which the "today" of God is written" (CCC, 2705).

When we meditate with Christ upon Sacred Scripture, we make discoveries about God and our life. The Word of God is alive. Every time we open Scripture, every time we hear it, every time we pray with it, God speaks something new to us. We can actually "hear," in a spiritual sense, the voice of God.

The Catechism goes on to instruct that: "There are as many and varied methods of meditation as there are spiritual masters. Christians owe it to themselves to develop the desire to meditate regularly, lest they come to resemble the three first kinds of soil in the parable of the sower. But a method is only a guide; the important thing is to advance, with the Holy Spirit, along the one way of prayer: Christ Jesus" (CCC, 2707).

We owe it to ourselves to not only *Pray40Days* but to pray regularly every day. To develop a prayer life that is sustained by some ritual, discipline, and order for our days. And though 90% of prayer is just being there, something wonderful happens when we engage all of our faculties. We encounter God and we let Him enter into our lives.

"Meditation engages thought, imagination, emotion, and desire. This mobilization of faculties is necessary in order to deepen our convictions of faith, prompt the conversion of our heart, and strengthen our will to follow Christ. Christian prayer tries above all to meditate on the mysteries of Christ, as in *Lectio Divina* or the rosary. This form of prayerful reflection is of great value, but Christian prayer should go further; to the knowledge of the love of the Lord Jesus, to union with him" (CCC, 2708).

CONTEMPLATIVE PRAYER: All of our prayer is a mixture of vocal, meditative, and contemplative, but the highest form and the deepest desire we have is for contemplative prayer. This is ultimately the closest to heaven we will ever experience on earth. It is not something that we can "make" happen; however, we can prepare ourselves to have this experience every time we pray with Scripture. We just need to be simply aware and mindful of God in our midst at every moment of our lives and focus on Christ.

The Scriptures encourage us to "*Pray without ceasing.*" (1 Thessalonians 5:17) but, in order to come to that type of reality, we need to at least pray "sometimes." In our busy, loud, and chaotic worlds, we need to foster times of silence. "Contemplative prayer is the simple expression of the mystery of prayer. It is a gaze of faith fixed on Jesus, attentiveness to the Word of God, a silent love. It achieves real union with the prayer of Christ to the extent that it makes us share in his mystery" (CCC, 2724).

"The choice of the *time and duration of the prayer* arises from a determined will, revealing the secrets of the heart. One does not undertake contemplative prayer only when one has the time: one makes time for the Lord, with the firm determination not to give up, no matter what trials and dryness one may encounter. One cannot always meditate, but one can always enter into inner prayer" (CCC, 2710). Though it is a challenge, we can always be present to God in the midst of our lives. Even when we suffer, we can be united with God in that suffering.

"Contemplative prayer is also the pre-eminently *intense time* of prayer. In it the Father strengthens our inner being with power through his Spirit 'that Christ may dwell in [our] hearts through faith' and we may be 'grounded in love'" (CCC, 2714).

"Contemplation is a *gaze* of faith, fixed on Jesus. "I look at him and he looks at me": this is what a certain peasant of Ars in the time of his holy curé used to say while praying before the tabernacle" (CCC, 2715).

"Contemplative prayer is *silence*, the "symbol of the world to come" or "silent love." Words in this kind of prayer are not speeches; they are like kindling that feeds the fire of love. In this silence, unbearable to the "outer" man, the Father speaks to us his incarnate Word, who suffered, died, and rose; in this silence the Spirit of adoption enables us to share in the prayer of Jesus" (CCC, 2717).

Silence and solitude are a necessary prerequisite for contemplative prayer. I encourage you to be in total silence during this type of prayer. Turn off your phones, communicate to others that you do not want to be interrupted, don't listen to any background music or noise, silence everything that you can, and be with Christ in the solitude.

"Contemplative prayer in my opinion is nothing else than a close sharing between friends; it means taking time frequently to be alone with Him who we know loves us" (Mother Teresa). Contemplative prayer is actually the simplest of prayers; it is essentially just being in the presence of God. I believe children do this all the time when they are playing. Adults do it, too, when they see a beautiful sunrise, or hold an infant, or pray before the Blessed Sacrament. What makes contemplative prayer difficult for us is learning how to spend time in silence and solitude. Contemplative prayer is not about accomplishing something or gaining some insight or solving a problem; it is about just receiving the gift of God's presence. It is very difficult for us to receive and not to do or accomplish something.

Contemplative prayer is a gift. It is allowing God to work in us, to be with us and to nurture us. In contemplative prayer, we take the time to be with the One we know loves us above anyone or anything.

PRAYER EXERCISES

GUIDED MEDITATION

Guided Meditation is a form of prayer that uses quiet reflection on a scene from Scripture or from everyday life. It is led by a person (guide) who describes the scene and the actions of those in the story. The purpose of guided meditation is to relax so that you are free to use your senses and to imagine a personal encounter with Jesus.

St. Ignatius was converted through meditation. He had been injured in the war where a cannon ball greatly disfigured his leg. He spent many months laid up in a hospital bed and was so bored that he found himself reading book after book. He loved reading books about chivalry and "knights in shining armor" and the tough guy getting the girls!

After reading every book on war and women that he could get his hands on, St. Ignatius was finally given two books that changed everything: "Lives of the Saints" and "The Life of Christ." A very interesting thing then occurred. The same creative imagination that he used to imagine himself in the scenes of war and women also helped bring to life something he once found so boring.

St. Ignatius' imagination took flight as he read "The Life of Christ" and the "Lives of the Saints." He said to himself that if St. Francis and other saints like him could do this, maybe he could, too. As he read more and imagined more, he discovered something very profound. In both cases, while he was reading and imagining, St. Ignatius found himself very excited, engaged, and inspired. But, there was a drastic difference. When he finished reading books about war and women, he realized that he was left feeling desolate, downcast, and sad. But, when he meditated on "The Life of Christ" and the "Lives of the Saints," he was excited, engaged, and inspired but he also remained in consolation for a long time afterward. Not only was he inspired during his meditation, it was a lasting inspiration. This "real" experience began his conversion and what would ultimately lay the foundation for the Spiritual Exercises and the use of imagination and meditation in prayer.

Maybe you have a vivid imagination, or maybe you think you don't. The truth is that we all have the God-given ability to "imagine." Some people think that if you are using your imagination, it is not "real." But our imagination is a gift given to us by God and can lead us to very "real" experiences of Him. It is a gift, but it can also be developed. Remember, there is a whole other level beyond the physical and our imagination can help take us there. If you have not used yours in a while, don't worry. It is there! We never lose our imagination. When we use our imagination -WOW - can God come to us in amazing ways.

CONTEMPLATIVE PRAYER

There are three ways that can help us focus on Christ and pray contemplatively: Word, Icon, and Nature (you can remember this by the acronym WIN).

WORD: When we pray with Scripture, we are concentrating our attention on Christ. We believe that the Word of God is alive and divinely inspired by the Holy Spirit. "The Sacred Scriptures contain the Word of God and, because they are inspired, they are truly the Word of God" (cf. *Dei Verbum*, n. 24). That means that every time we pray with Scripture, God is speaking to us. When you pray with Scripture and are present to God, He will be with you, right now at this moment, in a way that He never has been or ever will be again.

When we pray with Scripture contemplatively, we actually get to be with God. Right now, you can be with Him in whatever it is that you are going through. The Father wants nothing more than to spend time with you, to delight in you, to hold you, to rest with you, and to be with you.

"In Sacred Scripture, the Church constantly finds her nourishment and her strength, for she welcomes it not as a human word, "but as what it really is, the word of God." "In the sacred books, the Father who is in heaven comes lovingly to meet his children, and talks with them" (CCC, 104). St. Jerome once said that "ignorance of Scripture is ignorance of Christ" (CCC, 133).

As with all Christian prayer, our attention is focused on Christ. "*I am the way, the truth and the life. No one comes to the Father except through me*" (John 14:6). It is Christ, working through the Holy Spirit, who opens our hearts and minds through Scripture. So open yourself now to the wonderful experience of contemplation with the Word.

During contemplative prayer you simply need to rest with the Word. You don't need to do anything, produce anything, or come up with any insights or revelations (though they may happen). We are not trying to use our imagination, our intellect, understanding, questioning, dialogue, or any kind of vocal or meditative prayer. This is the highest form of prayer - contemplative prayer. So as we pray, allow yourself to be with Christ. Allow yourself to rest in His Word. As you pray contemplatively, you will probably be distracted. That is okay. You may be distracted a thousand times. But return a thousand and one times. The virtue is returning back to Christ, returning back to His Word, returning back to His voice that you hear proclaiming Scripture. But, have your Bible nearby with your Scripture passage opened so that you can go back and pray contemplatively with the Scripture as needed.

In praying contemplatively, read the passage in silence once very slowly. Then read it again slower, until you find a Word or a phrase that you feel God is speaking to you. Remain in silence repeating this Word over and over in your heart. If you get distracted, remember the virtue is returning back to the Word. Continue repeating the phrase over and over again until you come to a place of rest in the Word. Remain in silence, peace, and stillness for as long as the moment lasts. If there is fruit, remain with that Word or phrase. However, if you find the Word or phrase is no longer "working" for you, continue on until God speaks to you in another Word or phrase. It may help to speak it out loud if you are especially distracted. Repeat it over and over again until you become settled and remain in silence.

Contemplative prayer is an intense focused time on the Word. If you notice yourself moving back into vocal prayer or meditative prayer, gently try and let that go so that you can remain in this heightened state of contemplative prayer. Remember, as long as you remain in prayer, "all is grace." God will use it all to bring you closer to Him. The Holy Spirit will be your guide into this deep and abiding prayer with Christ and the Father.

ICONS: It might help if I first explain religious icons by using our modern understanding of icons. When you first heard the word icon, you may have thought of that little graphic or "icon" that is on your computer desktop. Actually, Microsoft Windows uses the term "icon" in a way that can help us understand what a religious icon does for us when we pray with it. When you open your main computer screen and click on an icon a new "window" opens up. You can then enter the program that the icon symbolizes and interact with that program. Just so, religious icons are said to be "windows into heaven." When we gaze upon an icon, a window into heaven opens up and we enter into this whole new world. Here we can be with and interact with the Father, the Son, the Holy Spirit, Mary and all the Saints and angels who are in heaven.

The history of icons dates back to the early church. Some even attribute the first icon to Jesus himself or to St. Luke. Icons were seen as an acceptable form of worship until around the 8th century when a heresy called Iconoclasm (the Greek word *Eikonoklasmos* means "image-breaking") developed causing a great disturbance in the church over the use of images. Some claimed that all images, statues, and even relics were a form of idolatry.

During that time, there was great persecution of Christians for their use of sacred images. Monasteries were burned. Monks were tortured, put to death, or exiled. It was a painful time in the Church. As with all heresies, it caused the church to articulate the truth. It wasn't until the 8th century at the Second Council of Nicea, however, that the church spoke in defense of icons clarifying the difference in the veneration given to God and that which is given to holy images, saints, or relics. As with anything, some things can be taken to extremes. It took a few centuries for icons to flourish in the church again but, by the 14th century, icons thrived once more in the Eastern church and in the Byzantine and Orthodox faiths.

Having said all that, why is it beneficial to pray with icons? Icons are the visual representation of the "Word." Just like Scripture is ever ancient and ever new when we pray with it, so, too, are icons ever ancient and ever new. Each time we gaze upon an icon in meditation or contemplation, God speaks to us. We have a glimpse into heaven. We can actually experience being with God right here in our world in His time and space.

"Christian iconography expresses in images the same Gospel message that Scripture communicates by words. Image and word illuminate each other. 'We declare that we preserve intact all the written and unwritten traditions of the Church which have been entrusted to us. One of these traditions consists in the production of representational artwork, which accords with the history of the preaching of the Gospel. For it confirms that the incarnation of the Word of God was real and not imaginary, and to our benefit as well, for realities that illustrate each other undoubtedly reflect each other's meaning'" (CCC, 1160).

It is important to understand that icons are different than paintings, statues, and other works of art. An icon is not a painting; it is the "written Word" of God in a visual form. What do I mean by this? Well, iconographers don't paint images, they write them. It is a completely different style or process than that of painting. To create an icon, the iconographer prays with Scripture, spends time in solitude, fasts, and follows a certain "form" in "writing" an icon. You will notice that figures in an icon look slightly distorted; this is intentional. An icon is not intended to be a literal representation of a scene, but of a glimpse into heaven.

The Catechism explains that: "The sacred image, the liturgical icon, principally represents *Christ*. It cannot represent the invisible and incomprehensible God, but the incarnation of the Son of God has ushered in a new 'economy' of images. Previously God, who has neither a body nor a face, absolutely could not be represented by an image. But now that he has made himself visible in the flesh and has lived with men, I can make an image of what I have seen of God . . . and contemplate the glory of the Lord, his face unveiled" (CCC, 1159).

"All the signs in the liturgical celebrations are related to Christ: as are sacred images of the Holy Mother of God and of the saints as well. They truly signify Christ, who is glorified in them. They make manifest the '"cloud of witnesses"' who continue to participate in the salvation of the world and to whom we are united, above all in sacramental celebrations. Through their icons, it is man '"in the image of God,"' finally transfigured '"into his likeness"' (CCC, 1161).

"The beauty of the images moves me to contemplation, as a meadow delights the eyes and subtly infuses the soul with the glory of God. Similarly, the contemplation of sacred icons, united with meditation on the Word of God and the singing of liturgical hymns, enters into the harmony of the signs of celebration so that the mystery celebrated is imprinted in the heart's memory and is then expressed in the new life of the faithful" (CCC, 1162).

Doesn't that make you want to learn more about icons and try praying with them?

NATURE: Praying with nature seems to be the most accessible form of prayer for people. I often hear people say, "I don't really like church, or the whole religion thing, but I find God in nature." It is true, they are finding God, but it is the same God that is found in Church. We have to be aware of this tendency known as Pantheism. The Church defines Pantheism as: "Pantheism: (Greek *pan* = everything and *theos* = God) the belief that everything is God or, sometimes, that everything is *in* God and God is in everything (panentheism). Every element of the universe is divine, and the divinity is equally present in everything. There is no space in this view for God as a distinct being in the sense of classical theism" (Vatican, 2016, para 7.2). The important thing to understand here is that while it is true that we do experience God in nature, we need to be careful to remember that God created nature and revealed Himself to us as the Trinity: the Father, the Son, and the Holy Spirit. *For creation awaits with eager expectation the revelation of the children of God* (Romans 8:19). Yes, nature gives us a glimpse of God the Father, but Jesus Christ through the Holy Spirit reveals His fullness. *We know that all creation is groaning in labor pains even until now* (Romans 8:22). All of creation is groaning to know what Jesus reveals in the Father. He reveals Him to us through Scripture, the Sacraments, and Tradition. Whenever we divorce ourselves from these we miss the fullness of God. We need to keep this in mind when praying with nature.

The Catechism explains that Creation can be a source of prayer for us. "Prayer is lived in the first place beginning with the realities of *creation.* The first nine chapters of Genesis describe this relationship with God as an offering of the first-born of Abel's flock, as the invocation of the divine name at the time of Enosh, and as '"walking with God.'" Noah's offering is pleasing to God, who blesses him and through him all creation, because his heart was upright and undivided; Noah, like Enoch before him, '"walks with God.'" This kind of prayer is lived by many righteous people in all religions. In his indefectible covenant with every living creature, God has always called people to prayer. But it is above all beginning with our father Abraham that prayer is revealed in the Old Testament" (CCC, 2569).

Like Abraham and Noah, we can be drawn into the Creator as we look upon creation and "walk with God." All of nature can be a sacramental leading us to the ultimate beauty of Jesus Christ. The Holy Father, Pope Francis (2015), in his encyclical letter, *Laudato Si'* "On Care For Our Common Home," teaches us how praying with nature is part of our Tradition: "What is more, Saint Francis, faithful to Scripture, invites us to see nature as a magnificent book in which God speaks to us and grants us a glimpse of His infinite beauty and goodness. *For from the greatness and the beauty of created things / their original author, by analogy, is seen* (Wisdom 13:5). Indeed, [His] *eternal power and divinity have been able to be understood and perceived in what he has made* (Romans 1:20). For this reason, St. Francis asked that part of the friary garden always be left untouched. That wildflowers and herbs could grow there, and those who saw them could raise their minds to God, the Creator of such beauty. Rather than a problem to be solved, the world is a joyful mystery to be contemplated with gladness and praise." (Laudato Si', para 12, 2015)

We have all experienced the wonder and awe of God in creation. I remember once walking out of a Walmart parking lot and seeing a beautiful sunset and thinking - I have to share this with someone. I called my mother and she was seeing the same sunset and thinking the same thing.

What was your moment of "awe" with God in creation? Maybe it was the first time you saw the ocean and were brought to an absolute peace and transcendence by the sound of the waves. It might have been a walk through an open field, the stars at night, a morning jog on a path through the woods, or a view from the top of a mountain. What a blessing it is when we stop to notice the beauty of creation around us!

Saint Bonaventure, a Franciscan Mystic, is one of the few saints that has a Theology of Nature. He boldly proclaims: "Whoever, therefore, is not enlightened by such a splendor of created things is blind; whoever is not awakened by such outcries is deaf; whoever does not praise God because of all these effects is dumb; whoever does not discover the first principle from such clear signs is a fool. Therefore, open your eyes, alert the ears of your spirit, open your lips and your spirit, open your lips and apply your heart so that in all creatures you may see, hear, praise, love, worship, glorify and honor your God, lest the whole world rise against you" (Cousins, 1978, p. 30).

St. Bonaventure goes on to show us that we can use nature as a form of contemplation and prayer: "Seen with the eye of contemplation, creatures are vestiges, that is, the very footprints of God; they are roads leading to God, ladders which we can climb to God; they are signs divinely given so that we can see God - shadows, echoes, pictures, statues, representations of God; creation is a book in which we can read God, a mirror in which the divine light shines in various colors" (Cousins, 1978). The Catechism reaffirms this: "God speaks to man through the visible creation. The material cosmos is so presented to man's intelligence that he can read there traces of its Creator. Light and darkness, wind and fire, water and earth, the tree and its fruit speak of God and symbolize both His greatness and His nearness" (CCC, 1147).

Finally, St. Bonaventure encourages us to move beyond our senses and experience the presence of the Father, the Son, and the Holy Spirit in created order. "But you, my friend, concerning mystical visions, with your journey more firmly determined, leave behind your sense and intellectual activities, sensible and invisible things, all not being and being; and in this state of unknowing be restored, insofar as is possible to unity with him who is above all essence and knowledge. For transcending yourself and all things by the immeasurable and absolute ecstasy of a pure mind, leaving behind all things and freed from all things, you will ascend to the super essential ray of the divine darkness" (Cousins, 1978).

So let us now experience this wonderful form of praying with God through the contemplation of nature. For "God himself created the visible world in all its richness, diversity and order. Scripture presents the work of the Creator symbolically as a succession of six days of divine "work," concluded by the "rest" of the seventh day. On the subject of creation, the sacred text teaches the truths revealed by God for our salvation, permitting us to "recognize the inner nature, the value and the ordering of the whole of creation to the praise of God'" (CCC, 337).

LECTIO DIVINA

Lectio Divina (which is a Latin phrase meaning Divine Reading) dates all the way back to the third century. Over the years, it was developed by some of the early Church Fathers, Saints of the Church, and religious communities such as: Origen, St. Ambrose, St. Augustine, St. Bernard of Clairvaux, Saint Benedict, St. John of the Cross, St. Teresa of Avila, the Desert Fathers who formed the first monasteries in the Eastern Church, the Carthusians, the Cistercians, the Benedictines, the Carmelites, and it had even been introduced to the Protestants by John Calvin.

It was not until Vatican II (in 1965) that one of the Church's most important documents emphasized the use of Lectio Divina. That document was "*Dei Verbum*" and is a dogmatic constitution or teaching on the Word of God. In 2005, Pope Benedict XVI reaffirmed the importance of Lectio Divina on the 40th anniversary of "*Dei Verbum*": "I would like in particular to recall and recommend the ancient tradition of Lectio Divina: the diligent reading of Sacred Scripture accompanied by prayer brings about that intimate dialogue in which the person reading hears God, who is speaking, and in praying, responds to Him with trusting openness of heart [cf. *Dei verbum*, n. 25]. If it is effectively promoted, this practice will bring to the Church – I am convinced of it – a new spiritual springtime."

Saint John Paul II, when he was pope, described how to enter into this ancient form of prayer. One condition for Lectio Divina is that the mind and heart be illuminated by the Holy Spirit; that is, by the same Spirit who inspired the Scripture and that the Scripture is approached with an attitude of "reverential hearing."

As is often said about Scripture, this type of prayer is itself "Ever Ancient, Ever New." The practice of Lectio Divina is best when it is experienced. The best way I can explain it is that it is an experience of prayer where you read Scripture in a prayerful and reflective way until God speaks to you through His Word. As we "hear" it over and over, meditate upon it, and contemplate it, the Word of God takes flesh in us. We become one with Christ. We experience this wonderful union with God the Father, the Son, and the Holy Spirit.

As with all prayer, the "way" that we do prayer is not important but, sometimes, especially for beginners, it is really helpful to have a structure and a routine to "get us into" prayer. Lectio Divina consists of four steps: *Lectio* (reading), *Oratio* (praying), *Meditatio* (meditation), and *Contemplatio* (contemplating).

Let's use eating as the analogy for this. *When I found your words, I devoured them; / your words were my joy, the happiness of my heart* (Jeremiah 15:16). *I am the living bread that came down from heaven; whoever eats this bread will live forever; and the bread that I will give is my flesh for the life of the world"* (John 6:51). Now, let's apply the four steps of Lectio Divina to eating.

Lectio (reading) is like looking at a meal that is placed before you - deciding which part you want to eat first, which looks the best, what you want to save for last, and taking that first bite.

Meditatio (meditation) is chewing on the food, tasting it, deciding whether you like it or not, or if you want more of it or want to try another part of the meal. This is often related to "chewing." Sometimes we eat our food so fast we don't even know what it tastes like; we can do the same to Scripture. For us to really meditate, we need to take it slow and notice all the textures and flavors of Scripture. The important thing here (or when doing any of the steps in Lectio Divina) is that we are not doing this on our own but instead are reading with God and pondering with God. Interesting enough, my last name "Denk" is a German word that means to think deeply or to ponder. This part comes naturally to me! But, if I do it alone, then it can become a rather dark and frustrating experience. This is why it is important to pray with God, with Scriptures, and always have Christ at the center. So "chew" unto your heart's content, but just remember you are "chewing" Scripture and not your own thoughts!

Oratio (pray) means speech, discourse, or dialogue. It is kind of like when we share a meal with someone (especially with God) and the conversation tends to flow naturally. During this step you not only savor the food but you savor the company and your heart naturally wants to say something and hear something in response. *Oratio* can be spontaneous prayer or a more formal vocal prayer that you write out or say to God.

Contemplatio (contemplation). There is nothing better after having a good meal then "resting" in the company you are with. Think about an Italian dinner or a Thanksgiving meal, where nobody gets up from the table right away. You tasted the food. You drank the wine. You talked, laughed, and loved. Now you just spend that last moment in silence, completely content, taking it all in, savoring it, enjoying it, just "being" there with the people that you love, with the God that you love.

The Catechism emphasizes that "Contemplative Prayer is *silence*... or silent love..." (CCC, 2717) in which the Father allows us to dwell in His Son, to become one with His Son, to be infused with the Holy Spirit and experience the closest thing to heaven that we can on this earth.

PRAYING LIKE A PIRATE

Praying like a pirate: ARRR!!!! This is a type of prayer that I learned from Msgr. John Esseff. In this prayer, you **A**cknowledge, **R**elate, **R**eceive, and **R**espond to God. In the first step of this type of prayer, you acknowledge whatever is in your heart. Whatever your desires or feelings are, acknowledge them. After you acknowledge, you will relate those feelings to God. Tell Him how you are feeling. After you acknowledge and relate, you need to receive God's message. This requires you to be silent to hear what God has to say. Once you receive God's message, you will want to respond to Him in some way. Perhaps it is saying, "Yes, Lord, I will do that," or "Yes, God, I can."

St. Teresa of Avila said that praying is a close and intimate sharing between friends. When you relate your feelings to God, you don't have to deal with the feelings on your own. You can hand them over to God who will then help you to understand them, process them, and actually take you to Himself in the process. It is important to know that all feelings are acceptable. There are no good or bad feelings. Sure some are more pleasant, and others are horrifying, but something wonderful happens when we share them with God. And the best part is that you don't have to do it alone! He is there with you every step of the way!

PRAYING WITH YOUR SENSES

St. Ignatius said that God takes on human flesh so that we can sense Him: *And the Word became flesh / and made his dwelling among us, / and we saw his glory, / the glory as of the Father's only Son, / full of grace and truth* (John 1:14). One of the gifts that we have been given is our senses. We take something into us by tasting, smelling, touching, seeing, and hearing. God came to us in the flesh so that we could "sense" or see Him. All three forms of Ignatian contemplation end with an imagined conversation between you and one or more of the characters in the passage.

The idea with this type of meditation or contemplation is to get us out of our thinking mind and into a way of concentrating with our senses. We use our senses both physically and imaginatively. There is something very sacred about calling upon the Holy Spirit to come to us in a way that we can sense through our imagination. God gave us the gifts of our imagination and our senses. This type of imaginative prayer can lead us into a deep contemplation and a very real "felt" experience of God the Father, the Son, and the Holy Spirit. Like the other types of prayer, this is just one exercise or structure to help us focus on and encounter the living Christ. In this spiritual tradition, there are two types of senses: the "ordinary" and the "spiritual."

What was from the beginning, / what we have heard, / what we have seen with our eyes, / what we looked upon / and touched with our hands / concerns the Word of life—/ for the life was made visible; / we have seen it and testify to it / and proclaim to you the eternal life / that was with the Father and was made visible to us—/ what we have seen and heard / we proclaim now to you, / so that you too may have fellowship with us; / for our fellowship is with the Father / and with his Son, Jesus Christ. / We are writing this so that our joy may be complete (1 John 1:1-4).

SEE: "*For the life was made visible; / we have seen it and testify to it / and proclaim to you the eternal life / that was with the Father and was made visible to us*" (1 John 1:2). Use your imagination to try to see everything in the Scripture passage. Let it come to life. Ask the Holy Spirit to help you to see.

HEAR: *"What was from the beginning, / what we have heard,"* (1 John 1:1). Try not only to hear the sounds of the people, places, and things but what they might be saying; what God may be saying to you.

SMELL: "*But thanks be to God, who always leads us in triumph in Christ and manifests through us the odor of the knowledge of him in every place. For we are the aroma of Christ for God among those who are being saved and among those who are perishing, to the latter an odor of death that leads to death, to the former an odor of life that leads to life*" (2 Corinthians 2:14-16). Smell and taste are so closely linked together. But it can be very beneficial to try them separately. St. Ignatius talks about the scent of God being very soft, gentle, sweet, and delicate. The phrase "stop and smell the roses" works well here. We have to slow down and be gentle and delicate with ourselves and with the Word of God so that we can smell the fragrant aroma of the scene.

TASTE: Again, the notion here is to savor and relish in the "Dolce" or sweetness of God's Word. "*How sweet to my tongue is your promise, / sweeter than honey to my mouth!*" (Psalm 119:103).

TOUCH: *"...and touched with our hands / concerns the Word of life..."* (1 John 1:1). Scripture is filled with our need to touch and be touched by God. This is what the Incarnation is. The Word became flesh so that we might experience God in the flesh.

When we use our senses and experience the Word of God, we can enter in a very real, profound, and tangible way into the scenes of the Gospel.

Often times people say they don't experience God in prayer, have never seen Him, or heard His voice. This is one of the ways that He can come to you and be very real to you.

When we pray with our senses and our imagination through the Holy Spirit, we can enter into God and allow God to enter into us. As with all prayer, the focus is never on us but on God and what God is doing in us and in our world right now. "Ignatian contemplation is focused, not on losing oneself in God, but on finding oneself in God. Contemplating is ordinarily understood as 'gazing upon' the divine. In this gazing, the emphasis is not on the relationship between oneself and God but rather is being absorbed in God, lost in God, taken up into God. An example of this kind of contemplation is centering prayer. For Ignatius, however, the focus is always on relationship... For Ignatius, 'contemplating the Gospel mysteries is the privileged way to come to know Jesus more clearly so as to love him more dearly and follow Him more nearly....'" (Fleming, 2008).

Prayer is ultimately about relating to God. We have all had the physical experience of using our senses and this prayer type will help you discover a whole other level with the "Spiritual Senses." Because we are physical beings, God wants to meet us in physical ways and also help us to experience the transcendent.

Finally, St. Ignatius encourages us to finish with a "Colloquy," which is simply sharing a conversation about your experience with the Father, the Son, the Holy Spirit, and Mary. This type of prayer can help us to really know God, fall in love with Him, and want to give the rest of our lives in service to Him when we experience His love in a very real way.

SCRIPTURAL RELAXATION

Faith and reason go together. We have learned much from the psychological discipline. One of the current approaches most translatable to prayer is Cognitive Behavioral Therapy (CBT) because it deals with our mind and body. A person can be aware of their thoughts and then change those thoughts through CBT. When the thoughts change, the behavior will follow. For example, if our thoughts tend to be negative, they will produce anxiety. When we are anxious, we behave like Martha. *Martha, you are anxious... Mary has chosen the better part* (Luke 10:41-42).

Jesus tells us over and over again "do not be afraid." One way to do that is to be aware of our thoughts and then change them. What better way to change our thoughts than to focus them on Scripture. *Have no anxiety at all, but in everything, by prayer and petition, with thanksgiving, make your requests known to God. Then the peace of God that surpasses all understanding will guard your hearts and minds in Christ Jesus* (Philippians 4:6-7).

From a Christian perspective, one of the most common phrases in Scripture is "do not be afraid" and is used throughout the Gospels. Ultimately, fear is a lack of trust in Christ and God's providence. We have a tendency to ruminate, to try and figure things out ourselves. We get trapped in our own thinking. With the wonderful advances in psychology and spirituality, we can, with the help of the Holy Spirit, change our thoughts from us figuring it out to God figuring it out for and with us.

What is wonderful about CBT is that it includes meditation, contemplation, and mindfulness. One of the greatest advances of our modern era is in the area of addiction and mental health. We have come to discover that spirituality is essential to the healing process. We have also come to acknowledge that the best approach to spirituality is one that encompasses our bodies, minds, and souls. We truly do believe in a holistic approach to spirituality. Not only our spirits, but our embodied spirits. Good holistic spirituality will treat your whole person, body, mind, emotions, and soul.

After consulting with some clinical psychologists from the Cleveland Clinic, I developed an exercise in which I combined clinically proven effective techniques with Scripture and what I have learned from the Spiritual and Mystical aspects of our Tradition. The focus is always on Christ doing the healing. The Word of God changes our self-thinking patterns. The goal of this prayer exercise is to help your body, mind, and emotions settle down and relax, to put you in a better disposition. As with all of these exercises, prayer is ultimately a gift from God and the exercises are a way to prepare us to receive Him. I hope that you find these scriptural relaxation exercises beneficial. That you may experience physical peace and emotional peace; and a deep abiding spiritual peace that only Christ can give.

As you do Scriptural Relaxation, remember you are in God's presence through His Word. Begin by reading the whole passage first, memorizing as much as you can to help you focus as you go through the relaxation. The steps are simple but remain focused. Find a place that's comfortable holding the book so that you can move on to each step easily.

You may find it more beneficial to listen to the audio versions of the Scriptural Relaxation exercises. The Scriptural Relaxation exercises can be done with the audio version by listening at TheProdigalFather.org/Pray40Days. (Also, see the website for more resources to assist you in all of the prayer types.)

Additionally, you can have someone you trust and feel comfortable with read the exercise to you. Or, you or someone you love - your spouse, child, or a friend can record the exercise to use for your prayer time. Make sure that person reads slowly and pauses often. This could be a wonderful treasure for you to have and to hold for years to come!

APPENDIX II

SCRIPTURE PASSAGES AND ICONS IN ***PRAY40DAYS***

OLD TESTAMENT

Genesis 18:1-15	Abraham's Visitors
Genesis 24:26	The man then knelt…
Exodus	
20:1-17	The Ten Commandments
3:5	Do not come near ...
Deuteronomy	
10:8	At that time ...
Numbers 20:6	But Moses and Aaron…
Psalm 23	The LORD is my shepherd…
Psalm 46	God is our refuge…
Psalm 55:17-18	But I will call upon God…
Psalm 63:2-9	Oh God, you are my God…
Psalm 119:103	
Psalm 139	LORD, you have probed me…
Wisdom 13:5	For from the greatness…
Daniel 6:11	Continued his custom…
Ezekiel 44:4-5	The LORD said to me…
Isaiah 43:1-5	Promises of Redemption and Restoration
Jeremiah	
1:4-9	The Call of Jeremiah
15:16	When I found your words, I devoured ...

NEW TESTAMENT

Matthew	
3:13-17	The Baptism of Jesus
6:7-11	This is how you are to pray ...
11:28-30	The Gentle Mastery of Christ
14:13-21	The Return of the Twelve and the Feeding of Five Thousand
15:29	Moving on from there Jesus ...
26:26-30	The Lord's Supper
5:45	He makes his sun rise ...
18:20	For where two or three …
19:29	And everyone who has given up ...
22:37	You shall love the Lord

Mark	
2:1-12	Healing of the Paralytic
4:35-41	The Calming of a Storm at Sea
6:45-52	The Walking on the Water
10:46-52	The Blind Bartimaeus
Luke	
1:26-38	Announcement of the Birth of Jesus
5:1-11	The Call of Simon the Fisherman
7:36-50	The Pardon of the Sinful Woman
10:41-42	Martha, you are anxious …
11:1-4	The Lord's Prayer
11:5-8	Suppose one of you has a friend ...
11:9-13	The Answer to Prayer
12:22-34	Dependence on God
15:1-7	The Parable of the Lost Sheep
15:11-32	The Parable of the Lost Son
17:15-16	And one of them realizing ...
18:18-23	The Rich Official
21:36	Be vigilant at all times ...
24:13-35	The Appearance on the Road to Emmaus
John	
1:14	And the Word became flesh ...
2:1-12	The Wedding at Cana
6:51	I am the living bread ...
8:1-11	A Woman Caught in Adultery
8:12	I am the light of the world ...
13:1-20	The Washing of the Disciples' Feet
14:1-31	Last Supper Discourses and The Advocate
14:6	I am the way ...
15:1-11	The Vine and the Branches
17:1-26	The Prayer of Jesus
19:17-30	The Crucifixion of Jesus
19:26-27	Woman, behold your son
21:15-19	Jesus and Peter
20:24-29	Thomas
21:1-14	The Appearance to the Seven Disciples
Romans	
1:20	His eternal power and divinity
8:19	For creation awaits…
8:22	We know that all creation…
8:35-39	What Will Separate us From the Love of Christ
1 Corinthians	
13:1-8	The Way of Love

2 Corinthians	
2:14-16	But thanks be to God...
1 John	
1:1-4	For the life was made visible
Ephesians	
1:3-12	The Father's Plan of Salvation
Philippians	
2:10	Then at the name of Jesus…
4:6-7	Have no anxiety…
Revelation	
3:15-18	I know your works ...
1 Thessalonians	
5:16-19	Rejoice always…Pray without ceasing
Icons	
Rublev Trinity	Figure 1
San Damiano Cross	Figure 2

SCRIPTURE PASSAGES BY PRAYER TYPE

CONTEMPLATIVE PRAYER

Genesis 18:1-15	Abraham's Visitors
Ephesians 1:3-12	The Father's Plan of Salvation
John 14:1-31	Last Supper Discourses and The Advocate
John 17:1-26	The Prayer of Jesus
Praying with Nature	
Praying with the Rublev Trinity	
Praying with the San Damiano Cross	

GUIDED MEDITATION

Luke 11:1-4	The Lord's Prayer
Mark 6:45-52	The Walking on the Water
Matthew 3:13-17	The Baptism of Jesus
Luke 7:36-50	The Pardon of the Sinful Woman
Mark 10:46-52	The Blind Bartimaeus
John 8:1-11	A Woman Caught in Adultery
Luke 24:13-35	The Appearance on the Road to Emmaus

LECTIO DIVINA

Psalm 23	
Isaiah 43:1-5	Promises of Redemption and Restoration
Luke 12:22-34	Dependence on God
Psalm 46	
Luke 15:1-7	The Parable of the Lost Sheep

1 Corinthians 13:1-8	The Way of Love
John 20:24-29	Thomas

PRAYING LIKE A PIRATE

Luke 1:26-38	Announcement of the Birth of Jesus
John 13:1-20	The Washing of the Disciples' Feet
Romans 8:35-39	What Will Separate us From the Love of Christ
Luke 18:18-23	The Rich Official
Luke 5:1-11	The Call of Simon the Fisherman
John 2:1-12	The Wedding at Cana
John 21:15-19	Jesus and Peter

PRAYING WITH YOUR SENSES

Luke 15:11-32	The Parable of the Lost Son
Matthew 14:13-21	The Return of the Twelve and the Feeding of Five Thousand
Matthew 26:26-30	The Lord's Supper
John 21:1-14	The Appearance to the Seven Disciples
John 19:17-30	The Crucifixion of Jesus
Mark 2:1-12	Healing of the Paralytic

SCRIPTURAL RELAXATION

John 15:1-11	The Vine and the Branches
Psalm 139	
Mark 4:35-41	The Calming of a Storm at Sea
Psalm 63:2-9	Ardent Longing for God
Matthew 11:28-30	The Gentle Mastery of Christ
Jeremiah 1:4-9	The Call of Jeremiah

BIBLIOGRAPHY

Denk, Michael. Christology in the Mystics: Coming to Know, Love, and Serve Christ through John the Evangelist, Teresa of Avila, and Ignatius of Loyola. Master of Arts Thesis, 2007.

Alison, James. Knowing Jesus. London: SPCK, 1993.

Arminjon, Blaise. The Cantata of Love. Ignatius Press, 1988.

Aschenbrenner, S.J. George A. "Becoming Whom You Contemplate."

Aschenbrenner, S.J. George A. "Consciousness Examen."

Aschenbrenner, S.J. George A. "Presumption for Permanence."

Aschenbrenner, S.J. George A. Stretched for Greater Glory. Chicago: Loyola Press, 2004.

Augustine. The Confessions of St. Augustine. Translated by Rex Warner. New York: Mentor, 1963.

Bailie, Gil. Violence Unveiled: Humanity at the Crossroads. New York: Crossroad, 1995.

Barnes, Michael. "The Presence and Absence of God."

Barron, Robert E. "Priest as Bearer of the Mystery."

Barry, S.J., William A. A Friendship Like No Other. Chicago: Loyola Press, 2008.

Barry, S.J., William A. Letting God Come Close. Chicago: Loyola Press, 2001.

Barry, S.J., William A. "The Experience of the First and Second Weeks of the Spiritual Exercises."

Barry, S.J., William A. and William J. Connolly. The Practice of Spiritual Direction. New York, NY: HarperSanFrancisco, 1986.

Bergan, Jacqueline Syrup. Praying with Ignatius of Loyola. Winona: Saint Mary's Press, 1991.

Bernard of Clairvaux. On the Song of Songs. Translated by Kilian Walsh. Kalamazoo: Cistercian Publications, 1980.

Bernard of Clairvaux. Selected Works (Classics of Western Spirituality). Paulist Press, 1987.

Bonaventure. The Life of St. Francis of Assisi. Translated by Henry Edward Cardinal Manning. Rockford: Tan Books and Publishers, 1988.

Bonaventure. The Soul's Journey into God, the Tree of Life, the Life of St. Francis Cousins. Translated by Ewert Cousins. New York: Paulist Press, 1978.

Brother Lawrence. The Practice of the Presence of God. Whitaker House, 1982.

Brown, Peter. Augustine of Hippo. Berkley: University of California Press, 1969.

Brown, Raymond E. The Gospel According to John. New York: Doubleday, 1970.

Brown, Raymond E. The New Jerome Biblical Commentary.

Buckley, Michael, S.J. "The Contemplation to Attain Love: Ignatian Election and Christian Choice."

Burns, J. Patout. Theological Anthropology. Philadelphia: Fortress Press, 1981.

Carroll, Eamon R. "The Saving Role of the Human Christ for St. Teresa." In Centenary of St. Teresa Carmelite Studies, vol. 3. ed. John Sullivan, 133-151. Washington, D.C.: ICS Publications, 1984.

Casey, Michael. Fully Human Fully Divine: An Interactive Christology. Liguori, MO: Liguori/Triumph, 2004.

Cassian, John and Colm Luibheid. Owen Chadwick. Conferences (Classics of Western Spirituality). Mahwah, NJ: Paulist Press. 1985.

Castellano, Jesus. "Christian, Human and Cultural Values in St. Teresa of Jesus." In Edith Stein Symposium/Teresian Culture Carmelite Studies, vol. 4. ed. John Sullivan, 110-124. Washington, D.C.: ICS Publications, 1987.

Chesterton, G.K. Saint Francis of Assisi. New York: Doubleday, 1957.

Clarke, O.C.D., John. Story of a Soul. Washington, D.C.: ICS Publications, 1999.

De Caussade, Jean-Pierre. Abandonment to Divine Providence. Ignatius Press, 2011.

De la Croix, O.C.D. Paul-Marie. The Biblical Spirituality of St. John. Staten Island: Alba House, 1966.

Delio, Ilia. Franciscan Prayer. Cincinnati: St. Anthony Press, 2004.

DeSales, Francis. Introduction to the Devout Life. New York: Doubleday, 2003.

Dubay, S.M., Thomas. Fire Within. San Francisco: Ignatius Press, 1989.

Dubay, S.M., Thomas. Happy are You Poor: The Simple Life and Spiritual Freedom. San Francisco: Ignatius Press, 2003.

Dubay, S.M., Thomas. Seeking Spiritual Direction: How to Grow the Divine Life Within. Cincinnati: Charis, 1993.

Dumm, Demetrius. A Mystical Portrait of Jesus: New Perspectives on John's Gospel. Collegeville: Liturgical Press, 2001.

Dunne, John S. "Insight and Waiting on God."

Dupre, Louis and James Wiseman. Light from Light: An Anthology of Christian Mysticism. New York: Paulist Press, 2001.

Dupuis, S.J., Jacques. Who Do You Say I Am. New York: Orbis, 1994.

Egan, Harvey. Ignatius Loyola, the Mystic. Wilmington: Glazier, 1987.

Egan, Harvey. Karl Rahner: Mystic of Everyday Life. New York: Crossroad, 1998.

Egan, Harvey. The Spiritual Exercises and the Ignatian Mystical Horizon. St. Louis: Institute of Jesuit Sources, 1976.

Fleming, S.J., David L. Draw Me Into Your Friendship: A Literal Translation and a Contemporary Reading of the Spiritual Exercises. St Louis: Institute of Jesuit Sources, 1996.

Gallagher, Timothy M. Discerning the Will of God: An Ignatian Guide to Christian Decision Making. New York: Crossroad, 2009.

Gallagher, Timothy M. Meditation and Contemplation: An Ignatian Guide to Prayer with Scripture. New York: Crossroad, 2008.

Gallagher, Timothy M. The Discernment of Spirits: An Ignatian Guide for Everyday Living. New York: Crossroad, 2005.

Gallagher, Timothy M. The Examen Prayer: Ignatian Wisdom for Our Daily Lives. New York: Crossroad, 2006.

Garrigou-Lagrange, Reginald. The Three Conversions in the Spiritual Life. Rockford: Tan Books and Publishers, 1977.

Gawronski, Raymond. Word and Silence: Hans Urs Von Balthasar and the Spiritual Encounter Between East and West. Grand Rapids: T. & T. Clark Publishers, 1999.

Gilson, Etienne. The Mystical Theology of Saint Bernard. New York: Sheed & Ward, 1955.

Granfield, O.S.B., David. “The First Principle of Christian Mysticism.” In Spiritual Direction Carmelite Studies, vol. 1. ed. John Sullivan, 213-228. Washington, D.C.: ICS Publications, 1980.

Haight, Roger. Dynamics of Theology. New York: Orbis Books, 1990.

Haight, Roger. The Experience and Language of Grace. New York: Paulist Press, 1979.

Hamm, Dennis. “Rummaging for God: Praying Backward Through Your Day.” America. [http://72.14.209.104/search?q=cache:4DbE4cS5230J:www.bc.edu/bc_org/uvp/mismin/intersec/programs/Examen_more.doc+rummaging+for+god&hl=en&ct=clnk&cd=2&gl=us], 1994.

Hathaway, Patricia Cooney. “The Mysticism of Everyday Life.” Church, Spring 1994, 18.

Hill, William J. The Three-Personed God: The Trinity as a Mystery of Salvation. Washington, D.C: The Catholic University Press, 1982.

Horn, John Phili. Mystical Healing: The Psychological and Spiritual Power of the Ignatian Spiritual Exercises. New York: Crossroad, 1996.

Ignatius of Loyola. The Spiritual Exercises of St. Ignatius. Translated by Louis J. Puhl. Westminster: The Newman Press, 1959.

Ivens, Michael. Understanding the Spiritual Exercises. Wiltshire: Gracewing, Cromwell Press, 1998.

Jalics, Franz. Contemplative Retreat: An Introduction to the Contemplative Way of Life and to the Jesus Prayer. Longwood: Xulon Press. 2003.

"Jesus Christ, the Bearer of the Water of Life: A Christian Reflection on the New Age." [http://www.vatican.va/roman_curia/pontifical_councils/interelg/documents/rc_pc_interelg_doc_20030203_new-age_en.html], 2003.

Johnson, Elizabeth A. Consider Jesus: Wave of Renewal in Christology. New York: Crossroad, 2002.

Jurado, S.J., Manuel Ruiz. For the Greater Glory of God. Maryland: The Word Among Us Press, 2002.

Kavanaugh, Kieran and Otilio Rodriguez. The Collected Works of St. Teresa of Avila: Volume 1. Washington, D.C.: ICS Publications, 1976.

Kavanaugh, Kieran and Otilio Rodriguez. The Collected Works of St. Teresa of Avila: Volume 2. Washington, D.C.: ICS Publications, 1980.

Kavanaugh, Kieran and Otilio Rodriguez. The Collected Works of St. Teresa of Avila: Volume 3. Washington, D.C.: ICS Publications, 1987.

Kempis, Thomas A. The Imitation of Christ. Notre Dame: Ave Maria Press, 1989.

Kysar, Robert. John: The Maverick Gospel. Louisville: John Knox Press, 1976.

LaCugna, Catherine Mowry. God for Us: The Trinity & Christian Life. San Francisco: Harper, 1973.

"Letter to the Bishops of the Catholic Church on Some Aspects of Christian Meditation." Pontifical Council for Culture, Pontifical Council for Interreligious Dialogue, Congregation for the Doctrine of Faith. [http://www.ewtn.com/library/CURIA/CDFMED.HTM], 1989.

Lossky, Vladimir. In the Image and Likeness of God. New York: St. Vladimir's Seminary Press, 2001.

Louth, Andrew. The Origins of the Christian Mystical Tradition. Oxford: Claredon, 1987.

Maloney, S.D.B., Francis J. The Gospel of John. Sacra Pagina Series, Volume 4. Collegeville: Liturgical Press, 1998.

Marmion, Declan. A Spirituality of Everyday Faith. Louvain: Peters Press, 1998.

Marsh, Robert R. "Looking at God Looking at You: Ignatius' Third Addition."

Martin, Ralph. The Fulfillment of All Desire. Emmaus Road Publishing, 2006.

Matthew, Iain. The Impact of God: Soundings from St. John of the Cross. London: Hodder & Stoughton, 1995.

McCreary, OFM Cap, Robert L. "The Humanity of Christ and Mysticism." Cleveland: This is a paper written for students at St. Mary Seminary, 1999.

McDermott, Brian O. "What is Apostolic Spirituality?" America, November 11, 2002, 18.

McGinn, Bernard. The Flowering of Mysticism: 1200-1350. New York: Crossroad, 1998.

McIntosh, Mark A. Christology from Within. Notre Dame, IN: Notre Dame Press, 1966.

Meissner, W.W. Ignatius of Loyola: The Psychology of a Saint. New Haven: Yale University Press, 1992.

Merriam-Webster Dictionary, 2016

Merton, Thomas. The Inner Experience: Notes on Contemplation. New York: Harper Collins Publishers, 2003.

Merton, Thomas. The Seven Storey Mountain. San Diego: Harcourt, 1999.

Metz, Johannes Baptist. Poverty of Spirit. New York: Paulist Press, 1968.

Morneau, Robert F. Spiritual Direction: Principles and Practices. New York: Crossroad, 1996.

Mother Teresa. A Simple Path. Ballantine Books, 1995.

Mott, Michael. The Seven Mountains of Thomas Merton. Fort Washington: Harvest Books, 1993.

Muto, Ph.D, Susan. "St Teresa of Avila: A Directress of Formation for all Times". In Centenary of St. Teresa Carmelite Studies, vol. 3, ed. John Sullivan, 3-187. Washington, D.C.: ICS Publications, 1984.

The New Interpreter's Bible: Luke – John. Nashville: Abington Press, 1999.

Nigro, Armand M. "Prayer – A Personal Response to God's Presence."

Nigro, Armand M. "Praying the Gospels."

Nigro, Armand M. "Praying with Scripture."

Nouwen, Henri J.M. Behold the Beauty of the Lord: Praying with Icons. Notre Dame, IN: Ave Maria Press, 1987.

Nouwen, Henri J.M. Lifesigns: Intimacy, Fecundity, and Ecstasy in Christian Perspective. New York: Doubleday, 1986.

Nouwen, Henri J.M. Making All Things New: An Invitation To the Spiritual Life. New York: Harper & Row, 1981.

Nouwen, Henri J.M. Out of Solitude: Three Meditations on the Christian Life." New York: Ave Maria Press, 1974.

Nouwen, Henri J.M. Reaching Out: The Three Movements of the Spiritual Life. New York: Doubleday, 1975.

Nouwen, Henri J.M. The Inner Voice of Love: A Journey through Anguish to Freedom. New York: Doubleday, 1996.

Nouwen, Henri J.M. The Return of the Prodigal Son. New York: Doubleday, 1992.

Oakes, Edward T. Pattern of Redemption: The Theology of Hans urs von Balthasar. New York: Continuum, 1994.

O'Collins, S.J., Gerald. The Tripersonal God: Understanding and Interpreting the Trinity. New York: Paulist, 1999.

O'Donoghue, Noel. Mystics for our Time. Wilmington: Glazier, 1989.

Paul-Marie of the Cross. "Characteristics of Carmel." In Carmelite Spirituality in the Teresian Tradition, 17-44. Washington, D.C.: ICS Publications, 1997.

Pennington, Basil M. Bernard of Clairvaux. New City Press, 1997.

Pennington, Basil M. The Song of Songs: A Spiritual Commentary. Woodstock, VT: Skylight Paths Publishing, 2004.

Philippe, Marie-Dominique. Mary, Mystery of Mercy. Battleford, Saskatchewan: Marian Press, 2002.

Pope Benedict XVI. "Deus Caritas Est.: Encyclical Letter to the Bishops, Priests, and Deacons, Men and Women Religious, and All the Lay Faithful on Christian Love." [http://www.vatican.va/holy_father/benedict_xvi/encyclicals/documents/hf_ben-xvi_enc_20051225_deus-caritas-est_en.html], 2005.

Pope Benedict XVI. "Message of His Holiness Benedict XVI for Lent 2007." [http://www.vatican.va/holy_father/benedict_xvi/messages/lent/documents/hf_ben-xvi_mes_20061121_lent-2007_en.html], 2007.

Pope Francis. "Encyclical Letter: Laudato Si of the Holy Father Francis on Care for our Common Home.", 2015.

Pope John Paul II. "Novo Millennio Ineunte." [http://www.vatican.va/holy_father/john_paul_ii/apost_letters/documents/hf_jp-ii_apl_20010106_novo-millennio-ineunte_en.html], 2000.

Pope John XXIII. Journal of a Soul. New York: Doubleday, 1964.

Pourrat, Pierre. Christian Spirituality, II. Westminster: The Newman Press, 1953.

Powell, John. Fully Human Fully Alive: A New Life through a New Vision. Chicago: Thomas More Association, 1976.

Powell, John. Unconditional Love: Love Without Limits. Chicago: Thomas More Association, 1995.

Powell, John. Why Am I Afraid to Love?: Overcoming Rejection and Indifference. Chicago: Thomas More Association, 1990.

Power, Dermont. A Spiritual Theology of the Priesthood: The Mystery of Christ and the Mission of the Priest. Washington, D.C.: Catholic University of America Press, 1998.

Puhl, S.J., Louis J. The Spiritual Exercises of St. Ignatius. Maryland: The Newman Press, 1959.

Rahner, Karl. "Ignatian Mysticism of Joy in the World." In Theological Investigations, Vol. III: The Theology of the Spiritual Life. New York: Seabury, 1974, 277-398.

Rahner, Karl. Spiritual Exercises. New York: Herder & Herder, 1965.

Rahner, Karl. Spiritual Writings. ed. Philip Endean. Maryknoll: Orbis Books, 2004.

Rahner, Karl. "The Three Kinds of Humility."

Rahner, Karl. The Trinity. New York: Crossroad, 1997.

Rahner, Karl. "Thoughts on the Theology of Christmas." In Theological Investigations, Vol. III: The Theology of the Spiritual Life. Baltimore: Helicon, 1967, 24-34.

Ratzinger, Joseph. "Surrendering to His Will."

Ratzinger, Joseph. The Ratzinger Report: An Exclusive Interview on the State of the Church. Ignatius Press, 1987.

Raub, John Jacob. Who Told You That You Were Naked?. New York: Crossroad, 1992.

Rohr, Richard. Adam's Return: The Five Promises of Male Initiation. New York: Crossroad, 2004.

Rohr, Richard. Everything Belongs: The Gift of Contemplative Prayer. New York: Crossroad, 2003.

Rohr, Richard. Great Themes of Scripture: New Testament. Cincinnati, OH: Saint Anthony Messenger Press, 1988.

Rolheiser, Ronald. Forgotten Among the Lilies: Learning to Love Beyond Our Fears. New York: Doubleday, 2005.

Rolheiser, Ronald. The Holy Longing. New York: Doubleday, 1999.

Rolheiser, Ronald. The Restless Heart. New York: Doubleday, 2004.

Rolheiser, Ronald. The Shattered Lantern. New York: Crossroad, 2001.

Rossetti, Stephen J. The Joy of Priesthood. Notre Dame, IN: Ave Maria

Press, 2005.

Rossetti, Stephen J. The Lost Art of Walking on Water: Reimagining the Priesthood. New York, Paulist Press, 2004.

Rossetti, Stephen J. When the Lion Roars. Notre Dame, IN: Ave Maria Press, 2003.

Ryan, John K. Introduction to the Devout Life. Harper Torchbooks, 1966.

Schillebeeckx, O.P., Edward. Christ the Sacrament of the Encounter With God. Franklin: Sheed & Ward, 1963.

Seelaus, Vilma. "Bluebeard's Palace and the Interior Castle: Contemplation as Life." In Carmel and Contemplation: Transforming Human Consciousness, Carmelite Studies, vol. 8, eds. Kevin Culligan and Regis Jordan, 101-113. Washington, D.C.: ICS Publications, 2000.

Seelaus, Vilma. "Teresa, Suffering, in the Face of God". In Carmel and Contemplation: Transforming Human Consciousness, Carmelite Studies, vol. 8, eds. Kevin Culligan and Regis Jordan, 137-205. Washington, D.C.: ICS Publications, 2000.

Seelaus, Vilma. "Transformation and Divine Union in the Carmelite Tradition." In Carmelite Prayer: A Tradition for the 21st Century, ed. Keith J. Egan, 139-161. New York: Paulist Press, 2003.

Sheed, Frank. To Know Christ Jesus. San Francisco: Ignatius Press, 1980.

Sheen, Fulton J. The Priest Is Not His Own. Ignatius Press, 2014.

Sheen, Fulton J. Treasure In Clay. New York: Doubleday, 1980.

Sheldrake, Philip. The Way of Ignatius Loyola: Contemporary Approaches to the Spiritual Exercises. St. Louis: Institute of Jesuit Sources, 1991.

Tetlow, Joseph A. Choosing Christ in the World. St. Louis: Institute of Jesuit Sources, 1999.

Tetlow, Joseph A. Ignatius Loyola: Spiritual Exercises. New York: Crossroad: 1992.

Thérèse of Lisieux. The Autobiography of St. Thérèse of Lisieux: The Story of a Soul. Translated by John Beevers. New York: Image Books, 1957.

Thérèse of Lisieux. Story of a Soul. Translated by John Clarke. Washington, D.C.: ICS Publications, 1996.

Thomas of Celano. The Life of Saint Francis. Translated by Christopher Stace. London: Society for Promoting Christian Knowledge, 2000.

Toner, Jules. Love and Friendship: Experience of Love/Personal Friendship: The Experience and the Ideal. Milwaukee: Marquette University Press, 2003.

Trapp, Daniel J. "Nuptial Love and Discerning Celibacy's Call: Loving as Celibates."

Vanier, Jean. Becoming Human. New York: Paulist Press, 1999.

Vanier, Jean. Community and Growth. New York: Paulist Press, 1989.

Vanier, Jean. Drawn Into the Mystery of Jesus through the Gospel of John. New York: Paulist Press, 2004.

Vanier, Jean. From Brokenness to Community. New York: Paulist Press, 1992.

Vaughn, John. Francis and Clare: The Complete Works (Classics of Western Spirituality). Mahway: Paulist Press, 1986.

Von Balthasar, Hans Urs. Credo: Meditations on the Apostles' Creed. Ft. Collins: Ignatius Press, 2000.

Von Balthasar, Hans Urs. Prayer. Ft. Collins: Ignatius Press, 1986.

Warner, Rex. The Confessions of Saint Augustine. Whitaker House, 1996.

Wikipedia. Figure 1, Rublev Trinity. https://en.wikipedia.org/wiki/Trinity_(Andrei, Rublev).2016.

Wikipedia. Figure 2, San Damiano Cross. https://en.wikipedia.org/wiki/SanDamianoCross.2016.